❧ THE SPACE THAT REMAINS

THE SPACE
THAT REMAINS

READING LATIN POETRY
IN LATE ANTIQUITY

Aaron Pelttari

CORNELL UNIVERSITY PRESS
Ithaca and London

First published 2014 by Cornell University Press

First paperback printing 2020

Library of Congress Cataloging-in-Publication Data

Pelttari, Aaron, 1982– author.
   The space that remains : reading Latin poetry in late
antiquity / Aaron Pelttari.
        pages cm. — (Cornell studies in classical
philology)
   Includes bibliographical references and index.
   ISBN 978-0-8014-5276-5 (cloth)
   1. Latin poetry– History and criticism. 2. Latin
poetry— Appreciation. 3. Authors and readers—
Rome. 4. Reader- response criticism. I. Title.
PA6051.P45 2014
871'.0109—dc23
                                        2014002762

ISBN 978-1-5017-5205-6 (paperback)

For Natalia

hanc praetexuit velut in musica concordiam dissonorum

he hid it like the harmony of music in dissonance

Marcob. *Sat.* 5.1.18

◢ Contents

✒ ACKNOWLEDGMENTS

In these days of tightened budgets and narrowed visions, I have been privileged with the opportunity to explore the history of Latin poetry. I am thankful to Cornell University and to the University of California, Santa Barbara, for the support that allowed me to complete this book. I am convinced that such studies are vital for a culture that is increasingly ignorant of its past, and it is my earnest hope that the reception of classical literature in late antiquity may show in some small way that the humanities can still have a bright future in our culture today. Learning about the classical world both deepens my understanding of history and broadens my enjoyment of literature. For that I am grateful.

I am also glad to acknowledge the personal debts accumulated in writing this book. The incisive reading of Éric Rebillard lies behind most of the structure and clarity that these chapters may have. I have been glad many times for his mentoring and friendship. Michael Fontaine, Joseph Pucci, and Hayden Pelliccia have also improved my work in a great many ways. Pucci is the kindest of readers, and Fontaine has a knack for finding just the right detail to adjust. Erik Kenyon, Zachary Yuzwa, and Jeffrey Leon read early drafts of each chapter. Talking over lunch about our writing remains one of my fondest memories of Ithaca. A number of other friends and colleagues read or discussed with me portions of my work at various stages in the writing of it. In particular, I am grateful to Kim Bowes, Charles Brittain, Kim Haines-Eitzen, Gavin Kelly, Cillian O'Hagan, Christopher Polt, Suzanne Rebillard, and Catherine Ware. The anonymous readers for Cornell University Press made a number of valuable suggestions. If there were space and my memory was better, there are surely many others who have influenced me. My notes will give some idea of how much I have learned from the writings of others. If I were not so stubborn, I surely would have benefited more from all this help. As it is, I alone am responsible for the infelicities and misjudgments that surely are here.

My greatest debt is to my wife, who encouraged me to begin, continue, and finish this project. I am thankful as well for the patience of both of my sons. David was born just as I was beginning to plan this book. Lucas was born as I was finishing the conclusion. They are both excellent readers, and their joy and energy are my constant inspiration.

All translations from the Latin are my own unless otherwise noted. The book's title comes from a line of Claudian's poetry discussed in the Conclusion (*Rapt.* 3.157). It recalls for me the room for reading that is latent in so much of the surviving late antique Latin poetry. I was probably influenced as well by the title of the English translation of Giorgio Agamben's *Il tempo che resta*, which I read as I was beginning to formulate my ideas. The subtitle "Reading Latin Poetry in Late Antiquity" refers both to the poetry produced in late antiquity and to the earlier Latin poetry that was read in and alongside this contemporary material. As I explain in the Introduction, the term "late antiquity" is limited here to the fourth century, arguably the most pivotal period in this time of changes. Nevertheless, my approach can only scratch the surface of all the poetry and contexts that survive from the fourth century. There is much more work to be done.

✒ ABBREVIATIONS

(Abbreviations for the titles of works of ancient authors are listed in the Index of Passages Cited.)

AE	*L'Année Épigraphique*
CC	*Corpus Christianorum, series Latina*
CIL	*Corpus Inscriptionum Latinarum*
MGH, AA	*Monumenta Germaniae Historica, Auctores Antiquissimi*
OED	*Oxford English Dictionary*
PG	*Patrologiae Cursus, series Graeca*
PL	*Patrologiae Cursus, series Latina*
PLRE	*Prosopography of the Later Roman Empire*
SEG	*Supplementum epigraphicum Graecum*
TLL	*Thesaurus Linguae Latinae*

THE SPACE THAT REMAINS

Introduction
Late Antique Poetry and the Figure of the Reader

Claudian began the *De raptu Proserpinae* by asking the gods of the underworld to uncover for him their deepest secrets ("vos mihi sacrarum penetralia pandite rerum / et vestri secreta poli," *Rapt.* 1.25–26). He imagines poetry as something hidden that needs to be uncovered. In contrast, Vergil began the *Aeneid* by asking the Muse to remind him of the reasons for Juno's hatred of the Trojans ("Musa, mihi causas memora," *Aen.* 1.8). In the *Aeneid*, the poet asks for a reminder or an explanation, not for a revelation of some deeper truth. Between the first century BCE and the fourth century CE, there occurred a broad shift in how poets conceived of the reader's role in making sense of the words on the page. In late antiquity, poets came to describe their material as needing interpretation, recovery, and activation. The figure of the reader structures the poetry of late antiquity and so it reveals how the formal aspects of their poetry worked for authors such as Ausonius, Claudian, and Prudentius. I focus on the long fourth century because that period saw the full development of an aesthetic sensibility characteristic of a late antiquity in which poets constructed their identity in and through their readers' presence.

From the third to the eighth century, around the entire Mediterranean, late antiquity was a period of transitions. In the Latin West, the fourth century saw the rise of a Christian aristocracy and of political centers beyond the city of Rome. In 410, Alaric I sacked the city of Rome itself. Augustine of Hippo says that he wrote *The City of God* in response to this setback, for the sake of contemporaries who were unnerved by the changes that they could see in their world. In contrast, Augustine's sermons reveal in a more neutral way the changing social realities for the entire population of Roman North Africa in the fourth century. The period as a whole saw the emergence of new social systems, new ways of structuring power, and new ways of imagining the world. Since Peter Brown's *The World of Late Antiquity: From Marcus Aurelius to Muhammad* (1971), there has been increased interest in how the medieval world emerged out of classical antiquity. In recent years, companions to the study of late antiquity have helped consolidate the scholarly gains of the last forty years.[1] In addition to social history, there has also been renewed interest in the literature and poetry of late antiquity. In the Latin West of the fourth and early fifth centuries, three poets stand out, diverse in their aims and methods but sharing many of the same expectations about their audience and readership. Of the three, Decimus Magnus Ausonius was the eldest. He was a professional rhetor from Bordeaux born around 310 and alive until the end of the fourth century. When he was appointed as the tutor to Gratian, son of the emperor Valentinian I, he found himself among the most influential men of his time. His poetic and literary sensibilities were an asset in the aristocratic circles that he came to inhabit. Claudius Claudianus was born in Egypt around 370 and came to Rome in the 390s, where he quickly found a place writing poems in praise of Honorius and his regent, Stilicho. Besides his political poetry, a number of shorter poems and several unfinished epics survive. Claudian probably died in 404. About the third poet, Aurelius Prudentius Clemens, we know less. He was from Spain and born in 348. He says in a preface that he once held a high office in the imperial administration. After leaving behind the things of this world, he dedicated himself to the writing of Christian poetry. The poems that survive show a highly skilled poet writing on all aspects of Christian life: lyrical poetry on the daily routines of worship, epic poems in praise of martyrs, and polemical works of theological and social commentary. These are the poets that we will come to again and again in the following pages, because they reveal together the literary transformations of late antiquity. Partly because of their differences, we can see within their poems the central importance of the reader within the textual world of late antiquity.

When I describe the reader as central to late antique poetics, I am making a comparative and historical claim. Leading scholars have suggested both

---

1. See S. F. Johnson 2012 and Rousseau 2009. G. Clark 2011 is from Oxford's series of Very Short Introductions.

that late antique aesthetics is a misleading category and that such literary-historical arguments are not worth making. Before Michael Roberts published *The Jeweled Style* (1989), it was common for authors writing in English to describe imperial poetry as decadent, as having declined from a high point under the rule of Augustus.[2] But rather than change or decline, some scholars have preferred to see a continuity between earlier and later imperial poetry. Thus J. B. Hall rejected Roberts's arguments concerning late antique style because some later authors (he names Prudentius and Claudian) "are fine writers, have something to say, and know how to say it."[3] In this view, all Latin poets of quality aspire to the same classical ideals. Hall implies that we would be better off to avoid talk of aesthetic change because some authors were still able to meet the standards of Vergil, or at the least of Statius. But if we remove historical change from our understanding of later Latin poetry, we remove the context that gave it life. If we describe ancient Latin poetry as an ideal space, essentially continuous from Livius Andronicus down to Claudian, we ignore the individual contours within that tradition. To be sure, no one has actually argued for continuity in so extreme a form as this.[4] However, I do think it important to balance explanations of similarity with arguments for difference. While the historical arguments in this study point to a series of differences between classical and late antique poetics, I would never want to suggest that there are not also important similarities. Indeed, if we knew more about the literature of the second and third centuries CE, we would probably be able to say more about the historical development of Latin poetry.[5] Nor do I want to suggest that late antique poetry is uniform. Ausonius and Claudian are quite different authors, and much work remains to be done on the relation between individual poets within late antiquity.

In describing an aesthetic peculiar to late antiquity, I employ a form of argument indebted to Hans Robert Jauss's reader-response criticism. In "Literary History as a Challenge to Literary Theory," Jauss proposed that criticism ought to reconstruct a work's "horizon of expectations" in order to "pose questions that the text gave an answer to, and thereby to discover how the contemporary reader could have viewed and understood

2. Rose 1936, Hadas 1952, and Williams 1978 are typical examples.

3. Hall 1991, 361. In contrast and on account of their stylistic preferences, Ausonius and Sidonius are "at best second-rate."

4. But Ernst Robert Curtius's magnum opus *European Literature and the Latin Middle Ages* (1953) remains an incomparably grand vision of continuity from the classical to the modern.

5. Cameron 1980 shows how little we know about the Latin poetry of the second century CE.

the work."[6] Michael Roberts expressed his debt to Jauss in the introduction to his treatment of late antique aesthetics,[7] and my own debt to both scholars should be obvious. Objections, however, have been raised about Jauss's literary-historical method. Charles Martindale suggested that Jauss's ideal reader should be rejected as a figment of the critic's imagination, and Stephen Hinds observed that every literary history is tendentious and partisan.[8] I do not dispute that a dogmatic account of the ideal reader would crowd out the pluralism inherent in any work's reception, nor do I contest that my account of late antique poetry must be tendentious even in ways that I do not realize. Nevertheless, whenever we describe a particular Latin poem, we necessarily set it, either explicitly or implicitly, in some narrative context. Therefore, while recognizing that late antiquity is a modern concept that necessarily obscures the particularity of each individual poem, I still use the term heuristically, to describe a set of common expectations shared by some contemporary poets.[9]

I have for the most part avoided consideration of the many ways in which late antique poets constructed their own identities against those of predecessors and contemporaries. Instead, I describe a set of literary techniques and poetic forms that construct the reader's involvement in the text. Every single technique that I discuss could be paralleled with earlier examples from classical Latin and even Greek literature. Even the figural poetry of Optatianus Porphyrius can be seen as an extension of the acrostics found in Aratus or Vergil. Nevertheless, the rising in the fourth century of an entire constellation of tropes that draw out the reader's involvement marks an important shift away from earlier, classical poetry. The shift toward this late antique aesthetic was a shift away from the direct precedents and exemplars that influenced the poets of late antiquity. For this reason, I do not apply to this period terms such as "neo-Alexandrianism," because they give the impression that the poetry of the fourth century is essentially continuous with earlier periods.[10] Although there are some very important similarities between Ausonius, Catullus, and Callimachus, the late antique poets do not seem to have been particularly influenced by the Hellenistic poetics of Callimachus or

---

6. Jauss 1982, 28.

7. Roberts 1989, 5–6.

8. Martindale 1996 and Hinds 1998, esp. 52–98. For a recent overview of reception theory, see Hexter 2006.

9. Jaś Elsner (2004) comes to a similar conclusion as regards the field of art history. Marco Formisano (2007 and 2012) also describes the textual system of late antiquity, but not in historical terms.

10. On the so-called neo-Alexandrianism of late antique poetry, see Charlet 1988.

Parthenius, perhaps because Catullus and Vergil had already appropriated their work for a Roman audience. I use the term "classical"—which can also be misleading—quite often in reference to Vergil and Horace, but also to describe any of the poetry that was identified in the fourth century as ancient and authoritative. I have always tried not to flatten the contours of classical poetry, but a different study could have followed the course of Latin poetry more fully along its many twists and turns. It has been my aim to mark only one turn, the transformation of Latin poetry within the fourth century.

That turn may be glimpsed briefly in two introductory passages, one written by a certain Nemesianus in the third century and the other by Claudian in the fourth. Each poet reflects upon the past, but they negotiate remarkably different sets of expectations. The *Cynegetica* of Marcus Aurelius Olympius Nemesianus, composed in either 283 or 284, begins with an extended *recusatio*, in which the poet promises to avoid the common path because the Muse will lead him through places untouched by any wheel ("qua sola numquam / trita rotis," *Cyneg.* 8–9). Nemesianus repeats a well-worn trope of both Greek and Latin poetry,[11] and he follows that topos of originality with a list of tired mythological themes, the poems that he will not sing. Niobe is an old story ("nam quis non Nioben numeroso funere maestam / iam cecinit," 15–16), as are the seventeen others that he mentions (17–45). Nemesianus concludes by noting that every story has been told already:

> Haec iam magnorum praecepit copia vatum,
> omnis et antiqui vulgata est fabula saecli.
>
> (*Cyneg.* 46–47)

> A multitude of great poets has already handled them,
> and every myth of ancient times has been made common.

Like the trope of originality, the listing of vulgar myths is also a commonplace. Vergil had given a shorter but similar list at the start of book 3 of the *Georgics*, which he begins by observing that everything was already common ("omnia iam vulgata") before going on, like Nemesianus, to cite examples (*G.* 3.4–8). The pseudo-Vergilian *Aetna* also begins with a *recusatio* of the tired stories that the poet will not recount (9–23). Even the cento *Hippodamia* enumerates the myths that the poet will not sing. Although Nemesianus ostentatiously refuses to write a traditional poem about mythology, he

---

11. Compare Verg. *G.* 3.291–93; Lucret. 1.926–27; and Call. *Aetia* 1, fr. 1.25–28 (Pfeiffer). Macrobius quotes the Vergilian and Lucretian passages at *Sat.* 6.2.2–3.

begins exactly where his predecessors had left off. He marks not the end but the survival of an earlier poetics.[12]

A genuinely new tradition would confront a different anxiety, as Claudian does in his preface to book 1 of the *De raptu Proserpinae*. Claudian transforms the topos of originality in order to mark his departure from classical epic. His preface describes the first sailor and explains how he came gradually to venture out into the open sea from shallower waters.[13] This is universally interpreted as an allegory of Claudian's poetic career: He is said to progress gradually from shorter, lighter poetry to the grander themes of epic, despite the fact that there is no agreement as to how the narrative matches Claudian's writings or when in his career it could have been written.[14] Whatever the biographical point, the preface imagines Claudian as a transgressive and original poet and thereby posits a gap between Claudian and the past. The preface both begins and ends with the poet's venture out onto the open sea:

> Inventa secuit primus qui[15] nave profundum
>   et rudibus remis sollicitavit aquas,
> qui, dubiis ausus committere flatibus alnum,
>   quas natura negat, praebuit arte vias,
> tranquillis primum trepidus se credidit undis
>   litora securo tramite summa legens;
> mox longos temptare sinus et linquere terras
>   et leni coepit pandere vela Noto;
> ast ubi paulatim praeceps audacia crevit
>   cordaque languentem dedidicere metum,
> iam vagus inrumpit pelagus[16] caelumque secutus
>   Aegaeas hiemes Ioniumque domat.
>
>   (*Rapt. 1,* praef.)

---

12. Thus I disagree with Martin Hose, who reads this passage as marking a crisis for traditional poetry (2007, 538–41). Hose does not take seriously enough the conventional nature of Nemesianus's *recusatio*.

13. Jason is surely the sailor who is meant (as stated by Charlet 1991, 4–5 and 83n1), although it is true that Jason was not the only one credited with that feat (on other possibilities, see Charlet 1991, 83n1; on the Hellenistic establishment of Jason as the first sailor, see Jackson 1997).

14. For the possibilities, see Felgentreu 1999, 162; Gruzelier 1993, 81; and Charlet 1991, xx–xxii.

15. J. B. Hall, with some of the manuscripts, prints these words in the order "primus secuit qui." For the reading "secuit primus qui," Charlet (1991, 83n1) marshals some manuscript support (unconvincing either way) and considerations of meter and rhythm (which are convincing).

16. Charlet (1991, 84n6) defends "pelagus" in place of Hall's "pelago."

He who first cut the deep on his newfound ship
    and who troubled the waters with his rough oars,
who dared to entrust his bark to the uncertain waves,
    and offered a path by art, where nature had denied a way,
he first entrusted himself to still waters,
    browsing the tips of the shore in a safe path;
soon he began to test the long bays and to leave land
    and to spread his sails before the smooth South Wind;
but when gradually his headlong audacity grew
    and his heart forgot its pale fear,
then wandering he bursts on the sea; and he follows heaven
    and tames the Aegean storms and Ionian sea.

The image of poetic production as a voyage is common throughout Latin poetry,[17] but this allegory can also be read as referring to the tradition. Claudian was initially only treading, or reading ("legens"), over the surface of the tradition. But as his audacity increased he forgot (literally "unlearned") the languishing fear that kept him close to shore. While the *primus qui* motif and the theme of the poet's originality were well-worn paths of Roman poetry,[18] Claudian imagines his invention as a transgressive act. In particular, Jason was a problematic exemplar because the invention of the arts was said to be spurred by greed and was often marked as a transgression of the natural, golden-age world.[19] In his *propemptikon* for Vergil (*Carm.* 1.3), Horace described the audacity of Jason in strongly moralistic terms. Therefore, if Claudian's poem is like the first voyage of the *Argo*, it is a reckless task that rewrites what had been a settled landscape ("sollicitavit aquas"). By comparing himself to Jason, Claudian describes himself as a poet who is transgressive of the natural order of poetry. Rather than expressing an anxiety that he has nothing original to say, Claudian conquers his (audience's) fear of actual originality. The figure of the first mariner makes a problem of originality rather than of conventionality. This figure works for Claudian and for his audience because it negotiates the poet's anxiety about working within and against the classical tradition.

Examination of the ways in which reading and authority were constructed in late antiquity makes it clear that late antique aesthetics are intimately conjoined to problems of interpretation, meaning, and communication. Therefore,

---

17. See Curtius 1953, 128–30.

18. See Hinds 1998, 52–56.

19. See Charlet 1991, 4–5.

I will explore the ways in which reading was constructed in late antiquity on the level of text, paratext, intertext, and commentary. In this way, I hope to contribute to the study of reading in the ancient world,[20] particularly to the study of the Reader as figured in and through poetry.[21] My Reader is not an individual or historical person but an abstraction drawn from the individual texts of late antiquity. I have been influenced by the work of Reinhart Herzog on exegetical Christian poetry (1975), by the articles of Patricia Cox Miller (1998) and Georgia Nugent (1990) on literary theory and late antiquity, by Joseph Pucci's work on the reader (1998), and by Marc Mastrangelo's observations on Prudentius and his reader (2008).[22] In approaching the figure of the reader, I have left aside the social and material realities of reading.[23] Further study could address how the relative absence of patronage affected the poetry of late antiquity or what effect the spatial separation of author and reader had upon the poetry of this period, in which an audience was no longer centered in Rome. But I have constrained myself here to investigating the reader as the figure who activates or realizes the meaning of poetic discourse. The poet writes for a reader who he expects will make sense out of the fragments of the text. My argument is that this imagined late antique reader played an active and influential role in the poem in ways that he had not in earlier periods. Again, I do not wish to imply that the reader played no role in earlier periods or that reading was unproblematic until the fourth century. David Konstan (2004 and 2006) has shown that the reader played an important role in Plutarch's views on poetry and in the poetry of Vergil. René Nünlist has shown that ancient literary theory, as embedded in Greek scholia, acknowledges the reader's role in filling in the gaps in a text (2009, 164–72 and 225–37). And Sean Gurd (2012) has shown that Cicero incorporated readers' suggestions into revised versions of his texts in such a way as to instantiate an open textual community. The reader had always been an important figure in the literature of

---

20. W. A. Johnson and Parker 2009 provides a series of exemplary essays on different aspects of reading in the ancient world, including an extensive bibliography organized thematically. For a good overview of reading from antiquity to the twentieth century, see Cavallo and Chartier 1999.

21. Citroni 1995 is an insightful study of the reader of ancient Roman poetry, from the time of the republic to the early empire.

22. Dykes 2011 also considers Prudentius and the reader of the *Amartigenia*, but he does not pay particular attention to the late antique aspects of Prudentius's poetry or audience. On the reader in the *Amartigenia*, Conybeare 2007 and Malamud 2011 are more approachable.

23. Dawson 1992 and W. A. Johnson 2010 have provided excellent studies of the social implications of reading in, respectively, Alexandria in the first to third centuries and Rome in the first and second centuries. Gamble 1995 and Haines-Eitzen 2000 survey the role of literacy within early Christianity.

classical antiquity. Nevertheless, in the fourth-century Latin West, the reader gained a new prominence that manifested itself throughout the literary system. Poets structured their work for its future activation, and they invited readers to participate in making sense of their texts. This shift marks the movement toward the new aesthetics that became dominant in late antiquity.

I have written for several distinct audiences beyond those already interested in late antique poetry. Historians who work on late antique religion and society have often taken literary approaches to their texts without, however, paying much attention to the poetry of the period. I hope that my work on the poetry of the fourth century will lead to a better understanding of late antique textuality in general. I have also had in mind those who work on Latin literature and for whom Macrobius, Servius, and Ausonius are usually sources rather than objects of interest in their own right. A better understanding of late antiquity may provide them with a new perspective on classical poetry and also help them to use these sources more carefully. Last, I hope that those interested more broadly in literature or reading will benefit from this focused treatment of reading on the cusp of the Middle Ages. I approach theoretical questions of interpretation and authority in a particular context, but I have also signaled some of the ways in which these problems have broader relevance. In trying to make myself clear to each of these audiences, I have undoubtedly said too little in some places for one group and too much in another.

Each of the following four chapters addresses a different aspect of the textuality of late antiquity. Chapter 1 discusses the broader context of reading by looking at the practice of interpretation. I examine how questions of reception and authority were handled by both readers of the Christian scriptures and by readers of Vergil. Jerome, Augustine, and Macrobius each celebrated their role as readers of these canonical texts, and they shared an approach to their texts that went beyond their religious and political differences. They celebrated the depths of their texts and the wisdom of their authors in a way that legitimized their own work of interpretation. This chapter provides a frame through which to understand the poets who played with the canonical texts, with their own status as authors, and with their contemporary readers. In addressing the role of the reader and the construction of classicism, I am indebted to Pucci (1998) and Catherine Chin (2008). By looking at how these writers viewed reading and textual authority, we see that they did not necessarily expect a contemporary author to be original. Instead, creative adherence to a continually renewed tradition was the hallmark of interpretation in late antiquity.

Chapter 2 uses Gérard Genette's idea of the paratext to interrogate the development of prefaces to Latin poetry. The prefaces of Claudian and Prudentius are shown to be distinct from earlier poetic forms, and the prose prefaces of Ausonius are addressed in terms of the poet's construction and imagined reception of his work. Because a paratext stands apart from the work, it allows the author a space in which to read his own poem. In this way, prefaces allow poets to enact for their readers one possible approach to the text. Claudian, Prudentius, and Ausonius use their prefaces to invite, to interrogate, or sometimes even to ward off the reader's influence over their text. In this chapter, I consider only prefaces, not titles or other such paratextual devices, because the preface allows the poet the most scope in which to create a paratextual frame around the text.

In chapter 3, I apply Umberto Eco's idea of an open text to a series of late antique poems. The figural poetry of Optatianus Porphyrius, the allegorical *Psychomachia* of Prudentius, and the sixteen surviving Vergilian centos create space for the reader to resolve the discrepancies and gaps within the text. I chose these poems because they are clear and powerful demonstrations of the openness of late antique poetry. By focusing on the reader, I show the level at which these works were meant to cohere. In this chapter, I do not discuss biblical poetry, although it does treat its source as an open text to be repeated. Because biblical poems are not technically different from the translations and secondary poetry that was always part and parcel of Latin literature, they are not the best of evidence for the turn towards the reader in the fourth century.[24] Like so many other texts from late antiquity, they reflect this turn, but they are not probative of it.

Chapter 4 is devoted to intertextuality. I focus on a characteristically late antique form of allusion. The allusions I study approximate quotations, for they set a fragment—typically of classical poetry—off against its new context within the late antique poem. These allusions can also be compared to centos because they aim to reproduce the exemplar in a new sense. Even when they were not writing centos, late antique poets employed such allusions to reveal themselves as readers of the classics and so to dramatize in this way the openness of their texts. This kind of allusive fragmentation resembles the use of spoliation and segmentation in the artwork of the fourth

---

24. For a very helpful survey of biblical poetry from the fourth to the sixth century, see Consolino 2005. Green 2006 is an excellent introduction to Juvencus, Sedulius, and Arator. Each of them provides an extensive bibliography. In his study of Sedulius's *Carmen Paschale*, Carl Springer includes a useful description of the relations between biblical poetry, rhetorical paraphrase, and earlier secondary poetry (1988, 3–16).

century, but I limit myself here to the poetic creation of textual continuity.[25] Such allusions are often participatory rather than emulative, but I should stress that I am not by any means trying to make a claim about every allusion in every late antique poem. Rather, I focus on this particular form because it reveals the reader at work activating the potential of the text. In order to clarify the scope of my argument, I include in this chapter a discussion of modern theoretical approaches to allusion in both classical and late antique poetry.

Some readers will no doubt recoil, with Jerome, against the strong versions of reading presented here. Others will embrace them as the only way to read. I hope that most will fall somewhere between these two extremes. And I hope even more that a fuller understanding of the context of later Latin poetry will aid its enjoyment. It is a nice irony that such tendentious readers as the late antique poets have so often been read through the lens of classical poetry. The view is different from the fourth century, and even our understanding of Augustan poetry is deeper for having explored its first, postclassical reception. For what makes a classic is a combination of its own presentation and its subsequent reception. In learning to read Ausonius, we also become better readers of Vergil. If I wanted a rationale, I would start there. But I have thoroughly enjoyed my time with these late antique poets, and their poems are well worth the trouble they take to understand.

---

25. On the fragmentations of late antique art and architecture, see Elsner 2000 and Hansen 2003.

❧ CHAPTER 1

Text, Interpretation, and Authority

In late antiquity, the readers of Christian scripture and of Vergil's poetry played a visible role in making meaning of the texts at their disposal. These readers of Vergil have often been charged with mindlessly yielding to a dogmatic belief in the poet's infallibility. Alan Cameron, for example, describes the explanatory notes of Servius and Macrobius as misguided attempts at defensive criticism, at saving Vergil from the charge of ignorance (2011, 590–94). But in describing their canonical texts as deeply meaningful, Augustine, Macrobius, and others made room for their own creative and positive interpretations. At the same time, late antique writers lent importance both to the work of exegesis and to the status of secondary authors. In this chapter, the construction of the culture's canonical works and the rise of a literature whose fundamental concern was the interpretation of that canon will serve as indexes to mark the privileged status of reading in late antiquity. Once this privileging of reading has been established, the cultural significance of Macrobius's or Augustine's exegesis will become evident. Rather than focus on the social or material conditions of reading in late antiquity, I approach reading as a literary activity. In this regard, I have benefited from the work of Joseph Pucci, who has shown that both Macrobius and Augustine legitimate the reader's involvement in the text (1998, 51–82). I build on his results in order to show that this legitimation is one of the ways in which late antique authors came to reflect upon the importance of their reading. Because the textual reverence of late antiquity conceals a powerful turn toward appropriation, the reader's role became more significant as the classical canon became more distant from the contemporary world.[1] Further, by construing writing itself as an act of reading, Macrobius and Jerome provided a theoretical basis for the reader's involvement in the text. I will begin with the exegetical programs of Jerome and Augustine before turning to the more literary reception of Vergil, in particular by Macrobius and especially in the *Saturnalia*.

⬥ Jerome and Augustine on the Interpretation of Scripture

Augustine wrote carefully about how and why he read the scriptures. Although he sometimes embraced the reader's free participation in making sense of the text, he also set strict limits on the proper interpretation of scripture. While Augustine admitted the reader's ability to understand something other than the author's intended meaning, the somewhat elder Jerome emphatically sought to restore the text's original sense. Both authors valued the work of reading. Jerome focused on the depths of scripture and on the writing of commentaries; his example will serve as a foil to Augustine's more theoretical focus.

⬥ Jerome and the Writing of Scriptural Commentary

Jerome was already famous as a scholar, commentator, and translator of the scriptures within his lifetime (c. 347–420).[2] A concern for historical context and for the literal interpretation of scripture was fundamental to his exegesis.[3] Although he drew on earlier Greek and Hebrew scholars (especially Origen), Jerome was an original thinker.[4] And despite his fondness for historical philology and a concomitant disdain for what he saw as

---

1. For an excellent study of textual reverence in general and of the grammatical fragmentation of classical texts in particular, see Chin 2008.

2. For a comprehensive study of Jerome and the scriptures, see Jay 1985. D. Brown 1992 and M. H. Williams 2006 consider Jerome's scholarship; Cain 2009 considers Jerome's self-fashioning in his letters, including that of his role as an exegete.

3. See M. H. Williams 2006, 116–23; and Jay 2004, 1104–5.

4. M. H. Williams 2006, 73–95; and Vessey 1993.

overly rhetorical interpretation, Jerome described the scriptures as a mysterious text whose sense remained to be uncovered by the diligent reader.[5]

In a letter to Paulinus (soon to be) of Nola written in 394 and destined to be used during the Middle Ages as a preface to the scriptures, Jerome explains the contents and proper interpretation of the scriptures. He quotes Psalm 118:8 on the inner wisdom of the sacred text:[6]

> "revela," inquit David, "oculos meos, et considerabo mirabilia de lege tua"; lex enim spiritalis est et revelatione indiget, ut intellegatur ac revelata facie dei gloriam contemplemur.
>
> (*Ep.* 53.4)

> "Unveil my eyes," says David, "and I will consider the wonders of your law." For the law is spiritual and requires unveiling in order to be understood and for us to contemplate the glory of God in his unveiled appearance.

Jerome describes Christ as the divine Wisdom and as the one who holds the key to scripture's unveiling (*Ep.* 53.4–5). His description of scripture borrows explicitly from Psalm 118; it also alludes to Paul's description of the veil hanging over the Hebrew scriptures, a passage that was often quoted by Christian exegetes.[7] Although Jerome was not the only author to describe scripture in this way, he does give special emphasis, in a relatively short letter, to the need for revelation. And when Jerome goes on to give Paulinus a brief overview of each book of the Old and New Testaments, he pays special attention to the mysterious sense of each text. In particular, he accentuates the hidden wisdom of the Apocalypse of John:

> Apocalypsis Iohannis tot habet sacramenta, quot verba. parum dixi et pro merito voluminis laus omnis inferior est; in verbis singulis multiplices latent intellegentiae.
>
> (*Ep.* 53.9)

---

5. See Jay 2004, 1105–7. For a concise, recent study of Jerome's allegorical interpretation and his commentary on Galatians, see Raspanti 2009. On Jerome's ideal of a *prudens lector*, see M. H. Williams 2006, 235–40.

6. In *Ep.* 58.9 (also to Paulinus), Jerome quotes the same verse, compares the inner truth of scripture to the inner core of a nut, and specifies that the writings of the evangelists and apostles are also veiled.

7. 2 Cor 3:14: "usque in hodiernum enim diem idipsum velamen in lectione Veteris Testamenti manet non revelatum, quoniam in Christo evacuatur."

The Apocalypse of John has as many mysteries as words. I have said too little, and every praise is inferior to the book's merit. Multiple meanings lie hidden in individual words.

The concealed meanings of scripture appeal to Jerome, and for him, even single words do not have a simple meaning.[8] Rather, he tells Paulinus that the simplistic surface of the text conceals a further meaning. The surface is simple so as to appeal to the unlearned; the learned, for their part, will understand scripture in a deeper way.[9] For Jerome, the hidden meanings of scripture obligate the reader to interpret this text in more than its literal sense, and the authoritative text accepts and even requires its reader's active participation. In this way, even a literal-minded exegete like Jerome emphasized the mystical aspects of scripture. In so doing, he suggested that the reader's participation (and especially the commentator's expertise) were necessary in order to elucidate the mysteries of scripture.

Jerome, who described scripture as a mysterious text, made a literary career out of scriptural exegesis. He was a student of the grammarian Aelius Donatus, and in many ways, his numerous scriptural commentaries follow the pattern set by commentators on classical texts.[10] However, unlike earlier commentators, Jerome viewed exegetical writing as the highest form of literature. In so doing, he canonized an ideal of literature as exegesis and so lent weight to the work of reading.

In 392 or 393, Jerome wrote a work on Christian authors, *De viris illustribus*, modeled on Suetonius's work of the same name.[11] In his prologue, Jerome explains that his goal is to review "all those who have published anything memorable on the holy Scriptures" ("omnes qui de scripturis sanctis memoriae aliquid prodiderunt"). He begins with Peter and ends with himself. His list includes poets, bishops, and exegetes. Thus, in Jerome's arrangement, "writing on scripture takes many forms and arises in many different contexts," but "all Christian writing worthy of the name is writing on

---

8. On Jerome's acceptance of multiple interpretations (not to be equated with a systematic, fourfold interpretation of scripture) and on Origen as his predecessor, see Jay 1985, 330–33.

9. "Ut . . . in una eademque sententia aliter doctus, aliter audiret indoctus" (*Ep.* 53.10). Elsewhere, Jerome says that both senses are edifying for both learned and unlearned alike (Jay 2004, 1107–8).

10. On the similarity between Jerome's commentaries and their classical predecessors, see M. H. Williams 2006, 102–9. In a polemical context (*Adv. Ruf.* 1.16), Jerome claims the traditional commentators (including Donatus) as his model. For an excellent overview of scriptural commentary in late antiquity, see Pollmann 2009.

11. Jerome mentions Suetonius's work in the prologue to *De viris illustribus*. In *Ep.* 112.3, he says that the title of his work should be either *De viris illustribus* (as it is commonly known today) or *De scriptoribus ecclesiasticis*.

scripture."[12] The common thread in Jerome's stance toward reading and his ideal of Christian authorship is the scriptural and exegetical thrust of his own scholarship.

In a follow-up to letter 53, Jerome invited Paulinus to begin writing works of scriptural exegesis. Upon receiving a panegyric (no longer extant) that Paulinus wrote in honor of Theodosius, Jerome praises his addressee's eloquence, but he longs for the chance to train Paulinus in the scriptures rather than have him continue in the poetic and rhetorical training that he has already received.[13] If Paulinus learns to understand the scriptures, Jerome says, there will be nothing "more beautiful, more learned, or more Latinate than his works."[14] Because Jerome goes on to compare Paulinus to a series of prose authors (Tertullian, Cyprian, Victorinus, Lactantius, and Hilary), he seems to have intended Paulinus to write exegetical works in prose rather than Christian poetry.[15] Further, Mark Vessey (2007) has shown that Jerome appropriated for his own scholarship the Horatian ideal of laborious art. But in place of Horace's *ars poetica*, Jerome substituted an *ars scripturarum*, the art of interpretation (*Ep.* 53.6). As Vessey says, "This substitution was not to be the labour of a day or of a single pair of letters. It was Jerome's life work, the combined effect of all his literary exertions" (2007, 40). By constructing an ideal of literature as scriptural writing, Jerome made the work of reading the central task of any (Christian) author.

Jerome himself wrote voluminous commentaries on the scriptures,[16] and he insists upon his role as commentator. In the preface to book 3 of his commentary on Galatians, Jerome apologizes for the rhetorical simplicity of his writing, in order to insist on the generic difference of commentaries:

> sit responsum me non panegyricum, aut controversiam scribere, sed commentarium, id est, hoc habere propositum, non ut mea verba laudentur sed ut quae ab alio bene dicta sunt ita intelligantur ut dicta sunt. officii mei est obscura disserere, manifesta perstringere, in dubiis immorari. unde et a plerisque commentariorum opus explanatio nominatur.
>
> (*In Gal.* 3, prol.)

---

12. I quote Vessey 2002, 56, on whom I depend in this paragraph.

13. *Ep.* 58.8.

14. "Si haberes hoc fundamentum, immo quasi extrema manus in tuo opere duceretur, nihil pulchrius, nihil doctius, nihilque Latinius tuis haberemus voluminibus" (*Ep.* 58.9).

15. This is the view put forward by Vessey (2007).

16. For a good overview of Jerome's commentaries, see Jay 1985, 69–80.

I would reply that I am not writing a panegyric or a rhetorical exercise, but a commentary; that is, my aim is not for my words to be praised, but for the admirable words of another to be understood in the same way as they were spoken. It is my job to discuss what is obscure, to pass over what is obvious, to linger in doubtful places. For this reason, most people call the product of commentaries an explanation.

Jerome asserts elsewhere the generic difference of commentaries, and he also states that his aim is to set out the meaning of his author rather than to speak on his own authority.[17] There is no reason to doubt that other commentators had the same aim or to think that Jerome was the first person to realize that a commentary was different than a panegyric. But for Jerome, the unique qualities of a commentary reveal their special value within the world of scriptural literature, as outlined in his *De viris illustribus*. In short, Jerome emphatically describes his work as a commentary, and he views his adherence to the text of the scriptures as the mark of his own value as an author.

Jerome, therefore, stands as the ideal author-as-reader. He wrote monumental commentaries on the individual books of the Old and New Testaments, and he defined (Christian) literature as a form of writing essentially indebted to the scriptures. In Jerome, the autonomy of the author yields to an avowed dependence on the scriptures as a source. Far from presenting himself as an autonomous author free to write on whatever topic he should choose, Jerome confined himself to explaining scripture and its meanings. This move, however, was hardly a limit on his literary output; as a reader, he retained the role of interpreter and gatekeeper of the canonical text. Thus, in writing commentaries, Jerome made the work of interpretation the source of his significant literary authority.

☙ Augustine and the Reader's Involvement

Whereas Jerome portrayed individual scholarship as the key to scriptural exegesis, Augustine viewed interpretation as existing within communities.[18] He thought that readers should attempt to recover the intention of the individual authors of the sacred text, but he also celebrated scripture's ability to

---

17. See Jer. *In Soph.* 3.14–18 (*CC* 76a, 708.549–54); *In Ion.*, prol. (*CC* 76, 377.20–378.24); *In Zach.* 2.7.8–14 (*CC* 76a, 806.218–22); *In Ezech.* 12.40.44–49 (*CC* 75.587.1151–53); *In Eph.* 2, prol. (*PL* 26, 701a); *In Is.* 5, prol. (*PL* 24, 155A); *In Is.* 8, prol. (*PL* 24, 281B–C); *Ep.* 49.17.7; and *Adv. Ruf.* 1.16. These passages were collected by Lardet 1993, 78; and Jay 1985, 70–71.

18. On Augustine's semiotics, see Markus 1996.

contain multiple meanings.[19] This apparent contradiction derives from a radical skepticism toward the possibility of human communication, coupled with a delight in the act of reading.[20] The primary texts in which Augustine discussed the ambiguities of reading are chapters 10–13 of *De utilitate credendi*, book 12 of the *Confessions*, and books 2 and 3 of *De doctrina Christiana*. Brian Stock (1996) and Isabelle Bochet (2004b) have treated extensively the roles that the processes of reading and the scriptures played in Augustine's thinking.[21] Augustine's theory of reading enabled him to find various meanings in his authors' words, and it shows how he thought of his own activity as a reader. And although Augustine's comments on reading are not entirely restricted to his discussion of Christian texts, the creativity of his reading is fully theorized only in his reading of the scriptures.[22]

In *De doctrina Christiana*, Augustine says that readers of scripture seek the intention of its various authors as a means to discover God's intention. He presents this as the normal course of events.

> quam [scripturam] legentes nihil aliud appetunt quam cogitationes voluntatemque illorum a quibus conscripta est invenire et per illas voluntatem Dei, secundum quam tales homines locutos credimus.
>
> (*doc. Chr.* 2.6)

> In reading scripture, they seek nothing other than to discover the thoughts and intention of those by whom it was written, and through them the intention of God, according to which we believe those men to have spoken.

Elsewhere in *De doctrina Christiana*, Augustine prescribes a reading directed toward the author's intention.[23] He thinks that it is the safest approach and the one most conducive to obtaining an accurate knowledge of the text.

---

19. On Augustine's legitimation of the reader's activity in the text, see Pucci 1998, 69–82. On Augustine's multiple interpretations of scripture, see Moreau, Bochet, and Madec 1997, 558–62, with further references.

20. On Augustine's philosophy of language, see Ando 1994. On God's role in effecting the reader's understanding, see Bochet 2004b, 25–89.

21. On Augustine and the scriptures, see also the essays in Bright 1999 and Nauroy and Vannier 2008. Bochet 2004a reviews fifty years of scholarship on Augustine's hermeneutics.

22. In *De utilitate credendi*, Augustine suggests that any text can be read usefully. On Augustine's reading of the philosophers, see Bochet 2004b, 331–500, along with Brittain 2011, who rightly points out that Augustine never advocated an intentional misreading.

23. *Doc. Chr.* 1.40–41. See also *Util. cred.* 11.

Despite his insistence on seeking an author's intentions, Augustine allows that reading need not depend upon correctly recovering the author's thoughts. In chapters 10–11 of *De utilitate credendi*, Augustine discusses readings that are ethically justified even though they do not accurately reproduce the intentions of the author. Augustine describes these readings as mistakes (*errores*), from the point of view of the reader; from the perspective of the text, he describes them as useful applications. He explains as follows those interpretations that are wrong but useful:

> tertium [genus errorum] est, cum ex alieno scripto intellegitur aliquid veri, cum hoc ille qui scripsit non intellexerit. in quo genere non parum est utilitatis, immo si diligentius consideres, totus legendi fructus est integer.
>
> (*util. cred.* 10)

> The third type of error is when something true is understood from someone else's writing, even when the author did not understand it. In this kind there is no little utility. Indeed, if you consider it carefully, the whole profit of reading remains intact.

Augustine therefore leaves open the possibility of useful readings unrelated to an author's intentions. In this model, reading is an ethical activity whose final aim extends beyond the recovery of those intentions.[24] Although Augustine would try to understand his text in the same way as its author, he goes on to say that it can be quite difficult to understand an obscure text and that in such cases a reader is constrained to believe the author to have been a good person and, therefore, to interpret the author as intending an ethical meaning.[25] That is, when communication breaks down, the reader ought to understand an acceptable meaning.

In book 12 of the *Confessions*, Augustine goes beyond his suggestion in *De utilitate credendi*. In an extended reading of the first verse of Genesis, Augustine strongly implies that a proper reading of the scriptures need not recover the individual author's intentions. Instead, he lays out a series of acceptable interpretations. Responding to critics who would accuse him of reading

---

24. For a similar statement on interpretations of the scriptures, see *De doctrina Christiana* 1.40. There, Augustine says that readers who understand the scriptures as teaching love of God and neighbor in some other way than the author intended are "neither seriously mistaken nor in any way deceiving themselves" ("non perniciose fallitur nec omnino mentitur").

25. *Util. cred.* 11.

philosophical meaning into the creation account, Augustine states that sometimes, in reading the scriptures, the honest interpreter will arrive at a meaning authorized directly by God, even if his meaning is not the one imputed to the text by its human author.

> quid, inquam, mihi obest, si aliud ego sensero, quam sensit alius eum sensisse, qui scripsit? omnes quidem, qui legimus, nitimur hoc indagare atque comprehendere, quod voluit ille quem legimus, et cum eum veridicum credimus, nihil, quod falsum esse vel novimus vel putamus, audemus eum existimare dixisse. dum ergo quisque conatur id sentire in scripturis sanctis, quod in eis sensit ille qui scripsit, quid mali est, si hoc sentiat, quod tu, lux omnium veridicarum mentium, ostendis verum esse, etiamsi non hoc sensit ille, quem legit, cum et ille verum nec tamen hoc senserit?
>
> (*Conf.* 12.27)

> What, I say, is the problem if I understand it differently than someone else understands him who wrote it to have understood it? All of us who read aim to discover and comprehend that which he whom we are reading wanted to be understood. And when we believe that he was truthful, we dare not think him to have said anything which we know or suspect to be false. Provided, therefore, that each of us attempts to understand, in the holy scriptures, that which he who wrote them understood in them, what's the harm if he should understand that which you, o light of all true minds, show him to be true? What's the problem, even if that person whom he is reading did not understand this, since he understood some other truth?

Although Augustine thinks that authorial intent should be sought, in the end he suggests that the exegete should also bring to the text his own knowledge and direct enlightenment. Thus Augustine admits a plurality of subjective readings, provided they respect authorial intentions and align with the truth.

At *Confessions* 12.42, Augustine again suggests that there is no reason not to interpret scripture in multiple true ways. If he were Moses, says Augustine, he would want his readers to interpret every possible true meaning.[26] Therefore, he thinks it right to believe that Moses intended all these possible meanings.

> ego certe, quod intrepidus de meo corde pronuntio, si ad culmen auctoritatis aliquid scriberem, sic mallem scribere, ut, quod veri quisque

---

26. Augustine also imagines himself as Moses at *Conf.* 12.36.

de his rebus capere posset, mea verba resonarent, quam ut unam veram
sententiam ad hoc apertius ponerem, ut excluderem ceteras, quarum
falsitas me non posset offendere. nolo itaque, deus meus, tam praeceps
esse, ut hoc illum virum de te meruisse non credam. sensit ille omnino
in his verbis atque cogitavit, cum ea scriberet, quidquid hic veri potuimus invenire et quidquid nos non potuimus aut nondum potuimus et
tamen in eis inveniri potest.

(Conf. 12.42)

For my part—I say this boldly from my heart—if I were writing anything authoritative, I would prefer to write in such a way that my
words would echo with the bit of truth that each person would be able
to receive from these things, rather than putting one true thought
openly so as to exclude the others whose error would not offend me.
I would not, therefore, want to be so rash, my God, as to believe that
that man [Moses] did not deserve this from you. He certainly intended in these words and considered, as he was writing them, whatever truth we could find in them and whatever we could not find or
could not yet find but is nevertheless discoverable in them.

In this case, Augustine says he is constrained to think that Moses really did
intend all of the true meanings in his text. If he were an inspired author,
Augustine would want to write a text that was open to multiple interpretations. Therefore, for Augustine, reading a divine text means that interpretation is limited only by an exterior truth. And Augustine legitimates
his own reading of Genesis by crediting Moses with every possible true
meaning.[27]

Although Augustine warns against the danger of unguided interpretation,[28]
he also celebrates the text's ability to yield multiple interpretations. In the
Confessions, he interprets the command in Genesis to "increase and multiply"
as a command to understand and expound the scripture fruitfully, that is, in
multiple ways (*Conf.* 13.36–37). In *De doctrina Christiana,* Augustine celebrates
this multiplicity as a divine gift; for while he specifies that the interpretation
of ambiguous passages should be guided by what is not ambiguous, he is also
glad that they may be resolved in more than one way:

---

27. But he also assumes at *Conf.* 12.43 that Moses intended only one meaning and states that he has
and should have attempted to recover that meaning.

28. *Doct. chr.* 3.39. The first book of *De doctrina Christiana* establishes charity as the rule of Christian
interpretation. On the ancient practice of determining the meaning of a text before interpreting
individual passages, see Young 1997, 29–45.

nam quid in divinis eloquiis largius et uberius potuit divinitus pro-
videri, quam ut eadem verba pluribus intellegantur modis, quos alia
non minus divina contestantia faciant adprobari?

(doc. chr. 3.38)

For in divine communications what could God provide more gener-
ously and more richly than that the same words be understood in multiple ways, to which other, no less divine words should bear witness
and whose approval they should effect?

According to Augustine, the ability to find multiple meanings in scripture is
a gift provided by God.[29] And reading is a pleasurable activity; it provides the
mind opportunity not only for discovery but also for exercise.[30] Augustine,
therefore, was glad to see that multiple interpretations could each be authorized by different parallel passages.

Augustine presented the scriptures as a diverse and multifaceted text
whose realization depended upon the involvement of its reader. Although at
times he prescribed a literal reading of the author's intention, he viewed
obscure and ambiguous passages as a blessing of divine providence. By understanding the author to have intended all true meanings, Augustine gave the
reader room to interpret the text. The limits of his concern for the author's
intentions are an indication of the pressure applied to the text by contemporary readers. Rather than reject nonauthorial readings, Augustine accepts
that authoritative texts accumulate meaning as they are read.

Despite his acceptance of the reader's involvement, Augustine formu-
lated in *De doctrina Christiana* a series of prescriptive exegetical rules to guide
his readers' interpretations. As Tyconius, a fellow African of the previous
generation, had done in his *Liber regularum*, Augustine attempted to set limits upon the practices employed by contemporary readers.[31] The exegetical
treatises of Tyconius and Augustine are the first such works to survive in the
Latin tradition.[32] Because of the difficulty of understanding scripture and
because of the proliferation of interpretive approaches, each author attempted to provide a theoretical framework through which to interpret the

---

29. On *doc. chr.* 3.38 and Augustine's idea of God's interior illumination, see Bochet 2004b, 48–50;
and Fuhrer 2008.

30. *Doc. chr.* 4.9.

31. The rules offered by Tyconius and Augustine also, of course, enable readers to construct new
meanings from the text.

32. This does not seem to be accidental. Tyconius and Augustine are the earliest *introductores scripturae divinae* cited by Cassiodorus (*Inst.* 1.10), as noted by Pollmann (1996, 32n1).

scriptures. In constructing interpretive systems, Tyconius and Augustine sought to control the influence of their readers.[33] Their works, therefore, reveal both the theoretical sophistication of reading in late antiquity and also the perceived need for a limit upon the interpreter's influence.

The *Liber regularum* was written in or around 383.[34] In the first paragraph of the work, Tyconius says that he found it necessary to write a book of rules in order to devise keys to open and lights to illumine the secrets of scripture.[35] These keys will guide the reader through the immense forest of scripture ("prophetiae inmensam silvam") and away from heresy ("ab errore").[36] After his preface, Tyconius offers seven typological schemata, or "rules," by which to interpret scripture.[37] For example, the rule "De Domino et corpore eius" explains that the referent of a given passage may be either Christ or the church. Thus Tyconius says that the messianic prophecy in Isaiah 53 refers in some lines to Christ and in others to the Church.[38] By understanding that the text switches between two different referents, Tyconius avoids readings that had given rise to Christological or ecclesiological controversies, and his rules can be read as a defense of Donatist ecclesiology.[39] In order to clarify contested passages, Tyconius imposed a definite structure on the reading of the scriptures.

Some of Tyconius's rules ("De specie et genere," "De temporibus," and "De recapitulatione") were drawn from his presumed rhetorical education, and Karla Pollman has suggested that synecdoche is the master trope behind Tyconius's reading (1996, 61–65). In borrowing from the rhetorical tradition, Tyconius reversed the direction of such tropes, from the production of texts to their analysis.[40] Quintilian and other authors had already explored the value of rhetorical analysis for the understanding of both prose and poetic texts, but Tyconius's treatise is different insofar as it is wholly devoted to

---

33. On the role of Tyconius's and Augustine's exegesis in the fight against heresy, see Pollmann 1996, 4–33. Jerome's interpretations were more closely focused, and the limits that he placed on interpretation were imposed by his scholarly and historical method, as outlined in *Ep.* 53.7.

34. Jean-Marc Vercruysse (2004) has published an edition of the *Liber regularum* with notes in the series Sources chrétiennes. Camastra 1998 and Bright 1988 are interpretive monographs. Pollmann (1996) devotes a chapter to Tyconius's work, and Babcock 1989 provides an English translation.

35. "Necessarium duxi ante omnia quae mihi videntur libellum regularem scribere, et secretorum legis veluti claves et luminaria fabricare" (*Prooemion*, 1–3 [Vercruysse]).

36. *Prooemion*, 3–9 (Vercruysse).

37. On the term *regula*, see Pollmann 1996, 33–38.

38. I.3–7 (Vercruysse), with Camastra 1998, 25–35.

39. Vercruysse 2004, 70–82; and Camastra 1998, 260–64.

40. See Pollmann 1996, 56.

discovering the meaning of a single text. Whereas interpretation had previously been a by-product of rhetoric, Tyconius used it as a means to the end of exegesis.

De doctrina Christiana, which was begun around 396 but not finished until 426–27, was one of Augustine's most influential works.[41] It is divided into four books. The first defines love of God and neighbor as the limit of Christian interpretation; the second lays out Augustine's theory of signs and surveys the knowledge useful for decoding the scriptures; the third discusses ambiguity; and the fourth covers the *modus proferendi*, that is the rhetorical exposition of scripture. Augustine incorporates Tyconius's seven rules at the end of his third book (3.42–56); and in general, the scope of his work is broader than that of Tyconius's treatise. Unlike Tyconius, Augustine sought to provide a comprehensive guide to the use of scripture, in ethics, in interpretation, and in preaching. Moreover, Karla Pollman has argued that Augustine envisioned a universal hermeneutics in which one's interpretation of scripture came to play the predominant role in one's own rhetoric.[42] By centering his treatise around the individual's use of scripture, Augustine provided a theoretical manual for his Christian readers. In this way, his work both sets limits on the ideal reader and marks Augustine's interest in the individual's use of scripture.

Both Tyconius and Augustine wrote treatises on the proper interpretation of the scriptures, because there was a perceived need for hermeneutical guidance. Jerome had sought to fill that need with scholarly expertise instead of theoretical reflection. In part, this need for hermeneutical guidance was related to a desire to set limits on what counted as Christian orthodoxy.[43] But the interpretations of these Christian authors were also something more than constructions of orthodoxy. While Augustine offered guidance in *De doctrina Christiana*, he also celebrated the fact that scripture could have different meanings for different individuals. Therefore, even after one obtained the correct notion of Christianity, reading the scriptures was still not a simple or transparent process. Rather, authors continued to expend time and energy reflecting on how it was that they read.[44] As we will see, these

---

41. On *De doctrina Christiana*, see Pollmann 1996; Stock 1996, 190–206; the essays in Markus 1996; and Moreau, Bochet, and Madec 1997.

42. Pollmann concludes as follows: "Augustin setzt in seiner Auslegungstheorie Auslegung und Sprache in eins, Auslegung ist *der* christliche Gebrauch von Sprache par excellence" (1996, 248).

43. On the fourth-century construction of orthodoxy, see Vessey 1996 and Rebillard 2000.

44. On the Bible as the focus of Christian writing in late antiquity see now Fuhrer 2013.

readers of scripture shared with contemporary readers of Vergil both a focus on the indirect meanings of literature and an interest in their own role
as interpreters.

Macrobius and the Reading of Vergil

Late antique readers of Vergil interpreted the poet within their own cultural and literary framework. They justified their interpretive work by describing Vergil as the supreme poet. By viewing him through their own
lens, they gained a model for the literature they would write. Thus the
Saturnalia of Macrobius is both an interpretation of Vergil and a literary statement in its own right. In the *Saturnalia*, Macrobius creates a theory of
authorship that privileges reading, and in so doing, he justifies his own
appropriative reading of Vergil. For, as reading becomes rereading, Macrobius's reverence becomes a justification for his realignment of Vergil's aims
and methods.

In extending to Vergil allegorical methods of reading already applied to
Homer by Greek authors, late antique readers of Vergil brought to Latin
literature a whole series of interpretive possibilities. Therefore, their frequently elaborate praise of Vergil should be understood as enabling their own
work as interpreters rather than as misplaced or unfounded adulation. In this
way, the late antique transformation of Vergil legitimates the reader's role in
making sense of the text.

Macrobius on Authority and Imitation

Macrobius Ambrosius Theodosius wrote the *Saturnalia* probably in the 430s
and probably after *In Somnium Scipionis*.[45] In the *Saturnalia*, he collects earlier learning and describes Vergil as an imitator of Greek and Latin poetry.
In so doing, Macrobius valorizes secondary authorship.[46] By describing
writing as reception, Macrobius lends weight to his and others' reading of
classical literature. Thus Macrobius's literary reverence is a form of appreciation for the work of reading.[47] In the preface to the *Saturnalia*, Macrobius

---

45. For a concise explanation of this order and dating, see Cameron 2011, 231–39, who provides
further references on the dating of Macrobius's life and works.

46. On the structure and purpose of the *Saturnalia*, see Kaster 1980. On Macrobius and the reader's
role in identifying allusions, see Pucci 1998, 64–69.

47. On Macrobius's literary reverence, see Chin 2008, 54–60.

sets out his approach to writing, and throughout the work, his treatment of Vergil implies a theory of writing as imitation.[48]

Macrobius begins the *Saturnalia* with a preface addressed to his son, Eustathius. He explains that the work is meant as a compendium of learning for his son's use, and he defends his habit of borrowing from earlier authors (*Sat.* 1.1.1–4). Eustathius should not consider it a fault, Macrobius says, if he copies the ideas and even the exact words of earlier authors.[49] Immediately after this pronouncement, Macrobius borrows a series of thoughts from Seneca's *Epistulae morales* 84. In so doing, he reveals the scope of his explicit statement on secondary writing.

In letter 84, Seneca advised Lucilius that he should take breaks from writing in order to read, since reading will refresh his mind.[50] Seneca then compares his task to the work of bees, to the stomach's digestion, and to the harmony of a chorus: bees collect pollen from various sources, the stomach breaks down and resynthesizes its material, and a chorus produces a single sound from numerous voices.[51] Seneca concludes that an imitated work should resemble its model in the way that a son imitates his father. That is, the resemblance should not be too exact:

> Etiam si cuius in te comparebit similitudo quem admiratio tibi altius fixerit, similem esse te volo quomodo filium, non quomodo imaginem: imago res mortua est.
>
> (*Ep.* 84.8)

> Even if the resemblance in you of someone else is apparent, someone for whom your admiration lies quite deep, I want you to be similar like a son, not like an image: an image is a dead object.

For Seneca, reading provides the raw material from which the author will construct his own work. But to ensure its originality, the secondary work must not become a copy.

In his preface, Macrobius borrows each of Seneca's comparisons, often transposing whole sentences at a time. The central point of Macrobius's preface is that the compiler must make the borrowed material part of a new

---

48. On the preface to the *Saturnalia*, see Lausberg 1991, De Rentiis 1998, and especially Goldlust 2010, 67–86. On the importance of imitation in the *Saturnalia*, see Vogt-Spira 2009.

49. "Nec mihi vitio vertas, si res quas ex lectione varia mutuabor ipsis saepe verbis quibus ab ipsis auctoribus enarratae sunt explicabo" (*Sat.* 1.1.4).

50. "Alit lectio ingenium et studio fatigatum" (*Ep.* 84.1).

51. On Seneca's comparison, see Castelnérac 2007 and Henderson 2004, 46–48.

whole, but the borrowings also reveal his more circumspect approach to imitation:

> ex omnibus colligamus unde *unum fiat, sicut unus numerus fit ex singulis. hoc faciat noster animus: omnia quibus est adiutus abscondat, ipsum tantum ostendat quod effecit.*

> (*Sat.* 1.1.8)

> From all sides we should collect *what will be one, just as one number comes to be from other individual numbers. Let our mind do this: let it hide everything from which it is helped; let it reveal only that which it produces.*

In this passage Macrobius apparently endorses the classical view represented by Seneca, according to which the secondary author creates a work that is distinctly his own. To what extent does Macrobius actually hold this view? I would submit that Macrobius's understanding of literary appropriation only becomes clear when we compare his passage with its source in Seneca:

> adsentiamur illis fideliter et nostra faciamus, ut *unum* quiddam *fiat ex* multis, *sicut unus numerus fit ex singulis* cum minores summas et dissidentes conputatio una conprendit. *hoc faciat animus noster: omnia quibus est adiutus abscondat, ipsum tantum ostendat quod effecit.*

> (Sen. *Ep.* 84.7)

> Let us assent to them faithfully and make them our own, so that *one thing should come to be* from many, *just as one number comes to be from other individual numbers* when a single notation collects lesser and different sums. *Let our mind do this: let it hide everything from which it is helped; let it reveal only that which it produces.*

Although Macrobius does edit Seneca and although he does go on to borrow a different analogy from Calcidius's translation of the *Timaeus*,[52] his view of imitation differs drastically from that expressed by Seneca in his letter to Lucilius. For Seneca, imitation requires a change in the actual material: by reshaping his material, the author conceals the borrowing ("ipsum tantum ostendat quod effecit"). Macrobius, however, does not conceal anything; he produces a compendium that incorporates Seneca's exact material, but in a new way. Macrobius changes the frame rather than the picture. The novelty

---

52. The borrowing from Calcidius was pointed out by Lausberg 1991, 175.

of Macrobius's approach is that verbal reproduction does not preclude actual artistry; and Macrobius's reception of Seneca is a literary act because it effects a new reading of Seneca's letter. Whereas Seneca insists that the secondary author must reshape the material at his disposal, Macrobius allows him to blend his reading and writing into one whole.

Insofar as Macrobius follows Seneca's advice to create a new work that is a unified whole, he distances his compilation from Aulus Gellius's *Noctes Atticae*. Gellius wrote his miscellany during the second century CE, but everything we know about him has to be inferred from his collection of literary memorabilia.[53] In his preface, Gellius explains that he gathered this material at random and by chance ("indistincte atque promisce") so as to create a storehouse of learning ("litterarum penus").[54] Macrobius also intends to create a storehouse of learning,[55] but he emphasizes the unity and structure of his work. He uses the same phrase ("indistincte atque promiscue") to describe the collection of his material, but he does so in order to explain that he has made his material fit together like the coherent members of a body ("in ordinem instar membrorum cohaerentia convenirent").[56] Macrobius rejects Gellius's chance in favor of Seneca's coherence. The deliberate planning of Macrobius's compilation reflects his shaping of the material at his disposal. Thus using someone else's words does not, in Macrobius's view, preclude him from writing a coherent and artistic work.

The implicit theory of Macrobius's introduction is expressed in the *Saturnalia* through the participants' reverence for the past. Robert Kaster described the dynamic relationship between the characters of Macrobius's dialogue and their past in his article "Macrobius and Servius: Verecundia and the Grammarian's Function" (1980). As Kaster explains, Macrobius's characters have a reverence for antiquity that does not preclude self-confidence or even criticism.[57] And the purpose of the *Saturnalia* is to effect cultural and social continuity through the memory of the past. The *verecundia* of Kaster's title, therefore, consists of the "willingness to preserve [the] past, and blend it with the present, expressing due *reverentia* for *both*" (1980, 231). This *reverentia* is a form of reading that both accepts the input of one's *auctores* and allows for their renewal. That is, Macrobius endorses a theory of originality that takes full account of the importance of the transmission,

---

53. On Gellius, see Holford-Strevens 2003.

54. *NA*, praef. 2.

55. *Sat.* 1.1.2.

56. *Sat.* 1.1.3. Goldlust discusses Macrobius's appropriation of this phrase (2010, 71–73).

57. Kaster 1980, esp. 230–32.

tradition, and reception (in a word, the reading) of the past for any consciousness of the present.

As Kaster notes, Macrobius describes Vergil's imitation of Latin and Greek authors in terms of a confident respect for the past (1980, 231). Books 5 and 6 of the *Saturnalia* set out Vergil's relation to earlier Greek and Latin authors. In these books, the "competitive element," that is, "the ἀγών emphasized by both ancient and modern readers," is "entirely absent" (1980, 232). As Kaster explains, the competitive element in *imitatio* is neutralized by Macrobius's interest in continuity rather than conflict.[58] Macrobius's approach to Vergilian *imitatio* is neatly revealed in his description of the *Aeneid* as a mirror of Homer and in a discussion of Vergil's borrowing from Pindar.

The image of the *Aeneid* as a mirror appears in books 5 and 6 of the *Saturnalia*. In book 5, the character Eustathius expounds upon Vergil's knowledge of Greek literature. After naming some of Vergil's principal models (Theocritus, Hesiod, Homer), Eustathius begins to detail Vergil's borrowings from Homer, and he compares the *Aeneid* to a mirror:

> quid quod et omne opus Vergilianum velut de quodam Homerici operis speculo formatum est?
>
> (5.2.13)

> What about the fact that the whole of Vergil's work is shaped as a kind of mirror image of Homer's?[59]

In this view, the *Aeneid* is a kind of Roman Homer, designed to reproduce its Greek original. Most of book 5 goes on to compare Homer and Vergil. Sometimes Eustathius prefers Vergil's version, and sometimes he prefers Homer's, but the focus throughout is on the community of authors rather than on any struggle between individuals.[60] In book 6, Rufius Albinus recalls Vergil's Latin models, works whose memory Vergil preserved in his borrowing.[61] He says that he will cite first the verses borrowed directly by

---

58. Thus Kaster's point is not invalidated by the fact that discussions of *aemulatio* and of the relative merits of Vergil and his predecessors are present in the *Saturnalia*, as discussed by Goldlust (2010, 270–82).

59. I borrow here the Loeb translation of Kaster (2011), with slight modifications.

60. Thus Eustathius thinks that Vergil would not mind being unable to match his *auctor*'s work: "et quia non est erubescendum Vergilio si minorem se Homero vel ipse fateatur, dicam in quibus mihi visus sit gracilior auctore" (*Sat.* 5.13.1). In contrast, Gellius enjoyed Roman comedy only until he read its Greek sources (*NA* 2.23).

61. "Transferendo fecit ne omnino memoria veterum deleretur" ("by incorporating [their work] he made it so that the memory of the ancients should not be wholly lost" 6.1.5).

Vergil and then the ones that Vergil borrowed with modifications; he does so in order that his audience might "recognize the model after which its mirror image was formed."[62] By describing Vergil's work as a mirror of Greek and Latin literature, Macrobius privileges the interpretive work of imitation. Rather than as an *agon* between opponents, literary history is imagined as the re-presentation of earlier *auctores*.[63]

The difference between Macrobius's approach and other more competitive approaches to *imitatio* is neatly revealed in his discussion of Vergil's borrowing from Pindar, a discussion which is itself borrowed from Gellius. After Eustathius finishes discussing Vergil's imitation of Homer, he goes on to survey Vergil's knowledge of other Greek authors.

> videamus utrum attigerit et Pindarum, quem Flaccus imitationi inaccessum fatetur. et minuta quidem atque rorantia[64] quae inde subtraxit relinquo, unum vero locum quem temptavit ex integro paene transcribere, volo communicare vobiscum quia dignus est ut eum velimus altius intueri. *cum Pindari carmen quod de natura atque flagrantia montis* Aetnae *compositum est aemulari vellet, eius modi sententias et verba molitus est ut Pindaro quoque ipso, qui nimis opima* et *pingui facundia existimatus est, insolentior hoc quidem in loco tumidiorque sit.*
>
> (*Sat.* 5.17.7–8)

> Let us see whether he touched on Pindar as well, whom Horace confesses to be impossible to imitate. I will leave behind everything "small and dewy" that he drew from Pindar. There is one passage that I want to share with you, the whole of which he tried almost to copy, because it is worth looking at more closely. *When he wanted to imitate Pindar's poem, which concerns the nature and the burning of* Mount Aetna, *he fashioned his thoughts and words in such a way that in this passage he should be more unusual* and *more inflated even than Pindar himself, whose speech is thought altogether rich and altogether extravagant.*

---

62. "Ut unde formati sint quasi de speculo cognoscas" (6.2.1). I use here Kaster's Loeb translation (2011).

63. On the idea of an *auctor* as source and on Vergil as an imitator in Macrobius, see D. Kelly 1999, 55–59. Macrobius's interest in reception explains the phenomenon too easily disparaged by Curtius (1953, 444): "[Macrobius's] conception of Vergil is surprisingly similar in approach to the medieval conception of poetry. He feels that he is no longer sharing in a living literature but that he is the conserver and interpreter of a consummated tradition. For him the classics are already 'the Ancients.'" On the difference between living and dead languages, see Agamben 2010, 45–60.

64. The phrase "minuta atque rorantia" is borrowed from Cic. *Sen.* 46.

Eustathius continues with a comparison of *Pythian* 1.21–26 and *Aeneid* 3.570–77. Although he offers a straightforward assessment of Pindar's and Vergil's lines, Eustathius does not doubt that recognizing the Pindaric in Vergil will only increase his listeners' appreciation for the Roman poet. This is the point of his introductory comments. He focuses on imitation and borrowing, and he says that this passage is worthy of closer inspection. Because Eustathius views imitation as a form of respect rather than as a competition, he does not need to criticize either poet.

Macrobius's approach in this passage becomes even clearer when set against its source. In the *Noctes Atticae*, Gellius recalled that Favorinus once praised Vergil's work, but with a qualification: whatever Vergil had finished was of the highest quality, but he asked on his deathbed that the *Aeneid* be burned because some passages were not yet worthy of his name.[65] Favorinus singled out for censure this same passage, in which Vergil imitated Pindar's description of Mount Aetna. The same passage that Macrobius's Eustathius used to highlight Vergil's interaction with Greek poetry had been used by Gellius's Favorinus to show the poetic imperfection of the *Aeneid*. By changing how this passage was introduced, Macrobius shifted the tone and focus of the entire discussion.

> in his autem, inquit, quae videntur retractari et corrigi debuisse, is maxime locus est, qui de monte Aetna factus est. nam *cum Pindari* veteris poetae *carmen quod de natura atque flagrantia montis* eius *compositum est aemulari vellet, eiusmodi sententias et verba molitus est ut Pindaro quoque ipso, qui nimis opima pinguique esse facundia existimatus est, insolentior hoc quidem in loco tumidiorque sit.*
>
> (*NA* 17.10.8)

> But in these, he said, which seem to have needed to be gone over again and corrected, an especial case is the passage concerning Mount Aetna. For *when he wanted to imitate* the ancient poet *Pindar's ode, which concerns the nature and the burning of* this *mountain, he fashioned his thoughts and words in such a way that in this passage he should be more unusual and more inflated even than Pindar himself, whose speech is thought altogether rich and altogether extravagant.*

Whereas Macrobius introduced this comparison as an example of Vergil's knowledge of Greek poetry, Gellius uses the same description to reject what

---

65. This is also the view of Macrobius's Evangelus, which we will come to presently.

he sees as Vergil's inferior poetry. Because they view imitation differently, the same words and the same description are quite different in each of their texts.[66] In Macrobius's conception of literature, tradition is quite as important as originality, and so the quintessential Roman poet serves as a gateway to ancient Greek and Latin literature.

By describing Vergil as a looking glass, Macrobius lends full weight to the ideal of writing as an act of reception. And by privileging Vergil's secondary poetics, Macrobius lends credibility to his own reading of the classical poets. For in Macrobius's view, writing is virtually inseparable from reading. Thus the *Saturnalia* celebrates the active participation of readers. They are essential to the preservation of any literary tradition, and authors are expected to be readers before they turn to writing their own texts. Rather than being viewed as passive reception, the reader's participation is an artistic and creative act of renewal. In this way, Macrobius envisions active reading as fundamental to any literary activity.

✒ Interpreting Vergil in Late Antiquity

Macrobius's notion of writing as reading lends a theoretical depth to late antique interpretations of Vergil's poetry. In late antiquity, Vergil came to be interpreted as containing all wisdom, in ways similar to how Homer had already been interpreted by Greek authors writing under the Roman Empire.[67] Domenico Comparetti, the nineteenth-century Italian scholar, misunderstood this phenomenon when he described late antique readers approaching Vergil's poems as though they were a puzzle waiting to be solved: "The art of the greatest of Roman poets seemed to these people a mystery, the clue to which could only be found in vast and recondite learning. Hence it was considered a sure proof of refined taste and superior erudition to be able to discover hidden in his verses scientific dicta and profound philosophical doctrines of every kind."[68] Whereas Comparetti considered these discoveries evidence of cultural decline, I take them as an index of the

---

66. On the role of context in determining the import of identical words, compare Jorge Luis Borges's famous character Pierre Menard, who sought to compose an early twentieth-century version of *Don Quixote*. Borges understood that the same words can be entirely different in a new context.

67. On the interpretation of Homer, see Struck 2004, Lamberton and Keaney 1992, and Lamberton 1986.

68. Comparetti 1997, 73. This edition is a reprint of the English translation of Comparetti's *Virgilio nel medio evo* with a new introduction by Jan Ziolkowski.

period's interest in the transitive power of interpretive reading. They mark a shift from authorial to readerly habits of interpretation and thus conceal the creativity of late antiquity under the guise of simple exposition.

While Homer had already been read as a divine poet, totalizing readings of Vergil—that is, allegorical interpretations that treat Vergil as a compendium of all learning—seem not to appear before the fourth century.[69] Thus both Seneca the Younger and Quintilian treat Vergil as the supreme Latin poet, but neither treats his poems as a profound text in need of universal interpretation. Seneca the Younger, in his *Epistulae morales*, contrasts two approaches to Vergil: the grammarian's and the philosopher's. Neither approach is allegorical.[70] The grammarian reads "fugit inreparabile tempus" (G. 3.284) and notes that Vergil uses the verb *fugere* every time he speaks of time's swift passing. The philosopher reads the same words and remembers the brevity of his own life.[71] In the same letter, Seneca gives a general plea for the ethical reading of poetry.[72] However, he gives no indication that either philosophers or grammarians were reading Vergil for abstruse, nonethical wisdom.[73] Quintilian, in the *Institutio oratoria*, compares Vergil to Homer, but he does not praise the two poets in the same terms. Homer is the "model and source of every part of eloquence."[74] Quintilian praises at length the marvelous qualities of Homer's work and asks whether it does not in fact exceed the measure of human genius.[75] For Quintilian, Vergil

---

69. For the reception of Vergil, Ziolkowski and Putnam 2008 and Courcelle 1984 are marvelous compendia. Rees 2004 collects a series of essays on Vergil in the fourth century. Zetzel 1981 and Timpanaro 2001 provide different views of Vergil's ancient textual critics.

70. Therefore Ziolkowski and Putnam (2008, 463) are wrong to group this passage with several others from Macrobius and Servius as treatments of "Virgil as philosopher and compendium of knowledge." Seneca offers only a philosophical reading of the poem and does not introduce a separate, allegorical meaning.

71. Sen. *Ep.* 108.24–25.

72. "Illud admoneo, auditionem philosophorum lectionemque ad propositum beatae vitae trahendam, non ut verba prisca aut ficta captemus et translationes inprobas figurasque dicendi, sed ut profutura praecepta et magnificas voces et animosas quae mox in rem transferantur" (*Ep.* 108.35).

73. In *Dial.* 10.9.2, Seneca introduces a quotation from Vergil with the words "clamat ecce maximus vates et velut divino ore instinctus salutare carmen canit." The word *velut* is essential. The verse introduced, which is on the brevity of life, is also quoted in *Ep.* 108. In both passages, it is read for its ethical content.

74. "Omnibus eloquentiae partibus exemplum et ortum dedit" (*Inst.* 10.1.46). Pseudo-Plutarch had already developed this view in his *Essay on the Life and Poetry of Homer*, on which see Keaney and Lamberton 1996.

75. "Quid? in verbis, sententiis, figuris, dispositione totius operis nonne humani ingenii modum excedit?" (*Inst.* 10.1.50).

was a Roman Homer; he was the second-greatest poet and the one who gave Latin poetry its beginning ("ut apud illos Homerus, sic apud nos Vergilius auspicatissimum dederit exordium, omnium eius generis poetarum Graecorum nostrorumque haud dubie proximus").[76] Their qualities, however, are distinct. Vergil's excellence is in his *labor*:

> Et hercule ut illi naturae caelesti atque inmortali cesserimus, ita curae et diligentiae vel ideo in hoc plus est, quod ei fuit magis laborandum.
>
> (*Inst.* 10.1.86)

> I swear, just as we yield to [Homer's] heavenly and immortal character, so is there more attention and diligence in [Vergil], because he had to work harder.

In the early empire, Vergil was the supreme Latin poet, but readers had neither mined his text for deeper wisdom nor treated it as a compendium of learning. These steps were taken in the fourth and early fifth centuries.

Tiberius Claudius Donatus—not to be confused with the famous grammarian Aelius Donatus who wrote commentaries on Terence and Vergil—wrote a lengthy rhetorical commentary on the *Aeneid* for his son, probably in the second half of the fourth century.[77] He treated the *Aeneid* as a compendium of rhetorical learning.[78] Although Claudius Donatus describes only the literal sense of the *Aeneid* and does not give physical or philosophical allegories, he claims that the work is a special text written in praise of Aeneas and, therefore, that it ought to be explained by rhetors rather than grammarians.[79] He counters criticisms of Vergil's poetry by claiming that all difficulties will be removed if only one remembers that Vergil's intention was to praise Aeneas, and he contrasts his own position with that of those who think Vergil's intention was "to take up some inner knowledge or philosophy as if he were its advocate" ("ut aliquam scientiae interioris vel philosophiae partem quasi adsertor adsumeret"). However, in the following sentence Claudius Donatus claims that the praise of Aeneas is so wonderfully composed that every kind of learning comes together in it and that

---

76. Quint. *Inst.* 10.1.85. Before Vergil's death, Propertius had already compared the *Aeneid* to the *Iliad*: "cedite, Romani scriptores; cedite, Grai: / nescioquid maius nascitur Iliade" (*Carm.* 2.34.65–66).

77. Murgia dates this commentary to between 363 and 395 because it draws from Aelius Donatus's commentary and because Claudius Donatus speaks of sacrifices in the present tense (2003, 47–48).

78. On Claudius Donatus's commentary, see Pirovano 2006 and Starr 1992. On the importance of epideictic rhetoric under the empire, see Pernot 1993.

79. *Interpretationes Vergilianae* 1.2.7–25 and 1.4.24–28.

from it one may learn everything necessary for life and action.[80] Indeed in the preceding paragraphs, he has already said that Vergil has shown himself a most skillful teacher ("peritissimus doctor") and useful for all sorts of people, including sailors, fathers, sons, husbands, wives, commanders, soldiers, citizens, patriots, those interested in religion and divination, and those who find themselves in various ethical dilemmas (1.5.4–24). Claudius Donatus does not think that Vergil was a philosopher, but he does think that the poet touches on all topics and is useful for all readers. Thus, although he presents himself as a more rational interpreter than some other contemporaries, Claudius Donatus asserts that the *Aeneid* is universal in scope. By reading the *Aeneid* as a storehouse for learning, he validates his own desire to search in the poem for rhetorical techniques and for every kind of rhetorical meaning. In this way, he shows the power of a universal reading of the *Aeneid*.

The grammarian Servius, who was born around 360 and probably wrote his commentaries on Vergil before 410, reads Vergil's poems as containing profound allegorical meanings.[81] In order to justify such readings, Servius's predecessor Donatus had called Vergil a divine poet and stated that he always touched on some truth.[82] While Servius implicitly accepts Donatus's opinion of Vergil, he usually focuses on the text itself and its multiple possibilities. In a brief preface to his commentary on book 6 of the *Aeneid*, Servius makes his understanding of the *Aeneid* explicit:

> Totus quidem Vergilius scientia plenus est, in qua hic liber possidet principatum, cuius ex Homero pars maior est. et dicuntur aliqua simpliciter,

---

80. "Interea hoc quoque mirandum debet adverti, sic Aeneae laudem esse dispositam, ut in ipsam exquisita arte omnium materiarum genera convenirent. quo fit ut Vergiliani carminis lector rhetoricis praeceptis instrui possit et omnia vivendi agendique officia reperire" (1.6.13–17).

81. On the date of Servius's birth, see Cameron 2011, 239–41; Kaster (2011, 1:xxxi) has renounced his earlier opinion that Servius was not born until the 370s. Murgia tentatively dates the commentary to before 410 (2003, 61–64). On Servius's career, see Kaster 1988, 356–59; on the social and intellectual context of Servius's work, see Kaster 1988, 169–97; on his teaching of Latin, see Uhl 1998; on the lack of a pagan agenda in Servius's commentary, see Cameron 2011, 567–626; for a detailed introduction to the context of Servius's work, see Pellizzari 2003; on Servius's allegorical interpretations, see Jones 1961.

82. The *DS* commentary *ad Aen.* 3.349 notes that what many take as fiction is supported by better geographic knowledge and then concludes: "unde apparet divinum poetam aliud agentem verum semper attingere" ("from this it is clear that the divine poet always touches on the truth, even when he is engaged in some other matter"). On the relation between the *DS* recension (a compilation dated to the seventh century) and the commentaries of both Donatus and Servius, see Goold 1970, 102–21. For a statement of Vergil's method similar to that given by Donatus, see Macrob. *Sat.* 3.4.5 ("suo more velut aliud agendo implet arcana"). Where it is impossible to determine whether Servius was following an earlier commentary, I credit him with the formulation given in his commentary because, like Macrobius, Servius borrows extensively but always constructs his own whole.

multa de historia, multa per altam scientiam philosophorum, theologo-
rum, Aegyptiorum, adeo ut plerique de his singulis huius libri integras
scripserint pragmatias.

(Ad Aen. 6, praef.)

Although all of Vergil is full of knowledge, in that category this book
has pride of place. The greater part of it is from Homer. And some
things are said directly, many things are about history, many others are
said through a profound knowledge of the philosophers, the theolo-
gians, and the Egyptians, to such an extent that many people have
written entire treatises about these individual aspects of this book.

Servius expects to find deeper meanings in his text, and that is exactly what
he does.[83] When Deiphobus asks Aeneas whether he came to the underworld because he was driven off course or because the gods told him to do
so ("pelagine uenis erroribus actus / an monitu diuum?"),[84] Servius says that
there are two ways of interpreting the first half of the question. In the first
interpretation, Deiphobus does not ask how Aeneas got to the underworld,
which is within the earth, but rather how Aeneas arrived at the entrance to
the underworld. The second interpretation finds a deeper meaning:

alii altius intellegunt: qui sub terra esse inferos volunt secundum cho-
rographos et geometras, qui dicunt terram sphaeroeide[85] esse, quae
aqua et aere sustentatur.

(Ad Aen. 6.532)

Others understand this more deeply: they want the ones below [<i>infe-
ros</i>] to be under the Northern Hemisphere,[86] in accordance with the
geographers and geometers, who say that the earth is spherical and
that it is supported on water and air.

On this reading, the <i>inferi</i> live in the Southern Hemisphere, and Aeneas really could have visited them by ship. This deeper reading understands Deiphobus's question as a covert allusion to Vergil's geographical learning.

---

83. Although Servius can also attribute what he sees as flaws in the <i>Aeneid</i> to its unfinished publication, as in his comment <i>Ad Aen.</i> 1.565. He also distinguishes at times between Vergil's use of words
and the usage that was "correct" in his own time (Kaster 1988, 169–97).

84. <i>Aen.</i> 6.532–33.

85. For the spelling of <i>sphaeroeide</i>, see Pelttari 2011a.

86. I do not know of any example of <i>sub</i> where the word means "on the other side of." I think,
therefore, that it is likely that <i>terra</i> in this first clause refers (illogically) to the Northern Hemisphere.

At times, Servius interprets the text of the *Aeneid* on multiple levels.[87] Rather than simply giving his reader various options on how to interpret the text, he also accepts some multiple meanings.[88] In his commentary on the twin gates of sleep, Servius gives for the passage intertextual, poetic, physiological, and oneiric interpretations. Thus Servius says first (*Ad Aen.* 6.893) that Vergil has followed Homer ("est autem in hoc loco Homerum secutus")— with the appropriate qualification that Homer has all dreams pass through the gates of both horn and ivory, whereas Vergil has the true dreams pass through the gate of horn but the false ones pass through the gate of ivory. Next, Servius says that the poetic sense is obvious ("poetice apertus est sensus"): Vergil wants his description of the underworld to be understood as fictional.[89] Then, there is a physiological sense ("physiologia vero hoc habet"): Horn is associated with the eyes, ivory with the mouth; false dreams pass through the gate of ivory because what we say with our mouth is less reliable than what we see with our eyes. Servius introduces his final interpretation as a further meaning ("est et alter sensus"). Those who have written about dreams say that those dreams which are likely to come true are associated with horn, whereas those dreams that are more extravagant than believable resemble ivory (because ivory is an extravagant material). Servius also accepts multiple meanings for other passages,[90] but this is the most extensive interpretation that he offers. Because Servius views the *Aeneid* as a profound work containing different sorts of learning, he accepts multiple interpretations of the text. In this way, he extends his reading of the *Aeneid* beyond the literal interpretations offered by earlier traditions. Thus the elevation of Vergil's text prepares the way for the supplemental readings that he proposes.

By the early fifth century, Vergil's authority had increased to such a point that in his commentary on the *Somnium Scipionis* Macrobius says the poet was free of all error. As Vergil came to be read as the source of Roman culture, he came to play the role that Homer had once filled for Roman as well as Greek literature. Macrobius consistently finds in Vergil a source of great learning and profound wisdom. In the *Saturnalia*, the symposiasts' authoritative reading of

---

87. Though he also at times rejects what he sees as superfluous allegories, e.g., *Ad Ecl.* 1.1 and 3.47.

88. Starr (2001) rightly takes the options presented by ancient commentators as revelatory of the reader's role in constructing the text. However, I am showing here that in some cases, late antique readers admitted a text's ability to contain multiple, noncontradictory meanings. In Greek, Porphyry had already interpreted Homer on multiple levels; see Lamberton 1986, 120–21.

89. For this understanding of Servius's "vult autem intellegi falsa esse omnia quae dixit," see Pollmann 1993, 244–47.

90. E.g., *Ad Aen.* 4.58, 4.244, and 6.719.

Vergil is explicitly contrasted with the character Evangelus's nonallegorical reading. And in his *In Somnium Scipionis*, a revealing digression offers several ways to save Vergil—whom Macrobius says was never wrong—from an apparent mistake. Rather than being a reflex of his unimaginative reverence for Vergil, Macrobius's reading of Vergil's poetry should be understood as an active and constructive approach to the past. For by treating Vergil as the most learned Roman poet, Macrobius created a literature to match the Greek interpretations of Homer's poetry.[91]

In the *Saturnalia*, the character Evangelus provokes the banqueters' discussion of Vergil by expressing his skepticism about their reading habits.[92] In book 1, Praetextatus gives a long speech explaining how the different gods are reflexes of the sun god Apollo. His speech occupies the first morning of the *Saturnalia*, when Macrobius's band of noble Romans has just begun to celebrate the holiday with learned conversation. Although the rest of the group is amazed by the speech and praises Praetextatus's memory, learning, and religion, the uninvited and uncouth Evangelus intrudes and accuses Praetextatus of misusing Vergil:

> equidem . . . miror potuisse tantorum potestatem numinum comprehendi; verum quod Mantuanum nostrum ad singula, cum de divinis sermo est, testem citatis, gratiosius est quam ut iudicio fieri putetur. an ego credam quod ille, cum diceret "Liber et alma Ceres"[93] pro sole ac luna, non hoc in alterius poetae imitationem posuit, ita dici audiens, cur tamen diceretur ignorans? nisi forte, ut Graeci omnia sua in immensum tollunt, nos quoque etiam poetas nostros volumus philosophari.
>
> (*Sat.* 1.24.2–4)

> I myself am impressed that you could comprehend the power of such great divinities; but as for the fact that you cite our Mantuan as a witness to details, when the discussion is on the divine, this is more a pleasant thing than something that could be thought discerning. Or should I believe that when Vergil said "Liber and kind Ceres" in place of "sun" and "moon," he did not do this in imitation of another poet, hearing it said in this way but not knowing why it was so?

---

91. On Macrobius's use in *In Somnium Scipionis* of Porphyry's Homeric exegesis, see Setaioli 1966.

92. On the character Evangelus, see Cameron 2011, 253–54; Kaster 2011, 1:xxxiii–xxxiv; and Goldlust 2010, 231–32.

93. *G.* 1.7.

Unless, perhaps, we also want our poets to philosophize, just as the Greeks treat all of their own literature as profound.

Evangelus reads Vergil as a poet indebted to other poets rather than as a theologian or philosopher, and he explicitly compares Praetextatus's reading of Vergil with the Greeks' reading of their own poets (Orpheus and Homer come readily to mind). When Symmachus asks whether Evangelus thinks Vergil suitable only for educating children or whether he thinks that he contains something deeper ("instituendis tantum pueris idonea iudices, an alia illis altiora inesse fatearis"),[94] Evangelus replies that Vergil would not have asked for the *Aeneid* to be burned if he had not known that it was flawed (*Sat.* 1.24.6). After Evangelus laughs at Symmachus's suggestion that Vergil was an orator no less than a poet, Symmachus finally realizes that Evangelus believes Vergil intended his work only as poetry ("Maro tibi nihil nisi poeticum sensisse aestim[a]tur").[95] The poetic sense is all that Evangelus accepts, and he reserves the right to criticize Vergil even on that level. Symmachus and the rest of his group are shocked, and they respond with a spirited defense of their poet.

Macrobius introduces Evangelus into his dialogue in order to explain and defend the interpretive methods of his group. To begin this defense, the character Symmachus accuses Evangelus of reading Vergil like a child at school.[96] Further, he quotes a letter from Vergil to Augustus in which the poet excuses the delays in the writing of the *Aeneid* as being caused by the various difficult studies to which he has turned.[97] Then, in a pivotal passage, Symmachus says that Vergil's excuse to Augustus is confirmed by the contents of his poem. Because the *Aeneid* is a profound text, Symmachus earnestly objects to the merely "grammatical" reading of Vergil:[98]

> nec his Vergilii verbis copia rerum dissonat, quam plerique omnes litteratores pedibus inlotis praetereunt, tamquam nihil ultra verborum explanationem liceat nosse grammatico. ita sibi belli isti homines certos

---

94. *Sat.* 1.24.5.

95. *Sat.* 1.24.8–10.

96. *Sat.* 1.24.5: "videris enim mihi ita adhuc Vergilianos habere versus qualiter eos pueri magistris praelegentibus canebamus."

97. *Sat.* 1.24.11: "de Aenea quidem meo, si mehercle iam dignum auribus haberem tuis, libenter mitterem, sed tanta inchoata res est ut paene vitio mentis tantum opus ingressus mihi videar, cum praesertim, ut scis, alia quoque studia ad id opus multoque potiora impertiar."

98. On the status of grammar in late antiquity, see Kaster 1988.

scientiae fines et velut quaedam pomeria et effata posuerunt, ultra quae
si quis egredi audeat, introspexisse in aedem deae a qua mares absterren-
tur existimandus sit. sed nos quos crassa Minerva dedecet non patiamur
abstrusa esse adyta sacri poematis sed arcanorum sensuum investigato
aditu doctorum cultu celebranda praebeamus reclusa penetralia.

(Sat. 1.24.12–13)

And the abundance of Vergil's subjects does not disagree with these
words of his.[99] Almost all the teachers pass by this abundance with un-
washed feet, as though a grammarian were not allowed to know anything beyond the interpretation of words. So those fine men have set
certain limits to their knowledge, as if it were some civic or religious
boundary. And if anyone should dare to pass beyond it, they are treated
as though they looked into the sanctuary of the goddess from which
men are banished. But we who disdain rude Minerva should not allow
the holiness of this sacred poem to be hidden; rather, let us allow the
inner place to be thrown open by investigating an approach to its secret
meanings, so that it may be celebrated by the veneration of learned men.

Symmachus could hardly make his point any clearer. He believes that Vergil
contains profound wisdom that the group ought to search out. Attention is
also drawn elsewhere in the *Saturnalia* to the hidden, deep, or profound
meaning of Vergil,[100] and this investigation of deeper meaning does seem to
have been Macrobius's preferred method of reading Vergil. He takes the side
of Symmachus against Evangelus in order to uncover the further layers of
Vergil's text.

After Symmachus explains his approach to Vergil, he proposes that the
group expound together the poet's profound wisdom. Symmachus will treat
rhetoric in Vergil, but he leaves oratory to Eusebius (*Sat.* 1.24.14). Praetextatus promises to show Vergil's knowledge of religion; Flavianus volunteers to
discuss augury; Eustathius will cover Greek poetry, astrology, and philosophy;
the Albini, Rufius and Caecina, take Vergil's antiquarianism; Avienus and
Servius are set to cover whatever falls between the cracks (*Sat.* 1.24.16–20).
And although there are significant lacunae in the extant text, each character
does go on to discuss his topic in the course of the work.[101] Vergil's manifold
wisdom is on full display, and it allows each participant to expound his own

---

99. That is, the letter from which Symmachus has just quoted.

100. *Sat.* 1.3.10, 1.17.2, 3.2.7, 3.2.10, 3.4.5, 3.7.1, and 3.9.16.

101. Kaster provides a helpful overview of the *Saturnalia*'s structure (2011, 1:il–liii).

wisdom through Vergil.[102] Moreover, the idea that Vergil is experienced in every discipline is repeated elsewhere in the *Saturnalia* and also in *In Somnium Scipionis*.[103] Thus, although the *Saturnalia* claims to be a description of Vergil's learning, it is actually a compendium of Roman culture. Macrobius's authoritative reading of Vergil provided him with the structure for his work.

The result of Macrobius's elevation of Vergil's poetry can be seen in a discussion of *Georgics* 1.237–39 from *In Somnium Scipionis*. In those lines, Vergil says that the zodiac passes through both temperate zones ("per ambas"). However, Macrobius has just shown that the zodiac actually never passes beyond the uninhabited torrid zone bounded by the tropics. Since Macrobius says that Vergil was never involved in any error ("Vergilius, quem nullius umquam disciplinae error involvit"),[104] he must search for an explanation for this apparent lapse. He offers two options: Vergil exaggerated; or Vergil wrote one preposition for another, as Homer often does.[105] Though Macrobius is not entirely satisfied with these options, he expresses his confidence that someone else could find a suitable solution:

> nobis aliud ad defensionem ultra haec quae diximus non occurrit. verum quoniam in medio posuimus quos fines numquam via solis excedat, manifestum est autem omnibus quid Maro dixerit, quem constat erroris ignarum, erit ingenii singulorum invenire quid possit amplius pro absolvenda hac quaestione conferri.
>
> (*In Somn.* 2.8.8)

> I cannot think of anything else in his defense beyond what I have said. But since I have shown what limits the path of the sun never crosses and since it is clear to all what Vergil said (whom we agree knew no error), it will be up to the ingenuity of each of us to find what else could be brought forward to resolve this question.

Because Vergil's texts are agreed to be inerrant, Macrobius thinks that there is an explanation for this apparent error. In the various explanations that he offers, he borrows Greek habits of reading Homer and applies them to

---

102. In response to Praetextatus's speech on religion in Vergil, the group equates Praetextatus's learning with that of Vergil: "omnes concordi testimonio doctrinam et poetae et enarrantis aequa[ba]nt" (3.10.1).

103. *Sat.* 1.16.12 ("omnium disciplinarum peritus"), *In Somn.* 1.6.44 ("nullius disciplinae expers"), and *In Somn.* 1.15.12 ("disciplinarum omnium peritissimus").

104. *In Somn.* 2.8.1.

105. *In Somn.* 2.8.2–7. Macrobius suggests that Vergil used *per* in place of either *sub* or *inter*.

Vergil's text. This passage shows most clearly that the exaltation of Vergil created the need for vigorous interpretation.

As we have seen, Macrobius imagined Vergil as a source of profound learning in both of his major works. Because Macrobius described Vergil as more than a poet, his own role as an interpreter came to be increasingly significant. Thus the exaltation of Vergil authorizes the *Saturnalia*'s expansive reception of Vergil. This point is neatly confirmed by Macrobius's creative commentary on Cicero's *Somnium Scipionis*.[106] In his *In Somnium Scipionis*, Macrobius idiosyncratically treats Cicero as an author who concealed wisdom beyond the literal meaning of his words.[107] It is surprising for a modern reader acquainted with Cicero's lucid prose to find Macrobius suggesting that he disguised his learning, but Macrobius's treatment of Cicero allowed him to write his own extremely ambitious commentary.[108] He ends his commentary by celebrating the perfection of the *Somnium Scipionis*. Cicero, he says, included in his narrative the three divisions of philosophy: the political aspects of Scipio's dream are ethical; details related to the cosmos describe the secrets of physical philosophy ("physicae secreta"); and the discussion of the motion and immortality of the soul ascends to the heights of rational philosophy ("ad altitudinem philosophiae rationalis ascendit").[109] The final sentence of Macrobius's commentary justifies his work:

> vere igitur pronuntiandum est nihil hoc opere perfectius, quo universa philosophiae continetur integritas.
>
> (*In Somn.* 2.17.17)

> Truly, therefore, it must be said that nothing is more perfect than this work, in which is contained as a whole the entirety of philosophy.

By reading Cicero's text as containing all of philosophy, Macrobius allows himself to treat all of philosophy within the limits of his commentary.[110] In

---

106. Favonius Eulogius (a Carthaginian and a student of Augustine) had also written a treatise on two aspects of Cicero's *In Somnium Scipionis* (its numerology and the harmony of the spheres), but he does not devote the same level of attention to Cicero's text as Macrobius does.

107. At *In Somn.* 2.12.7, Macrobius makes this explicit: "et quia Tullio mos est profundam rerum scientiam sub brevitate tegere verborum, nunc quoque miro compendio tantum includit arcanum quod Plotinus, magis quam quisquam verborum parcus, libro integro disseruit." Plotinus's treatise is *Ennead* 1.1.

108. We should also remember, however, that Augustine thought Cicero concealed Platonic wisdom within his Academic philosophy, on which see Brittain 2011, 84–89.

109. *In Somn.* 2.17.15–16. On the division of philosophy, see Hadot 1979.

110. This desire for perfection motivates the organization of Macrobius's commentary into two books of eight and seven sections each because this division mirrors the numerological perfection

the same way in which the *Saturnalia* treats the *Aeneid* as a compendium of Roman learning, *In Somnium Scipionis* treats Cicero's text as a compendium of philosophy. In both works, Macrobius increases his own status as reader by treating his author as a profound source of wisdom.

To sum up, the reading of Vergil's text as containing deeper wisdom was a significant act of appropriation performed by late antique readers. This shift was a strong act of reading, and it authorized readers to continue to look for and find further mysteries in Vergil. Allegorical interpretation proceeded from the late antique reader's desire to make Vergil meaningful. Therefore, although Comparetti was right that late antique readers sought to discover hidden learning in Vergil's verses, they did not really think his art a mystery. Rather, they were sure that their own goal was to expound a poetry whose aims seemed altogether familiar; they were more interested in seeing what they could make of Vergil than they were in adhering to the letter of his text.

⮞ A Shared Approach to Reading

Jerome and Macrobius described literature as a kind of meditation on preexistent texts. In this way, they legitimized the influence of strong readers on canonical texts. That is, they offered theoretical standing for the interpretive activity of their contemporaries. In approaching a series of diverse texts from late antiquity, I have shown that these works were shaped by the idea of reading as a strong and influential act. While I would not want to suggest that there were no differences between the particular uses of scriptural and poetic texts, the late antique turn toward reading is manifest in a number of similar ways in contemporary approaches to both the scriptures and Vergil's poetry. Readers lavished time and energy on extensive commentaries. They sought to recover hidden and secondary meanings beyond the plain or literal sense of the text. They interpreted their texts as the single source of all (relevant) learning. Rather than disparage or downplay their reliance on earlier texts, late antique authors gladly acknowledged their debt to the past. And rather than assert their prominence as authors, these writers pointed to the importance of reading in their own formation. They expected their readers to appreciate that their interpretations of the classics were actually shaping the tradition. In these ways, reading came to play a

---

of Scipio's age at the time of his death. Nino Marinone was the first modern reader to observe the numerological arrangement of the commentary (1990, 371–75).

constituent role in the literature of late antiquity, whether one read Vergil or the Christian scriptures. Moreover, in retrieving meanings for their texts, late antique readers called into question any simple relation between the written text and its proper meaning as the very richness of their texts led them to value their interpretations alongside the text's literal or surface meaning. Thus Augustine valued God's direct revelation in addition to the human author's original intention. Moreover, although they were interpreting their texts in new ways, these readers did not disregard their authors; rather, they celebrated their authors' wisdom and learning. Whenever they were not sure what the author intended, they first assumed that the author had to have been correct and then tried to understand in the text the meaning that made sense of their author. To have any hope of plumbing these depths, such readers would have to actively engage their texts. Therefore, the focus in late antiquity on authoritative texts conceals the reader's involvement in devising their particularly late antique reception.

❧ CHAPTER 2

Prefaces and the Reader's Approach to the Text

In late antiquity, prefaces played a significant role in mediating the presence of their texts. Jerome provides a vivid image for the function of prefaces. He does so within an explanation of Psalm 1, which was traditionally described as a preface to the whole book of Psalms.[1] He compares the Psalms to a large house with many rooms: each individual room has a door and a key (its title), and the house as a whole has one door (Psalm 1) and one key.[2] Thus Jerome imagines this preface as a *limen*, the boundary that both restricts and grants the reader access to the book. By creating an external space through which the reader approaches the text, a preface can permit, engage, or even forestall possible readings. Since Psalm 1 is the key that unlocks the meaning of the whole book, whoever understands that psalm will be able to understand the rest of the book. Thus Jerome explicitly describes the role played by prefaces in the mediation of textual meaning. Although authors earlier than Jerome employed prefatory material of various kinds, contemporary poets fully exploited the preface's paratextual potential. In so doing, they complicated any easy approach to the text.

---

1. For the titles of individual psalms and the part they played in exegesis, see Schröder 1999, 196–98. For Psalm 1 as a preface, see Jerome, *Commentarioli in Psalmos* (*CC* 72), 1; Origen, *Exegetica in Psalmos* (*PG* 12, 1080); and Hilarius, *Tractatus super Psalmos* (*CC* 61), "Instructio Psalmorum," 24.

2. Jerome, *Tractatus in Psalmos* (*CC* 78) 1.1.

Jerome's insight suggests that authors in late antiquity were aware of the importance of their prefaces. The extant prefaces to late antique poetry are paratexts, a category first defined by Gérard Genette in *Seuils* (1987; translated in 1997 as *Paratexts: Thresholds of Interpretation*). As Genette observes, texts are never found in the abstract; rather, they are read within an apparatus, a physical text, a series of markers, such as the name of the author, a title, or illustrations (1987, 7). As the name implies, a paratext is not actually part of the text. Rather, the paratext is precisely that which allows the text to be read as it exists "pour le *présenter*, au sens habituel de ce verbe, mais aussi en son sens le plus fort: pour le *rendre présent*, pour assurer sa présence au monde, sa «réception» et sa consommation, sous la forme, aujourd'hui du moins, d'un livre" (1987, 7). Insofar as a preface enables its text to be read, the preface becomes literary, despite the fact that prefaces often appear trite and hackneyed. As Genette puts it, "[L]a préface est peut-être, de toutes les pratiques littéraires, la plus typiquement littéraire, parfois au meilleur, parfois au pire sens, et le plus souvent aux deux à la fois" (1987, 270). In presenting their texts, prefaces declare that those texts are not self-explanatory, that they must be read and understood within a particular framework. And because the paratext establishes a liminal zone, it speaks to the reader more directly than does the text itself. For these reasons, the paratext is a privileged site of interaction between a text and its readers. Nevertheless, Genette described the preface as aligned with the author's subjectivity: "La plus importante, peut-être, des fonctions de la préface originale consiste en une interprétation du texte par l'auteur, ou, si l'on préfère, en une déclaration d'intention" (1987, 205). Because it stands apart from its text, a preface creates space both for the reader and for the author: the author, as if he were a reader, describes the meaning of his text; the reader finds in the preface a separable lens through which to view and understand the text. Thus prefaces enrich the reading of a text. They are often retrospective, written after the text: they grant it the quality of having been already read. Therefore, I will suggest that prefaces make sense when they are directed towards an audience interested in the creation of poetic meaning.

Genette's theory has shed new light on ancient practice, although Genette himself wrongly thought that authors and scribes could not distinguish text from paratext in a manuscript and, therefore, that significant paratexts were not to be found until after the introduction of the printing press.[3]

---

3. Genette 1987, 9 and, for the absence of prefaces in particular, 152–58. See also Rigolot 2000, where the (Renaissance's) development of the paratext is similarly linked to the emergence of literary subjectivity. Laurenti and Porqueras-Mayo 1971 is a helpful bibliography of prefaces in the

But even apart from prefaces, a series of other paratextual guides were employed in both late and classical antiquity.[4] At times, authors even commented directly on the apparatus of their texts; thus Ausonius claimed that the only thing he liked about his *Cupido cruciatus* was its title ("mihi praeter lemma nihil placet").[5] Although text and paratext were even more unstable then than they are now,[6] ancient authors did plan the presentation of their works; and they did append to them separate prefaces.[7]

In defining his topic, Genette distinguishes between the paratext per se and introductory material directly incorporated into the body of a poem. Thus the epic proem, in use since Homer, is both theoretically and actually distinct from the paratextual preface. Whereas the proem approaches complete assimilation to the continuous text, the preface stands apart and comments upon that text. In a preface, the author speaks in propria persona, rather than as "the poet" (i.e., the *ego* of "arma virumque cano" is the poet; the *ego* of "ille ego qui" is Vergil). In late antiquity, preface and proem stood side by side. Thus the epics of Claudian and Prudentius begin first with prefaces and then with separate proems constructed along traditional lines.[8] This doubling of introductory material makes it clear that for these poets the paratext operates differently from prefatory proems located within the strict boundaries of the text. Otherwise, the preface would be redundant

---

classical and vernacular literatures, although the field has seen a resurgence of interest since Genette 1987.

4. Fredouille et al. 1997 is a series of studies on ancient paratexts (not specifically poetic). Gutzwiller (2005) and Grafton and Williams (2006) discuss, respectively, the new Posidippus papyrus and the books of Eusebius and Jerome. Schröder 1999 is a thorough study of titles and other headings in Latin literature. Late antique illustrations of Vergil survive in both the Codex Vaticanus and the Codex Romanus; and Helen Woodruff (1930) has argued on stylistic grounds that illustrations of Prudentius's *Psychomachia* descend from a fifth-century archetype. Baraz 2012 studies Cicero's construction of philosophy in the prefaces to his philosophical works. I have not seen Jansen 2014.

5. Auson. *Cupido, Ausonius Gregorio filio sal.* Compare *Mart.* 14.2, in which the poet says that he has provided lemmata to the epigrams in this book so that the reader may skip the verses and read only the titles.

6. See Starr 1987, "The Circulation of Literary Texts in the Roman World."

7. On the various labels ascribed by the manuscripts to the prefaces of Claudian, see Felgentreu 1999, 59–66: *praefatio* is the most common title, followed by *prologus* and *prooemium*. Because paratexts were unstable even after the invention of the printing press, the fact that various manuscripts present different titular formulae should not call their basic authority into question. In any case, there can be no doubt about the first poem of Commodian's *Instructiones*, which is an acrostic that spells out the word *praefatio*.

8. For the distinction between preface and proem, compare Felgentreu 1999, "*Praefatio* und Proöm," 13–18. Raffaele Perrelli's otherwise helpful study *I proemi Claudianei: Tra epica ed epidittica* (1992) is vitiated by its failure to distinguish between Claudian's prefaces and his proems (see Felgentreu 1999, 10–12).

when followed by a proem. Because it is the distance of the paratext that makes room for an active reader, I focus in this chapter on those late antique prefaces that are fully paratextual.[9]

Rather than circumscribe himself within a closed text, the late antique poet freely admits the constraints on his authority and willingly engages the permeable limits of his poetry. A paratextual preface both addresses the reader from beyond the text itself and also allows the poet to authorize his own reading of a poem: a paratextual preface is at one and the same time both open and authoritative. In late antiquity, Claudian and Prudentius developed earlier prefatory forms into their own distinctly paratextual prefaces. Moreover, Ausonius wrote a variety of prefaces in verse and in prose, and he did so in such a way as to complicate the reading of his works. Though earlier poets had also written prose prefaces, Ausonius's prefaces directly confront the author's ambiguous link to his own work. We can see, therefore, that for late antique poets, these prefaces served to negotiate the active involvement of their readership.

The prefaces to late antique poetry reveal what was new about these poems, but they were not themselves entirely new. Although Augustan poetry is noticeably devoid of prefaces, both republican and post-Augustan poets used a variety of prefaces to introduce their work. In the following pages, I will draw a distinction between poetry that elides its own context and poetry that calls attention to its circumstances. This distinction gives us one way of defining classical and postclassical poetry. By considering the use of prefaces in earlier Latin poetry, I will both describe the various functions of these prefaces and also situate them within the tradition of Latin poetry. In various forms and in different ways, a number of Latin poets included prefatory material along with their work. Borrowing in some ways from their predecessors, Ausonius, Claudian, and Prudentius anticipated, in their prefaces, the gap between a written text and the subsequent process through which it would be read. Before coming to the use of prefaces in the fourth century, I will first describe a framework through which we can understand the traditional context in which the presence or absence of paratexts came to be significant.

---

9. Thus I do not discuss the introductory sections of either Juvencus's *Evangeliorum libri quattuor* or the *Cento Probae*. Although some of the manuscripts label these sections *praefationes*, they are in dactylic hexameter and more like proems than prefaces. The distinction between paratext and preface is, of course, ultimately unstable; nevertheless, the poles of the dichotomy are recognizable enough.

❧ Prefaces and Postclassical Poetry

Classical poets do not use prefaces; postclassical poets use prefaces to situate their work within a particular, ephemeral context. A classical text is timeless, set apart from the realia surrounding its original composition. Thus Horace proclaims his poetry a "monumentum aere perennius" (*Carm.* 3.30.1).[10] A postclassical text admits that it is secondary, that it can be read only within and against a certain framework. Of course, the categories "classical" and "postclassical" are contingent, contestable, and always determined by context.[11] Nevertheless, these two terms describe strategies according to which authors could and did construct their work in antiquity. And the choice to write prefaces or not is one way to trace the shifting tides of ancient poetry. Thus Vergil, Horace, and Propertius began their poems at the first line, without any authorial intrusion.[12] However, Catullus, Ovid (at least in the *Amores*), Persius, and Martial employed brief prefatory poems at the head of their books; to some degree, they eschewed classical poetics. In comedy, Plautus had employed prologues more freely than Greek playwrights, and Terence further distinguished his prologues from the dramatic action of the play. And although earlier poets had not done so, Martial and Statius used prose prefaces to introduce individual books of poetry. Thus it is possible, in various traditions of Latin poetry, to trace a movement from texts for which prefaces are either absent or unimportant to texts that are emphatically introduced by their prefaces. In this limited sense, we can say that Augustan poetry was classical and that post-Augustan poetry was postclassical.[13]

Since comedic prefaces were performed on the stage, they are not paratexts in exactly the same way as poetic prefaces. Nevertheless, their development at Rome reveals a trend toward the contextualization via preface of the literary work. And in any case, by the fourth century the prologues of Plautus and Terence were primarily read rather than performed.[14] Through their prologues—*prologus* is the name both for a prefatory speech and for

---

10. Oliensis 1998 surveys the ways in which Horace constructed an authorial persona, at times confidently and at other times more tentatively.

11. On the classicisms of antiquity, see the essays in Porter 2006.

12. Because they, like proems, are indistinct from the text itself, I exclude from consideration here the textually incorporated dedications that are common in classical poetry. For example, Horace addresses Maecenas at the beginning of his *Epodes*, *Carmina*, *Sermones*, and *Epistulae*.

13. It could have been otherwise. *Don Quixote*, the literary masterpiece of the Spanish Siglo de Oro, begins only after eleven epigrams, a preface, and a separate dedication.

14. Thus Ausonius advises his grandson to read ("perlege") the works of Menander and Terence (*Protr.* 45–60).

the specific character who came to deliver such speeches—Plautus and Terence presented a distinct character who offered commentary on the play and its production.[15] In Greek comedy, prologues were spoken either by a god or by a character from within the play. Although Plautus elsewhere uses prologues featuring gods and characters, in eight of his plays he employs a character *prologus* whose only role is to introduce the play from the outside as it were. Terence uses only this latter form of prologue, and he turns it into a forum for the author's polemical and metapoetic commentary.[16] Whereas other prefaces tend to blend into the play that follows, the *prologus* is set apart from the mimesis of the play and offers insight into its production.[17] Thus Plautus's prologue to the *Menaechmi* begins with a play on the poet's introduction:

Salutem primum iam a principio propitiam
mihi atque vobis, spectatores, nuntio.
apporto vobis Plautum, lingua non manu,
quaeso ut benignis accipiatis auribus.

(1–4)

Now first do I announce by way of beginning, spectators,
A kindly greeting for me and for you.
I bring you Plautus, by tongue and not by hand,
And ask you to receive him with kindly ears.

In this prologue, Plautus's ironic detachment marks his presentation of the play. Terence, however, is the one who fully develops this detachment and focuses on the circumstances of his play's performance rather than the background of his narrative.[18] For example, the manuscripts give two separate prologues to the *Hecyra*, which correspond to the playwright's second and third attempts to stage the play.[19] By distancing his prologues from the following mimetic productions, Terence created a space in which to attack his rivals and to defend himself. In his prologue to the *Eunuchus*, Terence ad-

---

15. On comedic prologues, see Raffaelli 2009, 13–125. For a study of the individual prologues of Plautus, see Abel 1955.

16. On the character *prologus* from Plautus to Terence, see Raffaelli 2009, 53–67.

17. Compare ibid., 59.

18. See ibid., 61: "Per riassumere con una formula, si può dire che mentre il prologo di Plauto è legato strutturalmente alla commedia, quello di Terenzio è legato non alla commedia, ma all'occasione teatrale, ad una specifica rappresentazione della commedia e soltanto a quella."

19. On a comparable prologue interpolated into Plautus's *Casina* for a performance of the play a generation after its original composition, see ibid., 60–63.

dresses a rival playwright who accused him of plagiarizing from Naevius and Plautus.[20] Terence denies that he even knew those earlier Latin plays, says that he borrowed instead from Menander, points out that comedy plays on stock characters, and concludes that poets always borrow from one another ("nullumst iam dictum quod non dictum sit prius").[21] Terence, therefore, turned the prologue into a statement on the play's production and presentation.[22] He did so after Plautus had introduced the *prologus* as a character distinct from the action of the play, which allowed him to write self-reflexive prologues. As Roman comedy negotiated its standing in relation both to its Greek past and its Roman present, Plautus and Terence innovated with prologues that would define their plays and win over their audiences.

Poets in antiquity used epigrammatic prefaces to introduce either an individual poem or a collection of poetry.[23] Although Catullus 1 is not an epigram per se, it introduces the poet's *libellus* as a Hellenistic (i.e., *lepidus*) book of poetry and dedicates it to Cornelius Nepos. While Catullus's hendecasyllabic poem situates his book within a particular context and before a particular audience, the meter and the manner of this poem reduce the paratextual distance between it and the poems to follow; that is, Catullus 1, like many other poems in this collection, is brief, learned, directed to a specific recipient, and personal. Catullus 65, however, is remarkable for introducing a single poem rather than a book or collection of poetry. In elegiac couplets, Catullus tells Hortalus that grief over the death of his brother has taken the Muses away from him; in his grief, Catullus sends to Hortalus a translation from Callimachus. Catullus 66 is then the poet's version of Callimachus's elegy on the lock of Berenice. Catullus 65, therefore, is a distinct introduction to the poem that follows. It is worth noting that both of Catullus's prefatory poems are directly linked to Hellenistic poetry.

Propertius and Tibullus began their elegies without introduction, but Ovid included a prefatory epigram at the head of the revised edition of his *Amores*.[24] In two elegiac couplets, Ovid allows his work to speak for itself ("Qui modo Nasonis fueramus quinque libelli, tres sumus"). Since the poet

---

20. On this prologue and Terence's relation to earlier comedy, see M. Fontaine 2013.

21. *Eun.* 41.

22. As a neat confirmation of the paratextual character of Terence's prologues, Raffaelli describes their transmission in the fourth- or fifth-century Codex Bembinus (2009, 110–25; for a full discussion, see Raffaelli 1980). In the manuscript, these prefaces are centered across two pages, with space remaining at the top and bottom of each page; the play begins on the following page, with normal spacing.

23. For a full survey of the various prefaces to Latin literature, see Felgentreu 1999, 39–57.

24. On this epigram, the personification of books, and epigrammatic prefaces in Greek poetry, see McKeown 1987–1998, 2:1–4.

has reduced the size of his work, he says that it will now be less of a bother to his readers. This witty preface creates space for the poet's ironic commentary on his *Amores*. Although it is a brief four lines, Ovid uses this preface to create his own persona and to explain why he has revised the *Amores*.

For his individual books, Martial wrote a number of prefatory epigrams. Thus Martial's book 1 begins (after a prose epistle) with four separate prefatory poems. The first poem of book 1 addresses the reader and celebrates the poet's fame ("toto notus in orbe Martialis").[25] The second poem offers directions on where to purchase Martial's works.[26] The third poem addresses the book and says that it would be safer for it to stay at home than to take to the open air ("aetherias volitare per auras"). The fourth poem addresses the emperor and declares that the poet's playful epigrams do not reflect the author's morality. By returning in multiple prefaces to the publication and reading of his epigrams, Martial draws attention to the particular context of his work. Even in this respect, however, Martial's prefaces are inseparable from the subsequent series of epigrams. The one blends into the other, and the distinction between text and paratext is not so strong as in Ovid's *Amores*.

If the fourteen choliambs of the Neronian satirist Persius are a preface,[27] the *Saturae* is the earliest example of a book of Latin poetry introduced in a meter set off from the rest of the work. The difference of meter is important, because it formally marks the limits of the paratext. Whereas there is no evidence that earlier satirists introduced their work in any comparable way, Persius offers a discrete commentary on the poetry that he has written. The author's preface is programmatic in that Persius rejects the poetics of Hesiod, Callimachus, and Ennius and then praises the role of poverty in compelling poets to sing.[28] The metrical distance of Persius's preface allows him to construct his own satiric persona, and to give that persona authority within the text. Once again, an imperial poet uses a preface to situate himself against an earlier tradition and within a particular cultural moment.

In addition to verse prefaces, imperial poets also wrote prefaces in prose, usually in epistolary form and directed to a specific recipient, but sometimes

---

25. Martial's epigrams often address their reader directly (e.g. 1.1, 1.2, 1.113, 2.8, 5.16, 10.2, and 13.3). Fitzgerald (2007, 139–66) discusses the various audiences of Martial's poetry and argues that Martial created for Rome the idea of an anonymous reader.

26. On the materiality of Martial's poetics, see Seo 2009.

27. One branch of the manuscript tradition places these lines after Persius's *Saturae*. Kissel, who thinks that the choliambs are in fact a preface, treats the question in detail in his commentary (1990).

28. See Reckford 2009, 52–55.

addressed to the general reader.[29] Archimedes introduced the epistolary preface to Greek literature, and the earliest extant and explicitly epistolary prefaces in Latin are from Seneca the Elder.[30] Quintilian mentions prefaces written by Seneca the Younger and Pomponius Secundus and concerned with tragic diction; therefore, these were presumably prefaces to their tragedies and in prose.[31] Although Terence's prologues are unexpected, it is even more surprising that imperial drama should have been introduced in prose. Yet prose prefaces to drama were common enough for Martial to present them as natural in comparison with his own prose prefaces.[32] Further, Suetonius quotes a few words from a preface written by Lucan that may have been in prose, although the fragment could also be metrical; in any case, it is unclear what work it would have introduced.[33] Book 10 of Columella's *De re rustica* provides a Vergilian treatment of horticulture and is introduced by an epistolary preface in prose. And Statius mentions an epistolary preface to the *Thebaid*, although that preface is no longer extant.[34] The only early imperial prose prefaces to survive introduce the *Epigrams* of Martial and the *Silvae* of Statius.

Martial uses epistolary prose prefaces to introduce books 1, 2, 8, 9, and 12 of his *Epigrams*. The epistolary preface to book 1 is addressed to the general reader rather than to a specific dedicatee.[35] In this preface, Martial acknowledges that epigrams are scurrilous and urges his reader not to be offended.[36] He ends his preface by comparing those who disapprove of his poetry to Cato the Younger, who attended the Floralia only to express his disapproval. Then Martial says that he will close his letter in poetry ("epistulam versibus clusero"): in four choliambs, he addresses "Cato" directly and asks

---

29. For an overview of prose prefaces to Latin literature, see Janson 1964. For a survey of prose prefaces up to Statius, see Johannsen 2006, 26–35. For prose prefaces to poetry from Statius to Ennodius, see Pavlovskis 1967. For a thorough study of Martial and Statius's prose prefaces, see Johannsen 2006.

30. See Janson 1964, 19–22 and 49–50, for Archimedes and Seneca, respectively.

31. Quint. *Inst.* 8.3.31, on which see Felgentreu 1999, 15.

32. In the prose preface to book 2 of his epigrams, Martial presents Decianus as being puzzled: "video quare tragoedia aut comoedia epistolam accipiant, quibus pro se loqui non licet: epigrammata curione non egent."

33. Suet. *Vita Luc.* (Reifferscheid, p. 50, 6–9); and, for the scholarship, Felgentreu 1999, 48–49.

34. Stat. *Silv.* 4, praef.: "Maximum Vibium et dignitatis et eloquentiae nomine a nobis diligi satis eram testatus epistola, quam ad illum de editione Thebaidos meae publicavi."

35. Some of the manuscripts give as a title "Valerius Martialis lectori suo salutem." Johannsen concludes that Martial's other epistles, like this one, are meant for the general public even though they are epistolary in form (2006, 238–39).

36. For a literary reading of this letter, see Fitzgerald 2007, 71–73.

why he would attend festivities that he could not enjoy, that is, why any humorless reader would open a book of epigrams. By concluding his preface in verse, Martial closes the gap between his prefatory epistle and the epigrams that are to follow. The preface to book 2 takes up the very impropriety of an epigrammatist writing in prose; Martial addresses his friend Decianus's question of why he is writing a prose preface and ends with the observation that the length of this letter will do the reader a favor, by boring him before he even gets to the epigrams.[37] The preface to book 8 dedicates that book to Domitian and reveals that, on account of his dedicatee, Martial will be more circumspect in this book than an epigrammatist would normally be. At the beginning of book 9, a short, extra-sessional epigram ("epigramma quod extra ordinem paginarum est") is introduced by a brief letter to Toranius.[38] The epigram and its introduction are notable both because they stand outside the normal order of the book and because the epigram was written to accompany a statue of its author and addresses the reader in the vocative. The preface to book 12 explains to Priscus why Martial has returned to Spain and has not published a new volume of epigrams in three years. In his prefaces, therefore, Martial provides a context in which to read his epigrams, but he uses them in only five books and indicates that they are a novel device. Their role is to offer a frame and a context in which to understand the poet and his work.

Each of the five books of Statius's *Silvae* is introduced by an epistolary preface in prose and addressed to the dedicatee of the book.[39] The prefaces to books 1–4 catalog the contents of each book,[40] while the epistle to Abascantus at the head of book 5 introduces only the first poem in that book.[41] Because Statius's prefaces catalog and explain the contents of each book, they are an important guide for their reader. They set out the relations of the poems to their dedicatee and to their original context.[42] Further, the preface to book 1 defends Statius's decision to publish the *Silvae*, on the grounds that Homer and Vergil both wrote lighter poetry (the *Batrachomyo-*

---

37. On this preface and Martial's ideal of *brevitas*, see Borgo 2001.

38. Johannsen (2003) argues that "extra ordinem paginarum" means that the letter was appended to the outside of the book scroll. Fitzgerald thinks that the letter was placed inside the book but at its head (2007, 150–52).

39. Newlands 2009 provides an excellent review of Statius's prefaces.

40. Pagán 2010 explores the importance of the literary catalog for Statius and Pliny the Younger.

41. For the likelihood that *Silv.* 5 was published posthumously and that Statius never wrote a proper preface to the book, see Gibson 2007, xxviii–xxx.

42. Rühl 2003 explores Statius's construction, via publication, of a literary context for what was originally occasional poetry.

machia and the *Culex*, respectively). Thus Statius uses his preface to present his work as in line with the lighter side of classical poetry.

In sum, Latin poets had long employed a series of paratextual prefaces to guide the reader into their poetry. Plautus and Terence wrote self-referential prologues, and republican and imperial poets wrote epigrammatic prefaces. In the first century CE, epistolary prose prefaces began to be written, in some cases in addition to separate epigrammatic prefaces. Comic prologues became more distinct from their plays as the tradition of Latin comedy developed; and the epigrammatic prefaces of Catullus, Ovid, Martial, and Persius describe, to varying degrees, the contingent character of their works. While there were Hellenistic precedents for these epigrammatic prefaces, the prefaces of Ovid and Persius were attached to books of elegiac love poetry and satire, genres that were developed only at Rome and did not, in earlier cases, include prefaces. In their prose prefaces, Martial and Statius rejected a classical poetics in favor of a more layered sense of the text's production and reception. In each of these cases, prefaces became more pronounced as the tradition turned toward a more explicit concern for introducing and mediating the text before its audience. In that sense, these paratextual prefaces are postclassical: Each of them draws attention to the space between its text and the tradition to which it belongs. Each of them situates that tradition within its own poetic moment and thus provide a subjective view of the following poem(s). In surveying these prefaces, I have shown that earlier Latin prefaces had always sought to complicate the presentation of the text. Next, I will show how late antique poets departed from earlier practice. That departure marks the development of a particularly late antique aesthetic, characterized by the reader's active involvement in the text and the poet's concern for the meaning and reception of the words on the page.

☙ The Allegorical Prefaces of Claudian and Prudentius

Twelve of Claudian's prefaces survive, all of them written in elegiac couplets. Each preface introduces an individual book of his hexameter poetry: panegyrics, invectives, epithalamia, and the epic *De raptu Proserpinae*.[43] Prudentius, in addition to a preface and epilogue to some unrecoverable edition of his works, wrote prefaces in various meters to his hexameter *Apotheosis*,

---

43. On Claudian's prefaces, see Zarini 2000, Felgentreu 1999, and Schmidt 1976. Parravicini 1914 surveys the prefaces of Claudian and other Latin authors.

Amartigenia, and *Psychomachia*, as well as one preface each for the two books of his *Contra Symmachum*. Each of these prefaces is allegorical in the sense that it provides an indirect introduction to the following poem. Claudian usually describes himself and his setting in terms of classical myth; Prudentius often fashions a scriptural allegory for his poem. There was no direct precedent for writing allegorical prefaces or even prefaces to individual poems.[44] Persius's choliambic preface was the only prior verse preface that was metrically distinct from its book of poetry. Other epigrammatic prefaces introduced collections of shorter poems rather than individual books of hexameter poetry. And while Greek panegyrical poems were introduced in late antiquity by prefaces in iambic trimeters, there is no evidence of a direct correlation one way or the other between those prefaces and Latin forms of the preface.[45] Although Prudentius and Claudian drew on various models, they innovated by writing prefaces that are distinguished by meter from the poems they introduce. In this way, they created for themselves a separable paratext. In writing such prefaces, they set out for readers their own approach to the text. At the same time, by marking the limits and circumstances of their texts, these prefaces repeat the earlier movement of other postclassical authors towards the contextualization of their work.

Most of Claudian's hexameter poems are introduced by a separate short poem in elegiac couplets, usually a mythical allegory that presents the protagonists of the panegyric through their resemblance to gods or heroes.[46] Claudian himself is often compared to the Muses or to Apollo. Two of Claudian's prefaces, *pr. III cons.* and *pr. VI cons.*, are descriptions of the circumstances of their recitation before the court and the assembled nobles. Like comedic prologues, Claudian's prefaces were originally written for a specific occasion, with the exception of the preface to book 1 (and probably also that to book 2) of the *De raptu Proserpinae*.[47] Thus Claudian's pref-

---

44. For a comparison of the prefaces of Claudian and Prudentius, see Herzog 1966, 119–35, along with Dorfbauer 2010. Herzog focuses on the allegorical technique underlying each set of prefaces. Dorfbauer questions Herzog's explanation of the origin of each poet's technique; he also shows that Prudentius's prefaces are more directly related to the subject of their poems, whereas Claudian's typically discuss either the poem's performance or Claudian's poetic persona.

45. On the Greek prefaces, see Viljamaa 1968 and Cameron 1970a. On a connection between the rhetorical *prolalia* and poetic prefaces, see Felgentreu 1999, 51–54 and 213.

46. See Felgentreu 1999, 187–89.

47. On the difference between oral and textual prefaces, see ibid., 212–13; and Dorfbauer 2010. On the performance of Claudian's panegyrics, see Gillett 2012. On the historical audience of Claudian's panegyrics, see Cameron 1970b, 228–52.

aces are usually not directly related to the content of their poem. Rather, they center upon the poet and his relation to the subject.

In his *Claudians Praefationes* (1999), Fritz Felgentreu provides a detailed study of Claudian's prefaces, but he does not set them within the context of late antique methods of reading.[48] Separately, Catherine Ware has shown how Claudian positions himself as an epic poet in his prefaces.[49] Without disagreeing in any way that Claudian appropriates the authority of his classical predecessors, I would point out that his prefaces work to guarantee the reception of his panegyrical poetry before a decidedly contemporary audience. They ask the reader to approach the text as though it were epic poetry and to accept the liberties that Claudian takes. By establishing the poet's authority in relation to the court, Claudian's prefaces guarantee that his poems will be read within their original context. In the same way in which they directed the initial, oral reception of his poems, Claudian's prefaces shaped the reception of his published work. For, in writing his prefaces, Claudian added to his poetry a further layer of interpretability. By presenting an authorial persona in his prefaces, Claudian both provided a lens with which to interpret his poetry and also revealed that the text could be read differently.

Claudian provided a simple allegorical preface to his *Epithalamium de nuptiis Honorii Augusti*.[50] The first sixteen lines of the twenty-two-line preface describe the wedding of Peleus and Thetis, the gathering of the gods and their feast. In their feasting, the gods turned to poetry and to Apollo:

> tum Phoebus, quo saxa domat, quo pertrahit ornos,
> > pectine temptavit nobiliore lyram:
> venturumque sacris fidibus iam spondet Achillem,
> > iam Phrygias caedes, iam Simoenta canit.
> frondoso strepuit felix hymenaeus Olympo,
> > reginam resonant Othrys et Ossa Thetin.
>
> > > (*pr. Nupt.* 17–22)

> Then Phoebus plied his lyre using the sublime plectrum
> > with which he tames rocks and draws out the woods:
> now he promises with his sacred strings the coming of Achilles,

---

48. The same is true of Zarini's (2000) overview of the prefaces to Latin panegyrical poetry.

49. Ware 2004; 2012, 59–66.

50. For a detailed overview of this preface, see Felgentreu 1999, 85–93.

now he sings of the Phrygian slaughters, and now of the
Simois.
His happy hymeneal sounds through leafy Olympus,
Othrys and Ossa echo in return that Thetis is queen.

This preface and especially these concluding lines draw a neat comparison
between Apollo and Claudian. Claudian presents himself as a divine poet in
order to guarantee that his praise of Honorius will be acceptable. Because both
the mythical setting and the meter of the preface are entirely distinct from the
poem that follows, Claudian's preface directs the reading of his poem from
beyond the strict limits of the text. Rather than being a part of the poem itself,
this preface tells us about Claudian and about one possible way to approach his
text. Therefore, in this preface, Claudian enacts the proper reading of the text.

The preface to *Panegyricus de sexto consulatu Honorii Augusti* produces a
somewhat more complex reading of that poem. It begins with the observation that all kinds of people dream about the things they think about during
the day.[51] After a priamel on the dreams of hunters, lawyers, charioteers,
and others, the poet declares that his own dream had set him on Olympus
singing of the gigantomachy before the feet of Jupiter. That personal revelation is explained in the final six lines of the preface, in which Claudian
surprisingly concludes that his dream came true:

additur ecce fides: nec me mea lusit imago,[52]
    inrita nec falsum somnia mittit ebur.
en princeps, en orbis apex aequatus Olympo,
    en, quales memini, turba verenda, deos!
fingere nil maius potuit sopor, altaque vati
    conventum caelo praebuit aula parem.

(*pr. VI cons.* 21–26)

Look, proof is given: my vision did not deceive me,
    nor did the false ivory send out an empty dream.
There's the prince, and the world's summit, made equal to Olympus;
    there, just as I remember them, is the venerable crowd of gods!
Sleep could not imagine anything greater, and this high court
    has given its poet an assembly equal to heaven.

---

51. For an overview of this preface, see ibid., 142–56.

52. Compare Narcissus from Ovid's *Metamorphoses*, who tells himself that he knows that his love is a
reflection: "iste ego sum! sensi, *nec me mea* fallit *imago*" (3.463). Claudian's self-assessment is fraught
with danger.

The gates of sleep are usually introduced to qualify as fictional a narrative sent through the gate of ivory. Claudian, however, turns the image around by saying that his dream is not one of the false dreams. His audience is thereby likened to the gods on Olympus, and Claudian to a poet singing of the gigantomachy. The panegyric that follows in honor of Honorius is Claudian's creative mixture of history and mythology. By presenting his recitation as a dream come true, Claudian argues for the paradoxical veracity of his figural narrative and invites the audience to lend him their belief. The poetic preface allows Claudian to deepen the reading of the poem, as he asks the reader to navigate his treacherous mixture of historical epic and panegyric.[53] Although this panegyrical poem is at times farfetched, Claudian asks his audience to understand it as a dream that is true.[54] Thus Claudian involves himself as poet in the reading of his work. While Hesiod and Ennius had also begun with their own divine visions, the separation of Claudian's preface creates a quasi-objective portrait of the author.

The prefaces of Prudentius also contain allegories that describe the author and his approach to the text, though his prefaces recall scriptural rather than mythical narratives to describe the text in question. His prefaces are in various meters; only one of the six prefaces to his hexameter poetry (the first preface to the *Apotheosis*) is in hexameters. The rest are marked by their meter as separate from the text.

Among Prudentius's prefaces, the preface to book 2 of the *Contra Symmachum* most clearly reveals the poet at work. Prudentius recounts the story of Peter walking on water, falling under the pressure, and being supported by Christ, as an allegory for Prudentius's perilous attempt to enter the storms of dialectic. That is, Prudentius has left the safety of silence, has attempted something of which he is incapable (i.e., arguing against Symmachus), and will fail in doubt if he does not receive divine assistance. That assistance from his divine addressee, however, will be a model for future readers. Thus he ends the preface by saying that he will fall unless he receives support:

> ni tu, Christe potens, manum
> dextro numine porrigas,
> facundi oris ut inpetus
> non me fluctibus obruat,

---

53. On this mixture, see Perrelli 1992.

54. Claudian's use of the verb *fingere* evokes the thin line that he walks.

sed sensim gradiens vadis
insistam fluitantibus.

(Symm. 2, praef. 61–66)

unless, powerful Christ, you stretch out
your hand in the favor of your will,
that the blast of his eloquent mouth
should not overwhelm me with its breakers,
but that I should gradually stand on
the flowing waters as though they were a path.

In the first place, there was a problem in composition: how could Prudentius succeed in writing his poem? As the preface unfolds, this becomes also a problem in reception: will the poem that follows be judged a success? This preface is distinguished from its text both by meter and by subject matter; in the first three lines of this book, Prudentius even alludes to book 2 of Vergil's *Georgics* and thus shows that the book proper begins only after the preface is finished. Thus the preface presents the poet from beyond the limits of his text.[55] From that space, Prudentius addresses his reader and presents a vision of the poem's success.

The preface to the *Psychomachia* is the most complex of Prudentius's prefaces. Here the poet prepares the reader to understand his *Psychomachia* as an allegorical story of the soul's victory over vice and of the following birth of virtue through Christ. The prologue begins by describing Abraham, who is praised because he showed that virtue must win, through battle, a gift pleasing to God. Prudentius says that Abraham gave himself as an example ("suumque suasor exemplum dedit") that the soul must conquer its own monsters before producing the sacrifice that will please God. The preface continues with a narrative of Abraham rescuing Lot in battle from hostile kings, meeting Melchizedek (a type of Christ) during his return from battle, being visited by the Trinity, and then becoming the father of the promised son, Isaac. The preface concludes with Prudentius's reading of the allegorical meaning of Abraham's life, in which Prudentius makes it clear that his preface's story contains a moral for the present day:[56]

---

55. For that reason, I do not understand Anthony Dykes's attempt to analyze the text and preface of the *Amartigenia* as a single poem (2011, 196–203). His emphasis on determining the genre of the poem obscures the distinction between text and paratext.

56. Compare *Am.*, praef. 25–26: "ergo ex futuris prisca coepit fabula / factoque primo res notata est ultima."

Haec ad figuram praenotata est linea
quam nostra recto vita resculpat pede.

(Psych., praef. 50–51)

This sketch was written down beforehand in view of the figure
which our lives would fashion in walking right.

Marc Mastrangelo has discussed the typological significance of this preface
and of these lines.[57] He argues that the poet engages his faith to read the
Old Testament as a model for the reader's present condition. As the following poem describes a battle between virtues and vices, the preface provides
the key to who will win. Thereby, the reader is able to understand Abraham's story as having significance both for the poem and for his life.
Through faith, the reader will follow the poet's example from the preface
and interpret the entire poem as an allegory applicable to his own situation.
Thus the preface prepares the reader for the figural reading that will produce an ethical response to the poem. Moreover, Jean-Louis Charlet, in his
article "Signification de la préface à la *Psychomachia* de Prudence," shows
that specific verbal echoes tie the preface to the poem as a whole.[58] Rather
than simply providing a self-enclosed narrative or miniature allegory, the
preface to the *Psychomachia* provides a story and an interpretation that are
related both to the narrative and to the method of the poem as a whole.
Because words, ideas, and structures from the preface are repeated in the
poem, the preface allows the reader to approach the text with a prior understanding of its contents and method. As the first reader of the *Psychomachia*, Prudentius uses the preface to construct his own reading of the text
and to invite the reader to follow him in it.[59]

Whereas the epigrammatic prefaces of earlier poets were programmatic
and often epistolary, the prefaces of Claudian and Prudentius contain brief
narratives that are allegorical of their texts. And while earlier prefaces usually
introduce collections of poetry, these prefaces introduce individual poems
and are expressly directed toward their reader's interpretation of the poem.
Claudian and Prudentius either describe themselves as authors or provide finished and coherent readings of their poems rather than explicitly addressing

---

57. Mastrangelo 2008, 84–93.

58. Charlet 2003, 244–48. Macklin Smith had already made this point (1976, 206–22).

59. On Prudentius's engagement with his reader's participation and what Mastrangelo calls the
"pact struck between poet and reader," which ensures that "[b]oth are part of making meaning
from the words on the page," see Prudent. *Am.* 624–25 and Mastrangelo 2008, 186n29, along with
5–7 and 19–21.

their readers or describing the reading of their poetry in general terms. Thus their allegorical prefaces enact a particular reading of the text and in this way the reader of an allegorical preface encounters a performance—the author's performance—of the reading of the text. We may infer that such performances became common at the end of the fourth century because the text was no longer expected to mean in a simple way. In writing such prefaces, these poets reveal that they did not expect their texts to be stable; rather, they knew that their readers would interpret them in various ways, and they attempted to direct those possible readings.

The Prose Prefaces of Ausonius

Ausonius wrote a series of epistolary prose prefaces to introduce his individual works. Like Martial and Statius, Ausonius presents his work through his prose prefaces. Unlike Martial and Statius, Ausonius purposefully creates distance between himself and his work and invites his reader to play an active role in his poetry. Thus Ausonius uses his prefaces to complicate any easy approach to his work. In so doing, he expands the scope of such prose prefaces and engages the permeable limits of his text in three important ways: (1) by describing the rules of his poetry, Ausonius opens the game to his audience; (2) by distancing himself from his poetry, Ausonius relaxes his own control over his work; and (3) by asking the reader to complete his poetry, Ausonius allows the reader to take control. Ausonius, therefore, employs the paratext to explore his status as author and to engage the reader in the interpretation of his text. For this reason, his prefaces had to be fully distinct from the texts that they present. Insofar as Ausonius does not attempt to justify himself or his approach to the text, his prefaces create space for a new kind of poetry, one that explores the potential of its own reception.

The Rules of the Game

In separate prose prefaces, Ausonius describes the rules that motivate the *Griphus ternarii numeri*, the *Technopaegnion*, and the *Cento nuptialis*. The *Griphus ternarii numeri* began during a banquet in Trier. Ausonius says in the preface that he had the idea to write a poem about things that come in threes, and that he finished it before dinnertime.[60] Then Ausonius suggests that some readers

---

60. Lowe (2012) offers a full reading of the *Griphus*. Hernández Lobato (2007) convincingly argues that the riddle points to the imperial family.

might criticize him for not including, in his ninety hexameters, everything that has to do with the number three. He responds by pointing out that he had composed his poem as a joke and over drinks, and that he had in any case introduced a great many things that come in threes. Even if someone could come up with more, no one could list everything ("alius enim alio plura invenire potest, nemo omnia"). Because *tres* or a derivative appears six times in just the first three lines of the poem, a reader would quickly guess the subject of the poem, even without the preface. Nevertheless, the preface makes the game behind the poem explicit. In doing so, it makes the work seem artificial or, rather, contingent upon a desire to follow the rules.

The *Technopaegnion* is a more complex exercise in ludic poetry. The work (it is called a *libellus*) consists of a series of poems in which each line ends in a monosyllable, an ending that is normally avoided at the end of Latin hexameters. In his first preface, Ausonius describes the general terms of this technical poetry and apologizes that there was no space for rhetorical embellishment. His second preface introduces just the first poem in the series and describes its challenge:

> versiculi sunt monosyllabis coepti et monosyllabis terminati. nec hic modo stetit scrupea[61] difficultas, sed accessit ad miseriam concinnandi ut idem monosyllabon quod esset finis extremi versus principium fieret insequentis. dic ergo "o mora" et "o poena"! rem vanam quippe curavi.
>
> (*Technop.* 2)

> These little verses begin with monosyllables and end with monosyllables. And the sharp difficulty does not end here, but my pitiable composition reached such a point that the same monosyllable that was the end of the last verse should be the beginning of the following one. So say, "What a waste" and "What a pain," for I spent time on empty material.

As in the preface to the *Griphus*, Ausonius makes the rules of the game explicit. The mock-serious reference to Cicero's "o tempora, o mores" establishes the playful tone. By describing the *Technopaegnion* in this way, Ausonius draws attention to his method of composition and away from the subject of his lines. Thus the poet steadfastly ignores Cato's advice: "rem tene, verba sequentur."[62] Instead of trusting that his poem will be understood on its own, Ausonius offers his own way of understanding its meaning.

---

61. On the aleatory connotations of *scrupeus*, see González Iglesias 2000.

62. Quoted by Iulius Victor in his *Ars rhetorica* (Giomini and Celentano) 3. The fragment is *Fil.* 15 (Jordan).

The *Cento Nuptialis* is the most extreme of Ausonius's ludic achievements. In its preface, Ausonius answers at some length the question of what a cento is ("cento quid sit"). In Chapter 3, I discuss in detail the rules of the cento and the contents of this preface. In short, Ausonius (1) describes the secondary and composite nature of cento composition, (2) outlines the metrical constraints on the cento poet, and (3) compares cento poetry to a popular game (*stomachion*) in which a player manipulates in various ways a series of geometrical shapes. In encountering Ausonius's description of cento poetry, the reader is asked to accept the same rules that motivated the poem's composition. The implication is that the poem would not make sense without those rules. This paratext thus provides the information that makes its text more fully readable.

While every paratext frames its work in some way, Ausonius uses the prefaces to his *Griphus*, *Technopaegnion*, and *Cento* to make explicit the verbal techniques that define their composition. In this way, he enables the reader to follow his lead, to participate in the same game. Unlike classical poets, who construct their meaning as direct and unproblematic,[63] Ausonius wrote a series of poems that directly address the manipulation of language and its meanings. To these poems, Ausonius appended prefaces that explain his techniques. Therefore, the poetry that Ausonius wrote gave him the opportunity to write not just programmatic prefaces but also interpretive prefaces. These prefaces expressly guide the reader into the structured form of his poetry.

✍ Distant Texts

In his prefaces to the *Cento*, the *Griphus*, the *Protrepticus ad nepotem*, and the *Bissula*, Ausonius draws attention to the distance between himself and the texts that he has written. Thus, in the preface to the *Cento Nuptialis*, he makes a point of mentioning that he composed the poem in a single day at the request of the emperor Valentinian.[64] When Ausonius later recounts the story to his friend Axius Paulus, he describes the poem in distant terms.

> hoc tum die uno et addita lucubratione properatum modo inter liturarios meos cum repperissem, tanta mihi candoris tui et amoris fiducia est ut severitati tuae nec ridenda subtraherem.
>
> (*Cento, Ausonius Paulo sal.*)

---

63. I certainly do not mean that classical poetry actually is direct or unproblematic; rather, it creates the impression of immediacy.

64. On the original performance of Ausonius's cento, see McGill 2005, 6 and 93–94.

It was finished quickly at that time, in one day with the nighttime included. Just now, after I had found it amid my scratch paper, I had so much confidence in your candor and affection that I would not hide from your judgment even something that is ridiculous.

By pointing out that this poem was written some time ago and that it has languished in his papers, Ausonius allows himself to look at the work objectively, to criticize it, and thus to reduce the immediacy of his own authorship.[65]

The preface to the *Griphus* begins with a similar revelation. The *Griphus* had also been around for a while before Ausonius pulled it out and sent it to the noble orator Quintus Aurelius Symmachus.

> Latebat inter nugas meas libellus ignobilis; utinamque latuisset neque indicio suo tamquam sorex periret.[66] hunc ego cum velut gallinaceus Euclionis situ chartei pulveris eruissem, excussum relegi atque ut avidus faenerator improbum nummum malui occupare quam condere.
>
> (*Griphus, Ausonius Symmacho*)

> There was hidden among my trifles an undistinguished little book; I wish it had stayed hidden and were not ruined by its own testimony, like a shrew mouse. When I, as if I were Euclio's chicken, had pulled it out of the dusty, decaying paper, I shook it off and read it over. And like a greedy moneylender, I decided to loan out rather than suppress my inferior coin.[67]

Euclio's chicken was beaten to death in Plautus's *Aulularia*, because he started scratching too close to the old miser's buried gold. Thus Ausonius's detachment from his work allows the poet to compare himself both to a chicken who happens upon a lost treasure and also to a greedy moneylender who cannot resist any opportunity. Rather than introduce a current work, Ausonius discovers a prior work, rereads it, and then sends it off to Symmachus with a new preface. Like the comedic prologues written for subsequent

---

65. On extravagant self-criticism in Latin prefaces, see Janson 1964, 124–41 and 145–49. On the author's reading of his own text, compare the insight of Jorge Luis Borges: "La prefación es aquel rato del libro en que el autor es menos autor. Es ya casi un leyente y goza de los derechos de tal: alejamiento, sorna y elogio" (1925, "Prologo," 5).

66. A close adaptation of Parmeno's exclamation at Ter. *Eun.* 1024: "egomet meo indicio miser quasi sorex hodie perii."

67. The opposition between *condere* and *occupare* probably also suggests the difference between composing a text and then using it.

productions of a play, Ausonius implies that this production (i.e., reading) will not be the same as the first time around.[68] Thus Ausonius draws attention to the distance between the initial creation of the text and the later readings to which it is subject.

In the preface to the *Protrepticus ad nepotem*, Ausonius turns to his reader's use of the text rather than his own rereading. The poem is addressed to a grandson who is also named Ausonius. The preface is addressed to the younger Ausonius's uncle Hesperius, whom Ausonius is about to visit. Ausonius tells his son Hesperius that he is sending the poem ahead of his visit so that he will have a chance to read it before they see each other. This is because he wants his son to be open in his judgment ("esset ut tibi censura liberior"). That judgment would be limited during a recitation for two reasons:

> quod aures nostras audita velocius quam lecta praetereunt et quod sinceritas iudicandi praesentia recitantis oneratur.
>
> (*Protrept., Ausonius Hesperio filio*)

> because what we hear passes by our ears more quickly than what we read, and because the sincerity of one's judgment is weighed down by the presence of the one giving the recitation.

Instead of privileging the presence of a recitation, Ausonius prefers that his son read the poem ahead of time and that he form a judgment in private. Whereas Ausonius points out that he wrote the *Cento* and the *Griphus* some time before their prefaces and so distances himself from those poems, here the poet distances himself from the subsequent reading of his work.

Ausonius describes his *Bissula* in more personal terms but also complains that Paulus has forced the poems out of hiding. In this case, the reader imposes a separation on the author and his text.[69]

> poematia quae in alumnam meam luseram rudia et incohata ad domesticae solacium cantilenae, cum sine metu <laterent>[70] et arcana securitate fruerentur, proferri ad lucem caligantia coegisti.
>
> (*Bissula, Ausonius Paulo suo s.d.*)

---

68. On the overlap between reading, performance, and ownership within the correspondence of Ausonius and Symmachus, see Pelttari 2011b, where I discuss several of Ausonius's prefaces.

69. For the stylized trope within prefaces of the dedicatee's insistence upon publication, see Janson 1964, 116–20.

70. *Laterent* is Peiper's plausible conjecture.

The little poems that I had composed for my girl were rough and begun as a comforting, indoor song. When they were <hiding> without fear and were enjoying their recondite safety, you forced them, dim as they are, to be brought out into the light.

Ausonius contrasts his own use of the poems with Paulus's appropriation of the work. Thus the poems' distance from their author becomes a trope for the reader's control of the text.

By distancing himself from his poems, Ausonius creates space for his reader. Although a prose preface is already distinct from the poetic text it introduces, Ausonius draws attention to the difference between himself as reader and his persona as author.[71] Whereas Martial and Statius describe in their prefaces a stable text, from its composition through its prefatory introduction and down to its reception, Ausonius imagines each step as critical. Publication is not unproblematic and may come about only because an author stumbles by chance upon an old work.[72] The reader of Ausonius's prefaces, therefore, will understand that an author is also a subjective reader and that once it is read, the text can no longer enjoy its hidden security.

✒ The Reader's Control

In addition to creating space for his reader, Ausonius also invites the reader to use and to activate his poetry. In prefaces to the *Bissula*, the *Technopaegnion*, the *Parentalia*, and the *Cento*, Ausonius directly addresses his reader and offers the reader either a share in or even control over his text. At the end of his prose preface to the *Bissula*, Ausonius tells Paulus to use the poems as his own:

> utere igitur ut tuis, pari iure, sed fiducia dispari; quippe tua possunt populum non timere, meis etiam intra me erubesco.
>
> (*Bissula, Ausonius Paulo suo s.d.*)

---

71. Ausonius takes the opposite approach in his preface to the *Cupido cruciatus*, in which he dissolves the difference between preface and text (see Nugent 1990, 41–42). Beyond Nugent's observations, "miratus sum" and "errorem meum" of the preface align Ausonius with the first and last characters in the poem's catalog of unfortunate lovers (I owe this observation to Joseph Pucci).

72. In V, the oldest of Ausonius's manuscripts, the *De herediolo* and the *Pater ad filium* are prefaced by brief notes that describe those poems in the third person and in the past tense. It has been thought that they are the work of an early editor. The former preface, however, uses Ausonian language ("honoratissimus," "villulam," "Luciliano stilo"), and the latter preface says the work was "incohatum neque impletum, sic de liturariis scriptum." It is just possible that Ausonius spoke of himself in the third person, but I think it more likely that these comments were abridged from Ausonius's prefaces. For what may be an abridged preface from the same manuscript, but to the *Ephemeris*, see Pucci 2009, 53–54.

So use them as your own, with equal rights but unequal confidence, since as yours they are able to meet their public without fear, as mine I blush at them even privately.

Ausonius wants Paulus to take responsibility for the *Bissula* because at least his own reading of the poems would be different if he were not also their author. As long as the poems enjoyed a secretive rest ("arcana securitas"), they belonged to Ausonius; but now they have been made public and are the responsibility of their reader.[73] Ausonius sets up a distinction between his poems and Paulus's: when they belong to Paulus, they are fearless ("tua possunt populum non timere"); when they belong to Ausonius, he can read them only with self-conscious embarrassment ("meis etiam intra me erubesco"). Ausonius suggests, therefore, that Paulus may mediate this poem to a broader audience. As the dedicatee imposes a filter on the text, so the reader will also come to determine their value.[74] More than simply acknowledging his own distance, Ausonius allows the reader privileged access to his poems.

Ausonius begins the *Parentalia* with a preface in elegiac couplets in which he describes the reader's access to the text as participation. Although the meter of this poem makes it continuous with the series of *Parentalia*, the invitation to the reader brings it in line with the prose prefaces considered here. Thus Ausonius thanks the reader for taking part in his mourning:

at tu, quicumque es, lector, qui fata meorum
    dignaris maestis commemorare elegis,
inconcussa tuae percurras tempora vitae
    et praeter iustum funera nulla fleas.

(praef. B 15–18)

But reader, whoever you are, in deciding
    to remember the deaths of my family in sad elegy,
may you pass with ease through the years of your life
    and weep at no funerals beyond what is right.

---

73. *Bissula, Ausonius Paulo suo s.d.*

74. It is worth noting that Ausonius usually dedicated his poems to friends and peers rather than patrons. Even the emperor Theodosius (to whom Ausonius dedicated a collection of his poems) addresses Ausonius in friendly terms. In an extant letter, Theodosius compares himself to the patron Augustus, but he also says that he is writing not as a king but rather through the private love he shares with Ausonius ("pro iure non equidem regio, sed illius privatae inter nos caritatis"). Green conveniently prints Theodosius's letter as an appendix to his edition of Ausonius (1991, 707). Because Ausonius did not usually address himself to patrons, he may have felt more freedom to actively engage his readers.

These *maesti elegi* are the laments of both Ausonius and the commiserating reader. By remembering with Ausonius, the reader becomes a mourner with the poet and a participant in his poetry.

Beyond asking the reader to participate in what is already present, Ausonius also invites his reader to activate what is at most only latent in the text. Thus the first preface to the *Technopaegnion* explicitly asks the dedicatee, Pacatus, to take part in enacting the work. The fate of the poem rests firmly in Pacatus's reading, for without him the poems are merely disjointed fragments:

> et simul ludicrum opusculum texui, ordiri maiuscula solitus: sed in tenui labor, at tenuis non gloria, si probantur. tu facies ut sint aliquid; nam sine te monosyllaba erunt vel si quid minus.
>
> (*Technop.* 1)

> All the same, I wove a playful work, although I am accustomed to beginning grander webs. But if they are approved, "my labor is in a small field, but the glory is not small." You will make them into something; for without you they will be monosyllables or less, were it possible.

Because the poem would be insignificant otherwise, Ausonius asks his reader to make something of it. The verbs in the future tense (*facies* and *erunt*)[75] mark the text's dependence on the moment at which it will be read.[76] Further, the quotation "in tenui labor, at tenuis non gloria" recalls Vergil's proem to Maecenas from book 4 of the *Georgics* (G. 4.6). In that proem, Vergil also describes his thin material, the work of bees, in wonderful terms ("admiranda tibi levium spectacula rerum," G. 4.3). Ausonius, therefore, makes a comparison between Vergil's work and his own venture into the smallest corners of discourse. Although the material is slight, the reader of the *Technopaegnion* will gather its disparate fragments and make them cohere in some meaningful way.

In the third prose preface appended to his *Technopaegnion*, Ausonius makes the reader's activity even more explicit. There, the incoherence of his poem will be remedied by the reader:

> sed laboravi ut quantum fieri posset apud aures indulgentissimas absurda concinerent, insulsa resiperent, hiulca congruerent, denique haberent

---

75. Although the future indicative may be used as a simple imperative, the futurity of the statement is important here.

76. In *The Corporeal Imagination*, Patricia Cox Miller notes the importance of this passage for an understanding of late antique aesthetics and for the role of the reader (2009, 52–53).

et amara dulcedinem et inepta venerem et aspera levitatem. quae
quidem omnia, quoniam insuavis materia devenustat, lectio benigna
conciliet.

(*Technop.* 4)

But I have worked so that—as much as is possible—in your indulgent
ears the dissonant should harmonize, the unsavory should be flavorful,
the gaping should be connected, and finally the bitter should have
sweetness, the tasteless grace, and the harsh should be smooth. And
although[77] their rough material disfigures it all, a kindly interpretation[78] will bring it together.

Ausonius delights in the oxymoronic description of his poems, but he does
not leave it at that. Rather, the oppositions inherent in his poems allow the
reader to actively reconcile their meaning. Ausonius, therefore, acknowledges that his text cannot determine its own meaning. In saying as much in
his preface, Ausonius declines to lay out a single configuration, via interpretation, of the text. Instead, he explains that his poetry will be transformed
through the act of reading.

As a final step beyond participation, Ausonius says that his reader should
decide whether or not his *Cento* even exists. In his preface to that poem,
Ausonius tells Paulus that although the lines and half lines of the cento are
drawn from Vergil, he has tried to make them his own in something more
than a trivial way. The decision as to whether Ausonius has succeeded in
composing a cento will depend upon Paulus. For, immediately after providing a list of the paradoxical qualities that he hopes to achieve, Ausonius asks
his reader to be the judge, or rather the paymaster, of his poem:

quae si omnia ita tibi videbuntur ut praeceptum est, dices me composuisse centonem et, quia sub imperatore tum merui, procedere mihi
inter frequentes stipendium iubebis; sin aliter, aere dirutum facies, ut
cumulo carminis in fiscum suum redacto redeant versus unde venerunt.

(*Ausonius Paulo sal.*)

And if all these things will seem to you to be just as prescribed, you
will declare that I have composed a cento. And, because I served at

---

77. In late Latin, *quoniam* is used like *quod* to introduce a noun clause (see Souter, s.v. *quoniam*). It
would seem that Ausonius here allowed the adversative sense of *quod* to color his use of *quoniam*.

78. This meaning of *lectio* is found in Latin from the fourth century on (see *TLL*, s.v. *lectio* I.A.b.β
[1082–83]).

that time under my commander, you will order my pay to come to
me among the crowds. Otherwise, you will cause my pay to be for-
feited, that—with the heap of this poem sent back to its own treasury—
the verses may return from whence they came.

As in the prefaces to the *Technopaegnion*, the future tenses (*videbuntur, dices,
iubebis, facies*) mark Ausonius's suspension of judgment. He is not prepared
even to assert that he has written a cento ("composuisse centonem") until
the poem is read and approved. The activation of the poetry, therefore, depends on the interpretation, via pronouncement ("dices"), of their dedicatee and reader. Should Ausonius fail, the lines will cease to be his and will
return the same as they were to their Vergilian home.

The concluding words of Ausonius's preface to his *Cento* echo the end of
the dedicatory epistle that Statius prefixed to book 2 of his *Silvae*:[79]

> haec qualiacumque sunt, Melior carissime, si tibi non displicuerint, a
> te publicum accipiant; si minus, ad me revertantur.
>
> (*Silv.* 2, praef.)

> Dearest Melior, if these, of whatever quality they are, do not displease
> you, they should be published by you. If not, let them return to me.

Like Ausonius, Statius submitted his poems to the judgment of their reader
and asked that they be published by their dedicatee or returned if found
unsuitable.[80] But Statius requested that the poems be literally returned.
Ausonius, on the other hand, turns that trope into a metatextual play on the
reader's judgment of his own intertextuality: Ausonius's clever request
makes the reader think about his text as a text. It makes the reader think
about the fact that his words are (in)distinct from the Vergilian poem, and it
invites the reader to critique Ausonius's use of Vergil. Ausonius uses the
formal apparatus of dedicatee and dedication as a pretext for his evocation
of the reader's role in making sense of the text.

I have argued that Ausonius uses his prefaces to break down the connection between author and text. He does this by setting out the rules underlying his work, by describing his work in distant terms, and by inviting his
readers to intervene in the text. By showing its dependence on the reader's

---

79. I owe this observation to Pavlovskis 1967, 546.

80. In their prefaces, authors often said that they were submitting their work for correction. On this
topos, see Janson 1964, 106–12 and 141–43. On Cicero's practice of submitting work for joint correction, see Gurd 2012, 49–76.

participation, Ausonius neatly circumscribes the text within its present station. Because the function of a paratext is precisely to circumscribe the text, every preface does this to some extent. But Ausonius downplays the immediacy of his poems in order to emphasize the processes of their mediation and eventual reception. To put it simply, Ausonius wrote prefaces because he enjoyed reading.

✒ Room for Reading

The heightened use of prefaces marks the importance of reading for the poetry of late antiquity. While Augustan poets avoided them, prefaces are often found attached to those Latin poems that draw on what I describe as a postclassical aesthetic. Earlier poets, however, tended either to write epistolary dedications or to treat prefaces as indistinct from the following text. As the reader's access to the text became more of a concern, late antique poets used their prefaces as a further level of mediation between themselves and their audience, which only served to make the text's interpretation more complex. These late antique prefaces should not be read as straightforwardly self-explanatory, and their presence creates room for interpretation. They are the first level of mediation between the text and its public, and they are the space in which reading is figured by the author and first enacted by the reader. Whatever clarity is provided by the prefaces of Claudian and Prudentius is fleeting because the preface itself is a text in need of interpretation. Ausonius, moreover, explicitly addresses his reader's active involvement and marginalizes his role as author. The prefaces of Ausonius, Claudian, and Prudentius both enact a particular reading of the text and invite readers to construct their own meanings for the text. Because late antique poets wrote with powerful readers in mind, they embraced the preface and its potential to dramatize the openness of their texts. In this regard, the preface marks the late antique turn towards an aesthetics focused upon the reader's work of interpretation.

➳ CHAPTER 3

Open Texts and Layers of Meaning

In the fourth century, a series of Latin authors wrote along multiple, distinct syntactic levels. The figural poetry of Optatianus Porfyrius destabilizes the idea of a univocal text. The allegorical poetry of Prudentius's *Psychomachia* points the reader to a deeper sense behind the surface of the text. The Vergilian centos blur the line between composition and reception. Without their reader, these poems collapse into dazzling but incoherent fragments, technically stunning but incomplete. They are open texts, as defined by Umberto Eco in *Opera aperta*,[1] his study of modernist aesthetics. By tracking trends in twentieth-century art, literature, music, science, and theoretical scholarship, Eco noted that modern thought inclined toward open structures, as it advocated ambiguity, uncertainty, and the direct involvement of its subjective observers. An open work—for my purposes, an open text—calls for "changing perspectives and multiple interpretations" (Eco 1989, 24). Eco was well aware that every text is open in a way. The only truly closed text is one that has never been read, a literally

---

1. *Opera aperta* was originally published in 1961, was revised in 1967 and again in 1976, and was then translated into English in 1989 in somewhat different form as *The Open Work*. Eco writes a brief history of *Opera aperta* in the preface to his 1976 edition, "Opera aperta: Il tempo, la società" (v–xxiii). David Robey's introduction to *The Open Work* includes brief comments on the selection of material in the English translation (Eco 1989, vii–viii).

closed book, while the only completely open work is pure potentiality, a blank sheet of paper. Further, a relatively closed text may be (mis)interpreted as though it were an open text (and the centonists' use of Vergil will be discussed presently).[2] Insofar as they are relative terms, the distinction between open and closed texts reveals a spectrum, on one side of which the poet welcomes the reader's direct involvement.

The open poetry described in this chapter operates through the layering of textual elements. By creating a poem that can be read in more than one way (i.e., on various levels), a poet allows the reader to inhabit the space between each layer. Because these layers are distinct, the reader must determine when and how they fit together. In articulating a different way to create and then read a poem, these poets negotiate the related problems of composition and interpretation.

Such experimental poems, concerned with the acts of writing and interpretation, run the risk of reducing the work of art to a statement on literary theory. Eco directly addresses the fact that open works can become little more than metapoetic commentary. He describes the reader who enthusiastically learns the new technique or method envisioned by a work, but then decides not to read it because "[h]e feels he has already gotten all there was to get from it, and fears that, if he bothered to read the work, he might be disappointed by its failure to offer him what it had promised" (1989, 170). However, insofar as an open work actually succeeds in stimulating the potential readings at which it aims, it will be more than a theoretical statement of poetics.[3] For that reason, I show through close readings not only the purpose of these open works but also how they actually produce their ends.

I will begin with Optatian's figural poetry because his poems provide the most coherent example of openness. Three layers stand in sharp relief on the page; insofar as they do not depend upon secondary meanings or intertextual designs, they are each self-contained. From there, I move to the *Psychomachia*'s personification allegory, which involves a secondary meaning in dialogue with the surface narrative of the poem. I then discuss the cento, which is in a way the most complex of these forms. The Vergilian centos transfer a more local sense of openness onto the literary past and thereby directly engage the history of Latin literature. In this way, they give a more expansive view of the openness of these distinctively late antique forms of textuality.

---

2. On the distinction between open and closed texts, see esp. Eco 1989, 24–43. Eco 1979, 56–59, provides a very concise statement of the problem.

3. This is also a point made by Eco (1989, 174–79).

✒ The Figural Poetry of Optatianus Porfyrius

Optatianus Porfyrius composed poems whose reading is intentionally complicated along several different axes. Some are pattern poems, whose shape
is outlined by the text of the poem. One is a Proteus poem, whose four
lines may be rearranged at the whim of its reader. And most of his poems
contain what he calls *versus intexti*, secondary lines encoded vertically or
diagonally along the page. The broad term "figural poetry" covers these various texts.[4] In each case, Optatian encodes a text whose potential is not ex-
hausted by a sequential reading from left to right. Because the reading of his
poems does not end at the same moment as the voice or eye reaches the last
word on the page, Optatian compels the reader to engage the multiple layers
of his text.

The manuscripts ascribe to Publilius Optatianus Porfyrius a *Panegyricus* in
honor of Constantine.[5] The date of his birth is reasonably assigned to between 260 and 270 on the basis of an honorific inscription found in the Pi-
azza Colonna in Rome and dated to the beginning of the fourth century.[6]
Along with being proconsul of Achaea,[7] Optatian was twice prefect of Rome
(during 329 and 333).[8] The only other contemporary reference comes from
Jerome, who says in his *Chronica* that "Porfyrius misso ad Constantinum
insigni volumine exilio liberatur."[9] Although the majority of Optatian's extant poems directly address Constantine and plead for his recall, the reason

---

4. The Latin *technopaegnia* has also been used, but it is found in antiquity only in the singular and as
the title of Ausonius's very different collection of poems.

5. Polara 1973, 1:viii–xvi. Polara follows Elsa Kluge in rejecting the title *Panegyricus* "perché il ter-
mine [*panegyricus*] indica sempre una singola composizione in versi o in prosa, e non può quindi
riferirsi ad una raccolta" (Polara 1974–1975, 3:283n63; Polara refers to Kluge 1922, 90). But *panegyricus* could be used as an adjective in Latin, as in Greek (see *TLL*, s.v. *panegyricus*, I.B), and an ellipsis
such as *liber* is easily understood. Moreover, since *panegyricus* was not a common title for a collection
of poetry in any period of Latin, there is no reason to impute the catachresis to a scribe rather than
to Optatian.

6. Timothy Barnes (1975) offers a speculative reconstruction of Optatian's life. Polara (1974–1975) is
more conservative but is certainly wrong to identify Optatian with the anonymous subject of the
horoscope detailed by Firmicius Maternus at *Mathesis* 2.29.10–20 (Kroll-Skutsch, pp. 81–84). As
Barnes (1975, 173–74) and Bruhat (1999, 4–7) have pointed out, this horoscope describes the life of
an individual who was born on either March 13 or 14, 303, which does not align with the other
details of Optatian's life

7. We know of this proconsulship from an inscription discovered at Sparta (*SEG* XI, 810 = *AE*
1931, 6).

8. Dated securely by the Chronographer of 354 (*Chronica minora* I [*MGH, AA* 9], p. 68).

9. Helm, Eusebius VII, 232. If Jerome's dating were correct, Optatian would have been recalled
from exile in 329. Jerome's dating is usually rejected on the grounds that it would place Optatian's
recall within the same year as his first tenure as prefect of Rome.

for his exile is unclear. Through datable internal references (above all to the *vicennalia* celebrated by Constantine in 325 and again in 326), the sending of the *Panegyricus* and the poet's subsequent recall from exile are placed variously between 324 and 326.[10] Beyond that, the precise dating of Optatian's life and career is problematic.

☙ Pattern Poems

Three of Optatian's poems take up the Greco-Latin tradition of pattern poetry.[11] Poem 20 forms the shape of a water organ (*hydraulus*); poem 26 forms an altar; and poem 27 outlines the shape of a panpipe. Before Optatian, Hellenistic pattern poems remain from one Simias of Rhodes, Theocritus (probably not genuine), and a certain Dosiadas; further, a separate *Altar of the Muses* is sometimes also attributed to this Dosiadas. In Latin, a short fragment survives from a *Phoenix* of Laevius (frag. 22 [Courtney]). These earlier pattern poems are polymetric. Differences in meter determine the length of each line and therefore the shape of their figure. Optatian, however, uses a different technique; he allows the number of letters to determine the length of a line and therefore the shape of the poem. Most notably, the twenty-six pipes of his water organ (*Carm.* 20) are formed of twenty-six hexameters, whose length increases regularly from twenty-five letters in the first line to exactly fifty letters in the final line.[12] By making regularly spaced letters the elements of his design, Optatian was able to create figures with a significant amount of regularity. Although Optatian's new technique shifts emphasis away from the sound of the words and onto the individual letters of which they are composed, in both Optatian and earlier poets the underlying goal of the form is the same, to compose an image from the contour of a poem.[13] Pattern poetry permits the reader a secondary approach to the text as it becomes both an image and a poem. In turning back to the tradition of pat-

---

10. See Polara 1974–1975, 3:282–84; Barnes 1975, 177–86; and Bruhat 1999, 270–72.

11. Book-length studies of pattern poetry are Kwapisz 2013, Luz 2010, Pozzi 2002, Ernst 1991, and Higgins 1987. Scanzo 2006; Bruhat 1999, 45–75; and Polara 1991 are discussions either focused on or largely devoted to Optatian.

12. Bruhat has suggested that Optatian's method of composing *versus intexti* within a rectangular grid derived from his experimentation with pattern poetry (1999, 172–74). Edwards (2005) separately concludes that Optatian's pattern poetry came before his *versus intexti*, although he does so on the basis of questionable judgments concerning their relative inability to "dazzle" Constantine.

13. For suggestive comments on the visual and musical aspects of Optatian's pattern poems, see Bruhat 1999, 66–67.

tern poetry, Optatian gave the form new relevance at the beginning of the fourth century.

✒ A Proteus Poem

Optatian's poem 25 is a brief four lines, at least on first reading. The subject of the poem is the poem itself.

> ardua componunt felices carmina Musae
> dissona conectunt diversis vincula metris
> scrupea pangentes torquentes pectora vatis
> undique confusis constabunt singula verbis
>
> the blessed Muses compose difficult poems
> they connect different chains from diverse verses[14]
> twisting the heart of their poet as they set their challenges
> each one will stand though the words be jumbled in every way

My translation makes no attempt to capture the poetry of the lines; rather, it gives only the bare sense. The lines say that the Muses compose their poems in distinct units and that they will remain even when the words are switched around. To take one example, the new line "ardua connectunt felices vincula Musae" retains the same metrical shape as each line of the original quatrain. As Optatian implies, his readers are able to create a new poem each time they revisit the text. Thus Optatian has written a Proteus poem;[15] and a full translation would have to retain the metrical play.

Different readers have followed different rules in composing their variants and so have calculated different numbers of possible outcomes. Jean Letrouit (2007) works through the various ways in which these lines may be combined. First, in a number of the manuscripts, eighteen variant quatrains follow immediately upon this poem. Each of these variants (1) retains *Musae*, *metris*, *vatis*, and *verbis* in that order and at the end of each line of the quatrain; (2) does not exchange words from the first and fourth feet with words from the second and third feet; and (3) does not use in any single line two dactyls that are both from the same metrical position in the original lines. On the

---

14. For *metrum* in this sense, see *TLL*, s.v. *metrum*, B.2.

15. On the name and form of Proteus poems, see Pozzi 1984, 147–51. Julius Caesar Scaliger mentions an analogous line he wrote "quem Proteum nominavimus" (*Poetices* 2.30). It is unclear whether the name antedates Scaliger. On the reception of Scaliger's line, see Higgins 1987, 183.

basis of a pattern within these variants, Polara emends the manuscript's text so that there are now two more quatrains (eighty lines) in his edition. The scholiast says that eighty-four different lines (not quatrains) may be composed from the original quatrain if the final words remain while the internal words are changed.[16] It is not clear how the scholiast arrived at such a small figure.[17] William Levitan calculates that if one follows the three restrictions found in the manuscript versions, 1,792 different lines may be composed from the original quatrain (1985, 251n17). Polara and Enrico Flores calculate that, following all but the third restriction (which Levitan was the first to formulate explicitly), 3,136 different hexameters may be composed (1969, 119–20). If one excludes the restriction (imposed by the scholiast) on exchanging the final words of one line with another final word, that number increases to 12,544. But there is no reason to follow the scholiast's rules, either in excluding the final word of each line or in counting the number of possible lines rather than the number of possible quatrains. Even if one does not change in any way the metrical shape of the quatrain, it is possible to compose 39,016,857,600 different quatrains from Optatian's original. If one retains the original order of the final word of each line, the number of total quatrains is reduced to 1,625,702,400. There is no way of knowing whether Optatian himself transcribed more than a single version of the poem. As far as I know, there has only been one attempt to compose all of the possible variants: in 1977 Levitan printed each of his 1,792 variants.[18]

I do not, however, want to give the impression that poem 25 is fundamentally a mathematical problem. In the first place, the poem (especially in those combinations in which a line ends "carmina vatis") alludes to Ovid's *Amores* 1.8.57–58:

> Ecce, quid iste tuus praeter nova carmina vates
> donat? amatoris milia multa leges.

---

16. "Hi quattuor versus omnes pari ratione conscripti sunt ita ut manente ultima parte orationis ceteras partes omnium versuum ordinibus tantum invicem mutatis vel ad directum vel ad reciprocum modum variare possis; ita dumtaxat, ut primae partes cum primis vel quartis versuum vices mutent, secundae cum secundis vel tertiis, et possis, si velis, nulla parte orationis addita ex his quattuor versibus mixtis octoginta quattuor facere ita, ut nullus sui similis sit." On the scholia to Optatian, see Polara 1973, 1:xxxii–xxxiii; and Polara 2004.

17. Perhaps the simplest explanation is that the scholiast found eighty variant lines in his source and mistakenly counted the original four ("his quattuor versibus") along with the lines that could be formed from them.

18. Levitan notes, "In December 1977, the entire set of permutations was programmed for computer by Glenn English of Austin, Texas, and printed for the first time in its history" (Levitan 1985, 252n20).

> Look, what can that poet of yours give you besides new
>   poems? You'll read many thousands from a lover.

In Ovid's poem, an old woman counsels a girl to distrust the futile songs of poets; Optatian's text allows that distrust to color its own configuration of *carmina* and *vatis*.[19] Thus the content of Optatian's poem directly confronts the difficulty of his poetry, the separability of the Muses' words, and the chance of combining them in various ways.

There is only one known predecessor of Optatian. Athenaeus (454f–455b) cites a *Hymn to Pan* by one Castorion of Soli (this is all we know of Castorion, and Athenaeus has no specific name for his kind of poetry). Athenaeus quotes five lines in iambic trimeter. He explains that each foot (whether composed of one, two, or three words) can be exchanged with the other feet in its line to form a series of different lines. However, because of restrictions of meter and syntax, many feet cannot be exchanged with feet from other lines; for that reason, Peter Bing (1985) has argued that the point of the poem is that Castorion has already selected the only combination of metra that is really adequate. Castorion is the first poet known to have composed a Proteus poem, but he seems not to have thematized the malleability of his words. It is possible that this passage tells us more about Athenaeus and his interest in poetic riddles (γρῖφοι) than about Castorion himself. Whether or not he knew of Castorion's poem, Optatian seems to have been the first Latin author to compose a Proteus poem, and he put effort into writing one that would be radically open to permutation.[20]

Although poem 25 is Optatian's only freestanding Proteus poem,[21] he was clearly concerned with offering his reader an open text whose potential remained to be explored and defined. Raymond Queneau, a modern proponent of the Proteus poem, confirms the reader's involvement in such poems in the preface to his "Cent mille milliards de poèmes." He introduces his work as one that "permet à tout un chacun de composer à volonté cent mille milliards de sonnets."[22] Like Queneau's sequence of sonnets, Optatian's poem 25 allows the reader to share in the work of composition.

---

19. This allusion to Ovid was first observed by González Iglesias (2000, 356) as part of a stimulating reading of this poem's intertextual links.

20. On a medieval Latin imitator of Optatian, see Polara and Flores 1969, 133–36.

21. The *versus intexti* of *Carm.* 6, 18, and 19 are miniature Proteus poems. On these poems, along with *Carm.* 25, see Bruhat 1999, 152–70.

22. "Mode d'emploi," in *Cent mille milliards de poèmes* (Paris: Gallimard, 1961); reprinted in a volume edited by the group Oulipo, *La littérature potentielle: Créations re-créations récréations* (Paris: Gallimard, 1973), 247–49.

✦ Versus Intexti

Most of Optatian's poems employ what he calls *versus intexti*,[23] secondary lines or poems inscribed within the fixed text of his poetry. Optatian's typical *versus intexti* poem is composed over a grid thirty-five letters wide by thirty-five letters high. The thirty-five hexameters of this typical poem are read from left to right, as they would be in any other poem. The secondary messages of the *versus intexti* are read diagonally, vertically, or horizontally along the grid. The lines of the *versus intexti* reveal in turn a third layer to the text as they shape a pattern or sometimes even the outline of another set of letters. The letters of the *versus intexti* were written in red pigment (*minium*) in order to distinguish them from the background of the text.[24]

The simplest of Optatian's *versus intexti* employ acrostics (at the beginning of each line), mesostics (in the middle of each line), and telestics (at the end of each line).[25] In these poems, the secondary text is read from top to bottom rather than from left to right. Optatian's other *versus intexti* are arranged in such a way that the selected letters are themselves figures. The figures outlined by these *versus intexti* may be divided into three groups:[26] geometric patterns,[27] images,[28] and letters.[29] The geometric patterns can be paralleled by patterns in mosaics contemporary with Optatian.[30] The images range from examples of clear mimesis to abstract symbolism. Thus the *versus intexti* of poem 9 outline a palm of victory in honor of Constantine; poem 19 contains the detailed outline of a ship; poems 2, 3, 6, 7, and 10 contain images that are symbolic and suggestive rather than strictly mimetic;[31] and two poems

---

23. *Carm.* 9 *v.i.* 5 and 3.17; compare *Carm.* 3.28. See also Bruhat 1999, 95.

24. As Optatian writes, "prodentur minio caelestia signa legenti" (*Carm.* 19.1).

25. These are *Carm.* 11, 13, 16, and 31, the last of which probably should not be attributed to Optatian (on which, see Polara 1973, 1:xxviii–xxix and 2:168–69). For a discussion of earlier acrostic poetry and Optatian's *versus intexti*, see Bruhat 1999, 85–95.

26. Of course, there is no clear line between these categories. For a thorough study of Optatian's poems and the categories into which they may be divided, see Bruhat 1999, 134–70.

27. *Carm.* 12, 18, 21, 22, and 23. Polara, however, doubts the authenticity of *Carm.* 22 (1973, 1:xxix–xxx).

28. *Carm.* 2, 3, 6, 7, 9, 10, 14, 19, and 24. Polara doubts the authenticity of *Carm.* 24 (1973, 1:xxix–xxx).

29. *Carm.* 5 and 8. *Carm.* 19 also incorporates an abbreviation (*VOT*) into its image.

30. Bruhat makes this connection for *Carm.* 7, 12, 18, 21, 22, and 23 (1999, 136–41).

31. Poem 3, for example, claims to describe the face (*vultus*) of Constantine (*Carm.* 3.1); because the *versus intexti* look nothing like a face, the comparison must be symbolic in some sense. Bruhat interprets the lines as two overlapping crosses and the imagery as Christian (1999, 141–46).

(14 and 24) present the chi-rho symbol.[32] Those *versus intexti* that outline letters spell out *AUG XX CAES X* and *IESUS* (*Carm.* 5 and 8, respectively). In two of his *versus intexti* (*Carm.* 16 and 19), Optatian goes so far as to make the individual letters serve double duty, being Latin in one direction and Greek in the other.[33] In these ways, Optatian breaks the word down, even to the shapes of individual letters, and compels the reader to reconstitute the text in its various directions.

Optatian claimed that his *versus intexti* were a new kind of poetry, and he is in fact the poet who transformed acrostic and labyrinthine poetry into texts that were alternate and yet continuous.[34] He speaks of his poetry as "nova carmina" (*Carm.* 3.24), "nova vincula mentis" (*Carm.* 10.18), "novi elegi" (*Carm.* 8.1), and "novae curae" (21.4).[35] In Poem 3, he describes his compositions in terms of this alternate text:

mentis opus mirum metris intexere carmen
ad varios cursus.

(Carm. 3.28–29)

It is a marvelous task for the mind, to plait a poem in verse along various paths.

The different paths of Optatian's poetry are significant in their own right, in the challenge they set for their poet, and in the opportunities they offer the reader.

Levitan introduces Optatian by drawing attention to this challenge. He writes, "Optatian is not a good poet; he is not even a bad poet. His poems are prodigies, monsters in the literal sense" (1985, 246). Levitan is right, but I would suggest that he downplays the degree to which Optatian's poems invite reading as well as wonder. His poems are admirable for their shape, their form, and their strange ingenuity. They offer a new vision of poetry, and their technical features can easily overwhelm the actual narrative. Nevertheless, even in their strangeness, Optatian's poems do invite a coherent reading along each of their individual layers.

Although poem 9 is not the most elaborate of Optatian's poems,[36] it reveals the technique of the poet and the options available to the reader. As with all

---

32. The chi-rho also appears, with other figures, in *Carm.* 8 and 19.

33. Thus the Latin *p*, for example, becomes *rho* in Greek.

34. On the originality of these poems, see Polara 1987, 168–71; and Bruhat 1999, 84–85.

35. For a partial list of Optatian's comments on his own poetics, see Polara 1974–1975, 4:104n193.

36. The most prodigious of Optatian's poems is surely poem 19, whose *versus intexti* outline a complex image of a ship, contain Greek, and also reveal a Proteus poem.

of Optatian's *versus intexti* poems, poem 9 may be approached on three levels. It may be read straight through from left to right; the reader may focus on the internal pattern of the *versus intexti*; and the reader may turn to the separate words of the *versus intexti*. Although the reader may approach these levels in any order, the readings cannot be simultaneous. I will describe these as the first, second, and third levels, although I do not want to imply that this order is preferable to any other.

On the first level, the reader approaches the text from left to right and discovers in the first two lines that it is a poem in praise of Constantine.

> Castalides, domino virtutum tradite palmam.
> Constantinus habet bellorum iure tropaeum.
>
> (*Carm.* 9.1–2)

> Castalians, give the palm of virtue to my lord.
> Constantine rightly possesses the trophy for his battles.

Optatian goes on to explain that Constantine has conquered his enemies, but with a clemency that returned the world to order (3–8). The middle of the poem (9–22) turns to the subject of poetry and specifies that Apollo and the Muses will grant Constantine a poetic reward. Thus lines 9–10 invoke the Muses again:

> Nunc mihi iam toto dociles Helicone Camenae
> mittite conpositas in tempora mitia palmas.

> Now send me, teachable muses, from all of Helicon
> palms shaped for gentle times.

Next, Optatian turns to praise of Constantine's sons Crispus (23–30) and Constantinus II (31–34). The poem ends with a brief prayer:

> Sancte pater, rector superum, vicennia laeta
> Augusto et decies crescant sollemnia natis.
>
> (35–36)

> Holy father, ruler of the heavens, may a blessed *vicennalia*
> spring forth for Augustus, and for his sons their *decennalia*.

In short, this poem is a brief panegyric on the occasion of Constantine's *vicennalia*.

The shape of the *versus intexti* sheds light on the first line of the poem. In red lettering, they outline a palm frond, a token of victory. This is the second level of the text:

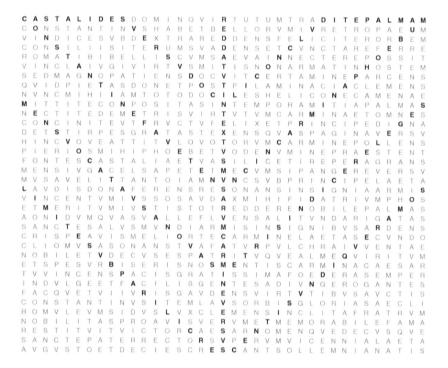

The image of the *versus intexti* is the palm that Optatian requests from the Muses. Or rather, this image is also the palm. The first reading of poem 9 (from left to right) already yielded a poem in praise of Constantine, a metaphoric trophy. The image outlined by the *versus intexti*, therefore, both represents the poem as a whole and is itself a gift, the picture of a trophy.

By tracing the *versus intexti* along their course, the reader enters the third level of the text; at that point, he discovers the following five hexameters:[37]

> Castalides, versu docili concludite palmam.
> Constantine, fave; te nunc in carmina Phoebum
> mens vocat, ausa novas metris indicere leges,

---

37. Though not necessarily in this order. Optatian's *versus intexti* generally proceed from left to right and from top to bottom, but that is not possible in every case.

limite sub parili crescentis undique ramos
reddat ut intextus Musarum carmine versus.

Castalians, enclose your palm in teachable verse.
Be kind, Constantine; my mind now calls you to my songs
to be my Phoebus, since it dares to impose new rules on meter,
in order that limbs growing on either side from an equidistant limit
may be produced in the Muses' song by my embroidered verse.

The praise of Constantine remains from the previous layers of the text, and Optatian continues to call on the Muses to enable his poetry. Also, he offers more explicit commentary on his poetic craft. Since he is setting new limits for his poetry, he calls his verse teachable ("docilis"). Just as the *versus intexti* reveal the parallel branches of a palm, Optatian the poet layers text upon text.

Poem 9 is eminently readable. Each level of the text stands on its own in praise of Constantine, and each level has some claim to prominence. Because there is no hierarchy amid the three layers of the text, readers are free to move from one to another and to devise their own connections (and connections there must be, since some letters belong to three different words). As in his other poems, Optatian here compels his reader to place these words within a coherent narrative.

In the abstract, Optatian's poems are, as Levitan suggested, prodigies that draw attention to the poetic text as a marvelous assemblage of letters. But Optatian's poems are more than poetic puzzles, and they are not mindless games or angst-ridden exercises.[38] Rather, they engage their reader to participate in and enjoy his poetry. Indeed, it is rewarding to read Optatian's poems closely, to move from one layer to another and to work out the possibilities inherent in his text. To read them as closed texts, determined by their author, would be to misunderstand the calling of Optatian's muse.

✒ Prudentius's *Psychomachia*

Prudentius's *Psychomachia* marks the beginning of what would become the medieval tradition of allegorical poetry. This is the consensus of literary historians and specialists. *The New Princeton Encyclopedia of Poetry and Poetics* calls the *Psychomachia* "the first full-scale Western personification allegory" (Preminger and Brogan 1993, 33), which echoes Macklin Smith's

---

38. Levitan compares Optatian to one of Samuel Beckett's despairing characters (1985, 266–68).

view that it is the "first sustained personification allegory."[39] Georgia Nugent describes it as "the first example of the genre of allegory as we know
it" (1985, 9). Michael von Albrecht says that it is "das erste vollständig
allegorische Großgedicht der europäischen Literatur" (1994, 1079). It must
be said, however, that neither personification nor allegory were new ideas.
Maurice Lavarenne makes the point quite strongly: "Prudence n'a . . . pas
innové en créant toutes les allégories de la *Psychomachie*. Sa tentative n'est
en somme que l'aboutissement logique d'une tendance de l'antiquité"
(1948, 24). Although Lavarenne is right that each element within the *Psy-*
chomachia draws on earlier Latin poetry, Prudentius's poem is the first epic
to employ allegory as its organizing trope. By activating a second, distinct
meaning beneath the surface of the text, Prudentius necessitates an active
reader and thereby participates in the trend toward the writing of open
poetry. Although the importance of Prudentius's allegory has been widely
acknowledged, it has not yet been understood within this contemporary
context.

☙ The Predecessors of Prudentius

Quintilian provides the fullest extant treatment from antiquity of the trope
of *allegoria* (*Inst.* 8.6.44–59). His definition is as follows:

> Allegoria, quam inversionem interpretantur, aut aliud verbis, aliud
> sensu ostendit aut etiam interim contrarium.

> *Allegoria*, which is translated as inversion, either expresses one thing
> verbally and something else in its sense, or sometimes it even expresses
> something contrary [to the explicit meaning of the words].

This trope is produced when the rhetor employs a series of continuous
metaphors ("continuatis tralationibus"). The variety of *allegoria* that expresses
an idea contrary ("contrarium") to its surface meaning is primarily represented by *ironia*. Quintilian's idea of allegory encompasses a broad range of
rhetorical moves, and his breadth is typical of ancient uses of the term.

Despite the breadth of his definition, Quintilian's first example is a poem
that commentators continue to regard as an intentional allegory, Horace's
Ode 1.14.

---

39. M. Smith, 1976, 3. In their introduction to *The Cambridge Companion to Allegory*, Rita Copeland
and Peter Struck also call the *Psychomachia* "the archetype of personification allegory" (2010, 6).

Prius fit genus plerumque continuatis tralationibus, ut "O navis, referent in mare te novi / fluctus: o quid agis? Fortiter occupa / portum,"
totusque ille Horati locus, quo navem pro re publica, fluctus et tem-
pestates pro bellis civilibus, portum pro pace atque concordia dicit.

(Inst. 8.6.44)

The former genus [of allegory] is most often formed from continued
metaphors, such as "New waves are going to carry you back to sea,
my ship: o what are you doing? With your bravery, get to port," and
the whole passage of Horace, in which he speaks of a ship instead of
the state, of waves and storms instead of civil wars, and of port instead
of peace and unity.

The two scholiasts to Horace, Pomponius Porphyrio and Pseudo-Acro, as
well as many modern commentators, agree with Quintilian that Horace's
ode is an allegory for the ship of state.[40] Of course, some readers do not
understand the poem as an allegory at all.[41] And still others read it as an allegorical description of the poet's love.[42]

In Quintilian's sense, any number of passages from Latin and Greek poetry
are allegorical; that is, they offer a second level of meaning beyond their surface narrative. In "Figures of Allegory from Homer to Latin Epic" (2003),
Andrew Laird has studied Vergil's allegorical description of Fama in order to
explore Greek and Latin authors' complex understanding of discourse in general and of epic language in particular. Further, Joseph Farrell, among others,
has argued that Vergil, in his composition of the Aristaeus episode at the end
of the *Georgics*, was influenced by allegorical interpretations of Homer.[43]
Plato's allegory of the cave was also composed with a secondary meaning in
mind, and Apuleius's story of Cupid and Psyche has a clear allegorical appeal. What is more, Prudentius himself composed a number of prefaces that
contain narratives allegorical of the poems they introduce.[44] Allegory, therefore, could be found both in discrete passages and (as in the case of Horace's
Ode 1.14) as the organizing principle of some classical poems.

---

40. See Nisbet and Hubbard 1970, 178–80.

41. For a survey of earlier antiallegorical interpretations, see Pilch 1929.

42. For bibliography up to 2006 and the argument that this poem refers to a woman rather than the
state, see Knorr 2006.

43. Farrell 1991, 256–72; see also Morgan 1999, 61–96.

44. See the discussion in Chapter 2.

Apart from the writing of allegory, allegoresis was a common form of interpretation in the classical world.[45] The earliest extant examples are from the sixth century BCE, when Homer was mined for insight into the physical world. The Derveni papyrus attests to a flourishing logic of allegory in the fourth century BCE; and the Stoics and then the Neoplatonists built up theoretical models to explain Homer's knowledge as either the traces of primitive wisdom or as the unconscious symbolism inherent in verbal reality. Robert Lamberton, in *Homer the Theologian* (1986), and Peter Struck, in *Birth of the Symbol* (2004), have studied these allegorical exegetes of Homer from the earliest exemplars to Proclus in the fifth century CE. As the title of Lamberton's book implies, these practitioners of allegoresis viewed Homer as a source of divine wisdom. Their task was to retrieve a deeper meaning from the text. It is notable that the tradition of Homeric allegoresis did not engender a separate tradition of allegorical poetry until late antiquity.[46]

Beginning with Philo, Paul, and then Origen, Jewish and Christian traditions of allegoresis grew up alongside Homeric allegoresis. Jean Pépin's *Mythe et allégorie* traces the reaction by Philo and the Christian allegorists to allegorical interpretations of Greco-Roman mythology.[47] Christian exegetes attempted to discredit the allegorization of mythology while simultaneously interpreting what they viewed as difficult passages in the Hebrew scriptures as allegories of moral or theological scope. As Francis Young has argued in *Biblical Exegesis and the Formation of Christian Culture*, Origen was the Christian author who systematized and "professionalise[d] the exegesis of scripture" (1997, 292). For, from Origen on, Christian exegetes borrowed the techniques of Homeric exegesis.

Christian exegetes adapted Homeric allegoresis in one important way. Beginning with Paul, they introduced the idea of types, which find their allegorical fulfillment in later historical figures. Typology, or figural allegory, as it is also called, is the form of allegoresis concerned not with a secondary meaning divorced from the surface of the text but with a secondary referent that is in some sense level with the primary referent.[48] While

---

45. The word "allegoresis" is a modern Grecism. In antiquity, either *allegoria* or such circumlocutions as *exegesis allegorica* were used in its sense. On *allegoria*, see J.-F. Thomas 2004, 88; for *exegesis allegorica* and similar circumlocutions, see *TLL*, s.v. *allegoricus*.

46. In his fourth chapter, titled "The Interaction of Allegorical Interpretation and Deliberate Allegory," Lamberton discusses Prudentius's *Psychomachia*, Heliodorus's *Ethiopica*, and Musaeus's *Hero and Leander* (1986, 144–61).

47. Maren Niehoff has studied Jewish exegesis at Alexandria in light of the Homeric scholia (2011).

48. See Auerbach 1944, Young 1994, Dawson 2002, and J.-F. Thomas 2004.

Homeric allegorists did not try to retain the surface narrative of their text,[49] Christian exegetes often (though not always) claimed both that events recounted in, say, the Pentateuch really happened and that they also referred to Christ or the Church or some other referent (their referentiality being determined by God as the maker of history). Of course, there is no clear line between allegory and typology; and what is now labeled typology was called *allegoria* in antiquity. In fact, the modern word "typology" was apparently not used until the 1840s.[50] Nevertheless, the distinction does give a name to the variety of allegoresis in which the secondary meaning is viewed as parallel to the primary meaning rather than as its replacement.[51]

Apart from the tradition of allegory, Prudentius's *Psychomachia* finds a precedent in the rhetorical use of personification. The English term "personification" (borrowed from the French *personnification*) makes a sharper distinction than the Greek *prosopopoeia*.[52] In ancient rhetoric, *prosopopoeia* describes either the introduction of absent, often deceased, persons (e.g., Cicero's performance as Appius Claudius Caecus in his speech *Pro Caelio*) or the invention of person and voice for an abstract concept (e.g., Cicero's invocation of the *Res Publica* in the *First Catilinarian*). Only the second variety of *prosopopoeia* is relevant to the *Psychomachia*, and this is precisely the meaning of personification. For that reason, I will discuss from now on personification and not *prosopopoeia*.

Before Prudentius, Latin poets employed personification in a number of ways.[53] Of course, in personifying abstractions, the Latin poets did not do anything that was absolutely new; Hesiod, for example, personifies a number of abstract ideas in his *Theogony*. Within the tradition of Latin epic, however,

---

49. But some Neoplatonist allegorizers unified the surface of Homer's text and its deeper meaning in a different way; Peter Struck speaks of Neoplatonic symbolic allegory as a sacramental act of interpretation (2004, 149, 204, and 247). While symbolism imagines an organic relation between the text and its referent, typology views the text and its referent as distinct entities within the same field of reference (e.g., as existing within the field of human history).

50. A. C. Charity says that the first use of *typologia* was ca. 1840 (1966, 171n2). The first entry under *typology* in the *OED* is from 1845. A certain Franciscus Xaverius Patritius, in his *De interpretatione scripturarum sacrarum* of 1844, 1:172, describes *typologia* as a "nomen a recentioribus scriptoribus inditum."

51. Dawson (2002) argues that the Christian interpretation of the Jewish scriptures was not, on the whole, supersessionist. I need not enter that discussion here because I want only to say that the possibility of typological interpretation was developed by the Christian exegetes who read in a single text two meanings that were both historical and distinct (i.e., nonsymbolic).

52. For a survey of rhetorical treatments of personification from antiquity to the twentieth century, see Paxson 1994, 8–34. Martin 2004 surveys the political uses of Rome personified up to the end of antiquity.

53. Maurice Lavarenne provides a concise survey of personification in Latin poetry (1948, 17–21).

personification is developed in a coherent manner. Vergil, in book 6 of the *Aeneid*, peoples the entrance to the underworld with a host of terrors.

> Vestibulum ante ipsum primisque in faucibus Orci
> Luctus et ultrices posuere cubilia Curae
> pallentesque habitant Morbi tristisque Senectus
> et Metus et malesuada Fames ac turpis Egestas,
> terribiles visu formae, Letumque Labosque;
> tum consanguineus Leti Sopor et mala mentis
> Gaudia mortiferumque adverso in limine Bellum
> ferreique Eumenidum thalami et Discordia demens,
> vipereum crinem vittis innexa cruentis.
>
> (Aen. 6.273–81)

> Before the first entry and in the very jaws of Orcus
> Grief and vengeful Cares have made their home,
> and there dwell the ashen Illnesses and sad Old Age
> and Fear and Hunger and ugly Poverty,
> (their shapes are terrible to look at) and Death and Labor;
> then there is Sleep, the cousin of Death, and Evil Joys
> of the Mind and War, who brings death from the opposite side,
> and the iron chambers of the Eumenides and mad Discord,
> who has fixed up her viperous hair with bloody bands.

Vergil's personified terrors surround the entrance to the underworld. They are modified by appropriate adjectives. But they do not act. As a further step in personification, Statius describes the attendants of Mars and gives them actions to fit their personalities. The scene is the reception that Hermes received when he arrived at the palace of Mars:

>   primis salit Impetus amens
> e foribus caecumque Nefas Iraeque rubentes
> exanguesque Metus, occultisque ensibus astant
> Insidiae geminumque tenens Discordia ferrum.
> innumeris strepit aula Minis, tristissima Virtus
> stat medio, laetusque Furor uultuque cruento
> Mors armata sedet.
>
> (Theb. 7.47–53)

>   Senseless Impulse jumps up from the front
> of the doorway, and there is blind Crime and red Passion

and bloodless Fear. And with a hidden sword Treachery
stands by and Discord holding its double-edged weapon.
The hall resounds with countless Threats. Virtue stands sadly
in the middle, and joyful Rage and armed Death
with her bloody face are sitting down.

In addition to the epithets and sparse description found in Vergil, Statius
grants his personifications their own meaningful verbs. And when personification employs description, it becomes a form of allegory; for example, the
description of Impulse jumping up means that impulsiveness is quick to act.
For his part, Claudian frequently employs personified figures, especially personifications of Rome.[54] He also describes, at the end of *De consulatu Stilichonis* 2, the cave of Time (*aevum*) in which Nature personified dwells. In that
passage, personification and allegory are drawn closer together as Nature
speaks in person within the allegorical frame provided by the cave of Time.

The *Psychomachia*, therefore, followed a long tradition of allegorization
and personification.[55] The rhetorical tradition of allegory provided Prudentius with a master trope by which he could describe one activity through
another; the techniques of allegoresis developed by Homeric and scriptural
exegetes provided him with an audience that was prepared to read epic poetry for its deeper sense; and the poetic tradition of personification gave
him the characters for his drama. Therefore, even though Prudentius's *Psychomachia* was the first personification allegory, it had roots throughout
Roman literary culture.

☙ The Allegory of the *Psychomachia*

The novelty of Prudentius's *Psychomachia* consists precisely in the fact that
he was the first to turn the techniques of personification and allegory into a
continuous and self-coherent narrative.[56] The *Psychomachia* is entirely structured around the personified virtues and vices who are its actors, and alle-

---

54. For a list of personifications in Claudian, see Beatrice 1971, 33n21.

55. Because it is distinct from the allegorical form of his poem, I have not even mentioned Prudentius's sources for what has become known as the *bellum intestinum*, the struggle of virtue against vice.
Beatrice (1971) discusses this aspect of the *Psychomachia* in detail, although he is too quick to dismiss
the classical (as opposed to Christian) sources.

56. For a contemporary political allegory in prose, see Synesius's *Aegyptii sive De providentia*, which
begins with an explicit reference to its own deeper meaning: ὁ μῦθος Αἰγύπτιος· περιττοὶ σοφίαν
Αἰγύπτιοι. τάχ' ἂν οὖν ὅδε, καὶ μῦθος ὤν, μύθου τι πλέον αἰνίττοιτο, διότι ἐστὶν Αἰγύπτιος. εἰ δὲ μηδὲ
μῦθος, ἀλλὰ λόγος ἐστὶν ἱερός, ἔτι ἂν ἀξιώτερος εἴη λέγεσθαί τε καὶ γράφεσθαι. Lamberton notes the
relevance of this text (1986, 144n1).

gory has become the device that allows this poem to exist. Prudentius elevates allegorical poetry to the genre of epic, as is made clear by his focus on a battle narrative, by intertextual links to the *Aeneid*, and by the invocation at the beginning of the poem.[57] Any discussion of the *Psychomachia*'s allegory, however, is complicated by the fact that Prudentius employs allegory in three distinct ways: the preface to the poem is both a typological interpretation of Abraham's life and an allegory for the poem as a whole; the narrative of the *Psychomachia* is structured through personification allegory (and it is this structuring that is most original from the viewpoint of earlier Latin poetry); and the poem employs typologies throughout in such a way as to involve the reader in its narrative. Each aspect of the *Psychomachia*, therefore, creates a poem whose interpretation remains to be completed as its allegory emphasizes the role of the reader.[58]

The first variety of allegory in the *Psychomachia* is found in its preface,[59] which announces the subject of the poem and provides a partial explanation of its narrative. The preface begins by recounting several scenes from the life of Abraham: the patriarch, with the help of 318 servants, defeats the kings who had captured his nephew Lot; and he is then visited by three strangers who prophesy that Sarah will give birth to Isaac. The preface ends with an allegorical interpretation of the story: the Christian defeats vice with the help of Christ;[60] and he then welcomes the three members of the Trinity, who herald a new birth of virtue in his life. This preface signals to the reader a broad outline through which to interpret the *Psychomachia*'s allegory. The allegoresis of Abraham, however, should be distinguished from the allegory of the *Psychomachia* proper. The *Psychomachia*'s allegory employs personified figures as its actors. The preface allegorizes Abraham as a model for the faithful reader by constructing his narrative as an analogue to the narrative of the *Psychomachia*. In this way, the reader is prepared to enter the text as Abraham went out to fight the pagan kings.[61] The reader who understands the allegory of Prudentius's preface is prepared to engage vice and receive his reward by applying the message of the *Psychomachia* to his life. In

---

57. On Prudentius as an epic successor to Vergil, see Mastrangelo 2008, 14–40, with further references. The title of Peuch's (1888) chapter on the *Psychomachia* was already "L'épopée allégorique."

58. Compare Quilligan 1979, 21: "The current fashion of 'foregrounding' the reader in the consideration of any text should not obscure the generic centrality of the reader that has always been particular to allegory."

59. On this preface as a preface, see the discussion in Chapter 2.

60. Mystically prefigured in the number 318, on which see Mastrangelo 2008, 55.

61. Compare ibid., 87–93, which describes Prudentius's construction of a faithful reader.

this respect, the preface of the *Psychomachia* is no different from Prudentius's other prefaces.

What is different about the *Psychomachia* is its second form of allegory. Rather than presenting his teaching directly, Prudentius employs personified figures to embody his point. The *Psychomachia* proper begins with a twenty-line proem in which the poet invokes Christ and announces that the key to the battle against vice is an accurate knowledge of both one's opponent and one's own side. From there, lines 21–725 describe the attacks of the vices and the final victory of the virtues. Lines 726–887 describe the speeches of Concordia and Fides and the building of a temple for Wisdom, and lines 888–915 give thanks to Christ for allowing the poet to understand the battle and for causing Wisdom to reign. Aside from the proem and the conclusion, in which the poet speaks in his own voice, the narrative is entirely given over to the actions and speeches of its personified figures.

Each of the seven pairs of virtues and vices receives individual treatment, and there is no simplistic structure which organizes their battles.[62] Rather, the narrative is tailored to each figure and builds up a comprehensive set of ambiguities of both a moral life and of language, which are resolved as Christ enters both the poem and the reader's soul. In the poem these ambiguities take the shape of Deception (Fraus) personified. Just as the ambiguities revealed by Fraus demonstrate the difficulty of constructing a coherent narrative out of incoherent language, Prudentius's allegory addresses the difficulties inherent in the referentiality of language.[63] Prudentius's allegorical personifications point to the separate and secondary meaning to which they refer, without losing their own substance within his narrative. Thus, in saying that the reader understands Prudentius's narrative on a second level, I do not want to suggest that the surface level of his text is emptied of its power. The virtues and vices are literary figures in their own right; it is just that the reader also interprets them as allegorical personifications. Because the reader must choose at each point whether to pursue the text's literal or allegorical meaning, the poem is continually open to the intervention of its reader.

The duel between Patience and Anger offers Prudentius ample space to employ his allegorical technique, and it clearly reveals the two levels of the text. The scene begins with a view of Patience, a modest figure:

---

62. Nugent demonstrates this in detail in the first part of her study of the *Psychomachia* (1985, 17–62).

63. Compare ibid., 90: "Although ambiguity does inevitably present a threat in the context of a semiotic system, the work of the psychomachic struggle is not merely to displace or conceal ambiguity, but to explore its limits and possibilities. Thus the problem of ambiguity is admitted into the poem in the form of *fraus*." Nugent's chapter on Fraus is entitled "Poetic deception in the allegorical system" (87–93).

Ecce modesta gravi stabat Patientia vultu
per medias inmota acies variosque tumultus
vulneraque et rigidis vitalia pervia pilis
spectabat defixa oculos et lenta manebat.

(*Psych.* 109–12)

And there was calm Patience, standing with a serious face
unmoved in the middle of the battle and amid the shifting tumult.
She watched the wounds and their vitals pierced through with stiff
    spears,
as she held down her eyes. And she remained calm.

After these lines, Prudentius describes Anger as impetuous, quick to act, and prone to frustration. After a few vain attempts on Patience, Anger becomes so frustrated that she grabs a spear from the ground and kills herself. Patience then proclaims her victory, in restrained terms:

quam super adsistens Patientia "Vicimus" inquit
"exultans vitium solita virtute sine ullo
sanguinis ac vitae discrimine. Lex habet istud
nostra genus belli furias omnemque malorum
militiam et rabidas tolerando extinguere vires.
ipsa sibi est hostis vaesania seque furendo
interimit moriturque suis Ira ignea telis."

(155–61)

Patience stood over her and said, "I won.
I defeated the vice in my normal strength and without any
risk of blood or life. My rule keeps
to this kind of war, in order to destroy by endurance
the furies and the whole army of evils and rabid violence.
Madness is her own enemy, and in her rage
she kills herself, and flaming Anger dies by her own spear."

"Vicimus" is very matter-of-fact, and the whole speech is particularly suited to Patience's virtue.[64] Whereas in earlier poets the actions and even descriptions of personifications are restrained, Prudentius describes his figures in full

---

64. For the contrast, compare Hope's response to her victory: "Extinctum vitium sancto Spes increpat ore: / 'Desine grande loqui, frangit deus omne superbum. / Magna cadunt, inflata crepant, tumefacta premuntur'" (*Psych.* 284–86).

and gives them actions and speeches to suit their personae. Each of these elements is allegorical of the abstraction described. That is, they refer to—or rather, construct an image of—the virtue patience. Of course, the surface of Prudentius's allegory is descriptive and compelling in its own right, but the poem invites its reader to associate these descriptions with a secondary field of reference. Like Optatian's figural poetry, Prudentius's *Psychomachia* constructs a text that may be read at more than one level. Each level of meaning is self-coherent, and at each point the reader may pursue one or the other or try to make them harmonize.

Just as the preface of the *Psychomachia* draws a typological connection between Abraham and the virtuous Christian, the speeches of the virtues and vices introduce a number of typological figures.[65] This is the third variety of allegory in the *Psychomachia*. The heroes from the Bible, who have already won their own battles, offer the reader a model for the struggles of life. Even more than that, Prudentius's typological figures involve his reader in a narrative that begins in the Old Testament but continues into the present moment of the text when the poem asks its reader to take sides in this battle. In that sense, the secondary level of Prudentius's allegory becomes continuous with the reader's identification with its typological figures. As Marc Mastrangelo says, the reader of Prudentius's allegory becomes the epic hero: "This typological connection underscores the poem's epic ambitions by recasting the epic hero not as a figure better than the reader but as the reader himself whose potential is actualized through the free choice of virtuous qualities."[66]

The typological identification between reader and figure is realized most clearly at the end of the poem, in the temple built for Wisdom. Faith speaks to the troops and recommends their final labor:

> unum opus egregio restat post bella labori,
> o proceres, regni quod tandem pacifer heres
> belligeri armatae successor inermus et aulae
> instituit Solomon, quoniam genitoris anheli
> fumarat calido regum de sanguine dextra.
> Sanguine nam terso templum fundatur et ara
> ponitur auratis Christi domus ardua tectis.
>
> .   .   .   .

---

65. These are discussed in detail by Mastrangelo 2008, 99–120; and M. Smith 1976, 178–94.

66. Mastrangelo 2008, 99. See also M. Smith 1976, 24–26; Jauss 1960; and Cotogni 1936.

Surgat et in nostris templum venerabile castris,
omnipotens cuius sanctorum sancta revisat!

(804–15)

O nobles, after war there is one task that remains,
an extraordinary job, one that Solomon instituted,
he who was at long last a peacemaker, the heir of a warrior
kingdom, who received a fortified palace
but went himself without weapons; for the tired hand of his father
smoked with the hot blood of the kings.
For when the blood has been wiped away, a temple is established
and an altar set up, the high home of Christ, with golden ceilings.
. . . .
Let a temple rise to be honored in our camp as well,
whose holy of holies the Omnipotent may visit again!

As Solomon once built a temple for Christ, so the virtues will once more
build a home for Christ (the following description of the jeweled temple is
reminiscent of the new Jerusalem described in the book of Revelation). As
the virtues build their temple, so do readers welcome Christ to reign in
their souls. (This final link is made abundantly clear in the epilogue and especially at the very end of the poem, when the poet says that the human
soul is at war until Christ comes and Wisdom reigns.)[67] The typological
allegory of the *Psychomachia* constructs the reader as an active participant in
its narrative, as the form of the poem compels the reader to consider the
meaning beyond its surface. In this way, typology and allegorical personification merge within Prudentius's description of these virtues, for they are
both informed by biblical exempla and potentially present within the soul
of the reader. This is the third way in which Prudentius uses allegory in the
Psychomachia; it is logically independent of his decision to compose the *Psychomachia* as a continuous personification allegory.

As we have seen, Prudentius's *Psychomachia* enables a secondary meaning
that is only suggested by its allegorical personifications and typological exempla. This allegorical epic brings together the formerly separate strands of
allegory and personification and makes of them the grounds for its own existence. In so doing, Prudentius elevates his reader to a place of prominence by
inviting the reader to reflect on the processes through which his text establishes

---

67. *Psych.* 908–15. M. Smith argues at length for identifying Wisdom with Christ (1976, 194–206).

its meaning. Whereas earlier epic poets had employed allegory as one trope within their text, it is present throughout this poem. The text presents two narratives that are internally coherent and yet distinct: the one on the surface of the text and the other on the level of allegory. By viewing this poem as an open text along its two layers, we see that Prudentius did not set out to create a final portrait of the struggle in the soul. Rather, he created a poem that remains to be actualized, both as the reader connects the secondary sense of the allegory and as the reader engages in his or her own personal psychomachia.

❧ The Latin Centos

Like the Greek κέντρων, the Latin word *cento* literally meant a patchwork rag, and from the third century CE on, it was used figuratively to denote a poem composed of the fragments of some earlier poem.[68] Unlike other imitative poetry, a cento retains the exact words of a predecessor. Unlike oral composition, the reproductions of a cento depend upon a fixed and verifiable text.[69] Epithalamia, narrative poems (Christian and mythological), and a tragedy all survive from antiquity in cento form. The cento, therefore, is a distinct literary form not because of its content but because each cento shares a technique of patchwork composition in which a previous poem is reduced to its constituent parts (e.g., the lines and half lines of dactylic hexameter) and then recomposed to a new end. Because the cento is a distinct literary form, the only poems that qualify as centos are independent works either entirely or very nearly composed from the exact words of a previous poem. This definition excludes such highly imitative works as the *Batracho-myomachia* and the *Concubitus Martis et Veneris*.[70]

Although we can date only a few of the centos, the broad outline of their history is uncontroversial.[71] The earliest centos of which we have sure knowledge were written toward the end of the second century, and the cento flourished in the fourth century and the beginning of the fifth.[72] Hosidius Geta's *Medea*, the earliest Latin cento, is from the end of the second or the begin-

---

68. On the word *cento*, see Salanitro 1997, 2319–21.

69. But Usher (1998 and 2003) provocatively compares the centonists and Homeric rhapsodes.

70. On the category of *pseudocentoni*, see Salanitro 1997, 2333–34 and 2356–57; and Bažil 2009, 46–47.

71. See Bažil 2009, 18–25; McGill 2005, xv–xvii; Salanitro 1997; and Polara 1989.

72. As observed by Salanitro 1997, 2335.

ning of the third century. The earliest Greek centos are from the same pe-riod.[73] The first Greek author to mention a centonic poem (though without using the word κέντρων) was Irenaeus. In a discussion of the misuse of scripture, he cites a short, ten-line Homeric cento on Heracles (*Adversus haereses* 1.9.4). Tertullian is the first Latin writer to speak of a cento (*De praescr. haer.* 39.3–5).[74] He refers to (1) an undefined group of *Homerocentones*, (2) a version of the *Pinax* of Cebes composed from Vergil by Tertullian's relative ("propinquus"), and (3) the recently composed *Medea* of Hosidius Geta. Tertullian presents centonic poetry as a recent phenomenon ("vides hodie ex Virgilio fabulam in totum aliam componi," *De praescr. haer.* 39.3). After the *Medea*, the next datable centos are the *Cento Probae* (fourth cen-tury), Ausonius's *Cento nuptialis* (ca. 374), and the Homeric centos of the empress Eudocia (fifth century). With the notable exception of the *Medea*, these are also the most extended and artistic centos from antiquity. The only other datable centos are the *Versus ad gratiam Domini* (sometime after the *Cento probae*)[75] and Luxurius's *Epithalamium Fridi* (late fifth or early sixth century).[76] Aside from the *De verbi incarnatione*,[77] the remaining ten extant, undated Latin centos were gathered in Africa during the first half of the sixth century and then preserved in the Codex Salmasianus. The cento, therefore, seems to have had a temporally limited existence in antiquity, appearing only in late antiquity and flourishing in the fourth century.[78] The brief appear-ance of the cento is not surprising, for Martin Bažil has observed that the cento is particularly dependent on aesthetic changes in the literary public (2009, 73). As this chapter shows, the relevant aesthetic change was the turn towards open poetry.

Vergil's ubiquitous authority made the cento possible in late antiquity. In particular, the role of Vergil's poetry in education produced a public that was familiar enough with his work to appreciate the centos that were pro-duced.[79] This is important because it means that the audience of the centos

---

73. On which see ibid., 2325–34.

74. I will discuss this passage in the following section "The Cento in late antiquity."

75. McGill 2001, 17n11.

76. On Luxurius, see Rosenblum 1961 and Kaster 1988, 415–17.

77. On this work see Bažil 2009, 218. It was transmitted in a single manuscript dated to the latter half of the ninth century.

78. On the afterlife of the cento in the high middle ages, see ibid., 231–42.

79. On the scholastic nature of the cento, see Lamacchia 1958. On the various uses of Vergil's po-etry in imperial culture, see McGill 2005, xvii–xxv. On the grammarian Servius's use of Vergil's poetry, see Kaster 1988, 169–96.

was capable of understanding their sophisticated interaction with the text of Vergil. And, if we needed evidence, this would show that the centos were not simple attempts at plagiarism. A cento usually depends on a recognized canon or a single authoritative text; in late antiquity, Vergil's poetry was both familiar and authoritative.[80]

↫ How to Read a Cento

A cento depends on its reader's familiarity with its source text. Giovanni Polara made this point when he wrote that the cento "non ha esistenza autonoma. Vive finché dura l'opera centonata: se questa si perdesse, non sarebbe piú riconoscibile come centone, e diverrebbe un testo qualunque, un banale, modesto «originale»" (1989, 274). An original may be read on its own, but a cento must be read through its source. Of course, every form of intertextuality depends on the reader's double awareness of both the primary text and its intertext(s). The cento, however, turns what is usually a secondary relationship into the motivating principle of its existence. For this reason, Françoise Desbordes concluded that the cento was particularly dependent on the active participation of its reader: "Le centon en *son* temps et devant *son* public, est une forme de l'art allusif qui compte avant tout sur la mémoire et la participation active du lecteur" (1979, 99). Scott McGill also noted the demands placed upon the reader of a cento: "Because the cento is the kind of *ludus* it is, the processes that lie behind its linguistic surface intrude more forcefully on the reading act than do the processes underlying the production of conventional poetry."[81] The cento asks its reader to constantly engage its source in order to follow the complexity of its composition.

In order to understand the complexity of a cento, we should think of it as having three distinct layers: the narrative surface of the text, its allusive engagement with the specific context of its source (microtextual allusion), and the abstract hypertextuality of its repeated words (macrotextual allusion).[82] The narrative surface of the text is the new poem created from the borrowed lines and half lines of its source.[83] The term "microtextual allusion" describes the circumscribed relation between individual fragments and their

---

80. It is worth noting that the Vergilian centos use only the *Eclogues*, *Georgics*, and *Aeneid* and never the pseudo-Vergilian poems (McGill 2005, 153n2).

81. Ibid., 9; compare Bažil 2009, 64–65. Hardie 2007 also shows the cento's need for a reader.

82. I borrow the terms "microtextual allusion" and "macrotextual allusion" from McGill (2005, 24–30).

83. On the importance of a cento having a coherent narrative, see ibid., 18–23.

original Vergilian context. "Macrotextual allusion" describes the relation between centonic composition and Vergilian poetry. That is, macrotextual allusion is concerned not primarily with the use of individual words but with the poet's wholesale transposition of Vergilian poetry. Because each line of a cento performs various functions at these different levels of reading, the reader must constantly choose which level to follow. Because a cento allows its reader to choose his own path through its text, a cento is an open poem.

In *Virgil Recomposed: The Mythological and Secular Centos in Antiquity*, McGill (2005) has noted the importance of the two levels at which a cento alludes to Vergil, and he provides convincing readings of the ways in which the mythological and secular centos actually operate as texts. My own approach to these centos is distinct from his in three ways. First, because I approach these texts through the reader, I present the reader's options as three levels of the text that are disconnected from one another and yet self-coherent. These separate layers are the organizing principle that structures the reader's approach to the text. Second, I approach the centos as open texts. They are meant to present their reader with possibilities, and at each moment, readers must choose how they will read the text. Third, I use these layers to show that the Latin cento marks a particular aesthetic moment in the history of Latin poetry, whereas McGill focuses on the reading of a cento as a timeless possibility. By approaching the centos as layered texts, I show that they are in fact open texts and that late antique poetry is marked by its turn toward openness. This feature of late antique textuality helps in turn to explain the cento's appeal to a late antique audience.

In order to show how each layer of the text actually works, I will present three readings of the proem to the anonymous *Hippodamia*.[84] In this proem, the poet invokes the Muses and declares the theme of his poem. I use this passage because it is an elaborate invocation—namely, that point at which a poet calls on the gods to give him authority and to inspire his poem—and, therefore, particularly suited to a discussion of the poetic layers of the text. I should stress, though, that any passage of any cento can be read along these lines.

First, the narrative surface of a cento functions in the same way as does that of any other poem. The poet has something to say, and he says it to the best of his ability. The invocation of the *Hippodamia* is immediately recognizable as such, for it employs the devices typically found at the beginning of a classical poem in epic meter: divinities addressed in the vocative case, imperatives enjoining the divinity to begin the poem, first-person

---

84. The *Hippodamia* has been edited by Paola Paolucci (2006) and discussed by McGill (2005, 85–88).

pronouncements of poetic intent, and the subject of the poem in the accusative case:

Pandite nunc Helicona, deae, nunc pectore firmo
este duces, o si qua via est, et pronuba Iuno;
pallida Tisiphone, fecundum concute pectus.
non hic Atridae et scelus exitiale Lacaenae:
hic crudelis amor. nunc illas promite vires,
maius opus moveo: quaesitas sanguine dotes
et scelerum poenas inconcessosque hymenaeos.

(1–7)

Now open Helicon, you goddesses, be strong now in heart
and be my guides, oh if there is any way, along with Juno the
    bridesmaid;
you, pale Tisiphone, stir up my heart and make it fertile.
The sons of Atreus are not here, nor the deadly crime of Sparta:
Here is a cruel love. Bring forward now that strength,
I start a greater work: a dowry sought by blood
and the payment for crimes and a forbidden marriage.

The poet employs various rhetorical figures: notably, anaphora with *nunc* in the first line and a brief priamel in lines 4 and 5.[85] In regards to content, the poet asks the muses of Helicon, Juno, and Tisiphone to lead him through his poem and to stir up his heart. Then the poet declares that this poem will be about love. After another request for strength and the statement that this is a greater work ("maius opus"), the poet expands upon the theme of his poem, the deadly chariot race in which Pelops defeated Oenomaus and won the right to marry Hippodamia. Although each of these seven lines is composed of half lines from throughout Vergil's poetry, they form a coherent text on their own.

In addition to telling his own story, the poet declares that this will be a greater work because he will not repeat the stale themes of the Trojan War. What does it mean for the centonist to construct a *maius opus* out of Vergil while at the same time rejecting epic poetry? McGill suggests that the *Hippodamia* is a post-Vergilian reinscription of mythological poetry (i.e., the poet restores what had been a trite and tired theme to new prominence).[86] In support of this view, McGill recalls *Georgics* 3.6–8:

---

85. On rhetorical figures in the centos, see McGill 2005, 14–16.

86. Ibid., 85–86. McGill's fourth chapter, "Omnia Iam Vulgata," considers the mythological centos of Vergil and borrows its title from Verg. G. 3.4 (ibid., 71–91).

cui non dictus Hylas puer et Latonia Delos
Hippodameque umeroque Pelops insignis eburno,
acer equis?

Who has not talked about the boy Hylas and Latona on Delos
and Hippodamia and Pelops, who is famous for his ivory shoulder
and keen with horses?

Since "umeroque Pelops insignis eburno" is used at *Hippodamia* 150, we can be sure that the centonist remembered Vergil's rejection of Pelops and his famous chariot race. However, the poet of the *Hippodamia* has a story to tell and a new poem to write, and he is quite willing to reject Vergil's authority. For that reason, the poet invokes the gods to aid him in his task (and Juno and Tisiphone are quite the gods to invoke)![87] On its surface, a cento is simply a poem, and the poet of a cento makes use of the figures employed in any other poem in order to produce poetry. The reader of a cento, therefore, may always enjoy its surface and narrative apart from its intertextual and ludic foundations.[88]

Second, the reader of a cento may compare each fragment to its context in the source text. In a microtextual allusion, the centonist alludes to a specific passage in his source, in the same way as any other poet would. The difference in a cento is that it is entirely possible to read every fragment as an allusion. In practice, of course, most readers will not see a microtextual allusion in every line. Nevertheless, the presence of microtextual allusions allows the reader to pursue this possibility.[89] And the openness of centonic poetry depends on the fact that a reader must constantly choose which path to follow. Below is the same passage from the *Hippodamia*, with the source for each hemistich cited:

Pandite nunc Helicona, deae (*Aen.* 7.641),[90] nunc pectore firmo
(*Aen.* 6.261)

---

87. On the role of the underworld in initiating the action of the *Aeneid* as well as subsequent, post-Vergilian epic, see Hardie 1991, chap. 3, "Heaven and Hell," 57–87.

88. That late antique readers did in fact view the centos as discrete texts is neatly confirmed by the fact that two centos (Luxurius's *Epithalamium Fridi* and Pomponius's *Versus ad gratiam Domini*) imitate earlier centos (Ausonius's *Cento nuptialis* and Proba's *Cento*, respectively). In reusing a previous cento, these centonists reveal that their poetry could and did function as literature in the same way as any other poem. On the intertextual link between Luxurius and Ausonius, see McGill 2005, 104–5. On Pomponius and Proba, see McGill 2001 and Bažil 2009, 209–18.

89. McGill (2005) pursues a microtextual reading of sections of each secular cento.

90. = *Aen.* 10.163.

este duces, o si qua via est (*Aen.* 6.194), et pronuba Iuno (*Aen.* 4.166);
pallida Tisiphone (*G.* 3.552),[91] fecundum concute pectus (*Aen.* 7.338)!
non hic Atridae (*Aen.* 9.602) et scelus exitiale Lacaenae (*Aen.* 6.511):
hic crudelis amor (*Aen.* 6.24). nunc illas promite vires (*Aen.* 5.191),
maius opus moveo (*Aen.* 7.45): quaesitas sanguine dotes (*Aen.* 7.423)
et scelerum poenas (*Aen.* 8.668) inconcessosque hymenaeos (*Aen.*
     1.651).

When the first line of the poem is read microtextually, the reader recalls that
"pandite nunc Helicona, deae" was spoken at two points in the *Aeneid*. At
7.641, the poet invokes the Muses at the beginning of his catalog of the Italian forces; at 10.163, the poet invokes the Muses at the beginning of the
catalog of Etruscan ships. The original contexts correspond closely to the
centonist's invocation, and so the fragment seems to fit naturally within its
new context. At *Aeneid* 6.261 ("nunc animis opus, Aenea, nunc pectore
firmo"), the Sibyl calls on Aeneas to prepare himself for their descent to the
underworld. On the microtextual level, "nunc pectore firmo" alludes to
Aeneas's mysterious and poetic descent. Perhaps, one may think, the *Hippodamia* will also engage the limits of poetry. "Nunc illas promite vires"
works somewhat differently. In the *Aeneid*, it comes from the ship race during the funeral games of book 5. Mnestheus urges his men to recall the
strength they showed at the most difficult points in their journey from Troy.
The *Hippodamia* poet, however, calls on his muses to bring forth their ability
to inspire cruel love. The referent of "illas" is different, and the subject of
"promite" has changed. Here we have an example of antanaclasis, the figure
of speech in which a word or phrase is repeated in a different sense.[92] On
the microtextual level, the reader explores the poet's use, reuse, and misuse
of Vergilian fragments.

Third, the centonist alludes on the macrotextual level to the differences
between his own aims and Vergil's poetry. Because a cento constantly repeats the exact words of its source, it always allows its reader to consider its
poem as a ludic exercise in poetic memory: the poet approaches Vergil as an
open text, and the reader enjoys the extreme manipulation of the cento's
source.[93] The difference between Vergil's text and its reshaping within a
cento stands out most clearly at those points at which the centonist departs

---

91. = *Aen.* 10.761.

92. Polara uses the term "antanaclasis" to characterize the allusivity of the cento (1981 and 1989,
266–69).

93. McGill notes that the cento approaches Vergil as an open text, that the cento is an extreme form
of intertextuality, and that it is ludic in nature (2005, xvii–xviii, 23, and 7–10).

most drastically from Vergil's poetry. Therefore, the parodic[94] and transformational[95] centos most clearly reveal the dynamics of macrotextual allusion. But because a centonist revises the meaning of each fragment that is incorporated into the cento, the reader of a cento will consistently think of the work as a specifically hermeneutic game. In that way, a cento constantly alludes to its source macrotextually, and a reader may always pursue its meaning on the macrotextual level.

On the macrotextual level, the first line of the *Hippodamia* ("pandite nunc Helicona, deae, nunc pectore firmo") leads the reader to reflect that the meaning of *nunc* is entirely dependent on its context. Further, the centonist's invocation of the Muses is also in a way an invocation of Vergil, for the centonist's material comes from Vergil rather than from any divine Muse. Moreover, the phrase "maius opus moveo" takes on new meaning when the cento is read as a cento. Whereas a surface reading of the text takes "maius opus moveo" to be a claim to poetic primacy and a microtextual reading of the same line notes that the phrase came from Vergil's invocation at the beginning of the second half of the *Aeneid*, a macrotextual reading of the phrase considers the irony of the centonist's claim to be writing a greater poem while at the same time using Vergilian fragments to do so. Thus the macrotextual level is distinct from the microtextual level insofar as a macrotextual reading stands back from the text and negotiates the cento's relation to its Vergilian source. And even when a particular fragment bears no relation to its context in Vergil, it may allude to the fact that a cento is always a secondary text.

In short, the reader of a cento must constantly navigate the three layers of its text: its surface and its microtextual and macrotextual allusions. Although my analysis has treated each aspect separately, the actual reading of a cento will constantly switch among them. While microtextual allusion revolves around the pastness of the Vergilian words, macrotextual allusion concerns their present instantiation: the tension between source and text is brought into high relief. Centonic poetry forces the reader to play a strong and active role in the poem because it presents a text that is always open to a multiplicity of readings.

---

94. The parodic centos are the *De panificio* and the *De alea*, which are discussed by McGill (ibid., 55–64 and 64–70, respectively). Also parodic are the portions of Ausonius's *Cento nuptialis* and Luxurius's *Epithalamium Fridi* that describe the sex of their newlyweds (ibid., 103–8).

95. The Christian centos transform Vergil in terms of content (Bažil 2009); Hosidius Geta's *Medea*, Ausonius's *Cento nuptialis*, and Luxurius's *Epithalamium Fridi* transform Vergil in terms of genre (McGill 2005, 31–52 and 92–103).

✒ The Cento in Late Antiquity

In the previous section, I described the reading of a cento in modern terms. In this section, I analyze the presentation and reception of centos in late antiquity. The most extended discussion of centonic poetry comes from the prefatory letter that Ausonius wrote for his *Cento nuptialis*. Ausonius gave special attention to the cento's ludic and paradoxical qualities. Centos were also discussed in relation to Christian exegesis: Tertullian and Jerome dismissively compared heretical interpretations of the scriptures to centonic poetry, while both Proba and an anonymous scribe presented her cento as a positive improvement upon the text of Vergil. Both contemporary critics and proponents of the cento recognized that it was an extreme form of appropriation. The macrotextual level of the cento, its ability to play with the hermeneutic possibilities of a poetic text, is a common thread throughout their responses. As a group, they are most concerned with how centos both treat Vergil as an open text and elicit a parallel response from their readers.

Ausonius's prefatory epistle to Axius Paulus (1) describes his cento as an affront to Vergil's dignity, (2) considers the cento's ability to reshape Vergil's text, (3) compares the cento to a game called *stomachion*, and (4) recounts the contradictions inherent in the text of a cento.[96] I will consider these four aspects of Ausonius's letter in this order.

Ausonius tells Paulus that his cento imposes a shameful meaning on Vergil. In an apology at the beginning of his letter,[97] Ausonius recounts his displeasure:

> piget equidem Vergiliani carminis dignitatem tam ioculari dehonestasse materia.
>
> (*Cento, Ausonius Paulo sal.*)

> For my part, I am annoyed at having dishonored the grandeur of the Vergilian poem with so playful a subject.

In the prose *parecbasis* that introduces the final section of the cento (on Gratian's sexual relations with Constantia), Ausonius repeats the same regret:

> cetera quoque cubiculi et lectuli operta prodentur, ab eodem auctore collecta, ut bis erubescamus qui et Vergilium faciamus impudentem.
>
> (*Cento, Parecbasis*)

---

96. This letter is discussed by McGill 2005, 1–11 and 18–21; and Pollmann 2004.

97. On the penchant of authors to include apologies and *recusationes* in their prefaces, see note 66 in Chapter 2.

the remaining secrets of the bedroom (and the bed) will be revealed, [in pieces] gathered from the same author. I must blush twice, since I am also making Vergil immodest.

In both passages, Ausonius expresses his regard for the chaste poet's honor.[98] His regret, however, is muted both by the fact that he did in fact send his poem to Paulus and by his subsequent observation that its contents were taken directly from Vergil (and therefore that he should not be held responsible for any obscenity).[99] But what concerns us here is that Ausonius attributes to his work the ability to alter Vergil. Ausonius's cento produces a reading of Vergil's work that changes the grandeur of that previous poem ("Vergiliani carminis dignitatem dehonestasse") and makes Vergil immodest ("Vergilium faciamus impudentem"). Ausonius tells Paulus that his cento will change the way that other readers look at the *Aeneid*. By borrowing the exact words of a previous source, the cento shows that its source is liable to external influence.

If Ausonius's cento lowers the register of Vergil's poetry, it also reshapes its source into something new. That is, his cento works both backward to affect its source and forward to create a new poem. Ausonius makes this point by contrasting the text as it was in its source and as it now is in his cento (the oxymoronic quality of Ausonius's description will be considered later):

> accipe igitur opusculum de inconexis continuum, de diversis unum, de seriis ludicrum, de alieno nostrum, ne in sacris et fabulis aut Thyonianum mireris aut Virbium, illum de Dionyso, hunc de Hippolyto reformatum.
>
> (*Cento, Ausonius Paulo sal.*)

So take my little poem. It's continuous, from unconnected pieces; it's one, from separate pieces; it's playful, from serious pieces; it's mine, from someone else. You'll no longer be amazed, in the mysteries and myths, by either Thyonianus[100] or Virbius[101] (the former was reshaped from Dionysus, the latter from Hippolytus).

---

98. On Ausonius's use of Vergil Parthenias, see McGill 2005, 108–14.

99. "Et si quid in nostro ioco aliquorum hominum severitas vestita condemnat, de Vergilio arcessitum sciat" (*Cento*, Green 1999, 154).

100. On the uncertain source of this epithet, see Green 1991, ad loc.

101. On Virbius, see *Aen.* 7.765–69.

"Continuum," "unum," and "nostrum" make the cento sound like a rather stable and ordered text. Thyonianus and Virbius very neatly illustrate Ausonius's point because the preposition *de* emphasizes that these are not the same characters but new characters drawn out of the old figures.[102] Put differently, it is their identities and not merely their names that have been changed. Like Thyonianus and Virbius, the cento has its own unity. As McGill has pointed out in reference to this passage, "[T]he patchwork text is not another of the same thing, but a different entity made out of the same material" (2005, 19). Despite the obvious secondariness of his cento, Ausonius is also aware that it is a new poem, in its own way self-coherent.

As Ausonius continues to explain the cento, he compares it to a game known to him as *stomachion*[103] and elsewhere as *loculus Archimedius*.[104] The game is played with fourteen pieces of various geometric shapes; the point of the game is to arrange the pieces so as to form different figures (Ausonius lists as examples a war elephant, a wild boar, a flying goose, a gladiator in arms, a sitting hunter, a barking dog, a tower, and a drinking cup). The pieces of this game are like the fragments of Vergil's text;[105] their rearrangement produces new figures, and the skill of the player or poet consists in his ability to combine the given material. Thus Ausonius compares the cento to a game that creates almost limitless possibilities within a constrained system.[106] Like a *stomachion* player, the poet enjoys the ability to reconfigure Vergil's poetry. And the composition of an experienced player, Ausonius says, is a marvelous thing.[107]

Ausonius describes the final goal of his game in contradictory terms:[108]

> hoc ergo centonis opusculum ut ille ludus tractatur, pari modo sensus diversi ut congruant, adoptiva quae sunt ut cognata videantur, aliena

---

102. This point was made by McGill (2005, 19). Marcellus Empiricus also used Virbius as a metaphor for textual reassembly, as noted by Formisano (2007, 284).

103. This name for the game is attested in Ausonius's letter, in the title of Ennodius's *Carm.* 2.133 (Hartel), and in a short treatise by Archimedes on the various combinations of its figures. For Archimedes, see J. L. Heiberg, ed., *Archimedis opera omnia cum commentariis Eutocii*, 2nd ed. (Leipzig: Teubner, 1913), 2:416–24. Green (1991, ad loc.) correctly prefers *stomachion* to the *ostomachion* presented in one of the manuscripts, but he needlessly prints the word in Greek characters.

104. This name is used by Marius Victorinus in his *Ars grammatica* (Keil 6:100–101) and in a *De metris* falsely ascribed by the manuscripts to Atilius Fortunatianus (Keil 6:271–72; on the text, see Herzog and Schmidt 1989, § 525.3).

105. On this game and the ludism of the cento, see the discussion in McGill 2005, 8–9 and 20–21.

106. As Reviel Netz and William Noel note in their book on the Archimedes codex, there are 17,152 different ways just to form a square out of the fourteen *stomachion* pieces (2007, 255).

107. "Peritorum concinnatio miraculum est." On the importance of *concinnatio* for Ausonius's poetics, see Sánchez Salor 1976, 175–82.

108. For Ausonius's delight in the oxymoronic qualities of his poetry, see also *Technop.* 2 and *Technop.* 4.

ne interluceant, arcessita ne vim redarguant, densa ne supra modum
protuberent, hiulca ne pateant.

(Cento, Ausonius Paulo sal.)

Therefore, this little centonic work is handled like that game, so that
in the same way divergent meanings should come together, so that
what is adopted should seem to be genuine, so that what is foreign
should not show, so that what is forced should not prove my violence,
so that what is thick should not stand out too much, so that what is
gaping apart should not be exposed.

It is possible to read this oxymoronic language as mere rhetorical embellishment and to conclude that Ausonius meant to say only that the cento should
present a coherent text whose clean surface belies its underlying fragmentation. Since, however, Ausonius allows the contrary terms of the hypotext to
intrude upon his description, they should not be dismissed. The contradictions within the cento appeal to Ausonius. He goes out of his way to say that
even the best-constructed cento is made of diverse pieces that did not belong
together. Because a cento both appears genuine and is adopted, it allows its
reader to pursue both aspects of the text. Ausonius concludes his preface by
saying that if he succeeds in achieving these goals, Paulus will declare that he
has composed a cento. If Paulus judges them a failure, the verses will return
from whence they came, that is, back to the Vergilian text.[109] In Ausonius's
view, a cento is a ludic exercise that both presents a new poem and creates a
sense of wonder at the centonist's ability to reshape the original work.

The other late antique authors whose writings about the cento have sur-
vived also focus on the form's ability to rewrite its source. Unlike Ausonius,
they present centonic poetry as a serious form of interpretation and not as a
playful game (although, of course, Ausonius's game is also serious in a sense).
I will first discuss the negative responses of Tertullian and Jerome and then
the more constructive comments of Proba and her scribe.

Tertullian compares the centonist's technique both to Marcion's choice
to excise portions of the scriptures and to Valentinus's reinterpretation of
scripture (De praescr. haer. 38.7–10). He says that these interpreters of the
Bible use their text in the same ways as some other proponents of secular
literature ("saeculares scripturae") use Vergil and Homer:

vides hodie ex Virgilio fabulam in totum aliam componi, materia secundum versus et versibus secundum materiam concinnatis. denique

---

109. This passage is discussed at the end of Chapter 2.

Hosidius Geta[110] Medeam tragoediam ex Virgilio plenissime exsuxit. meus quidem propinquus ex eodem poeta inter cetera stili sui otia Pinacem Cebetis explicuit. Homerocentones etiam vocari solent qui de carminibus Homeri propria opera more centonario ex multis hinc inde compositis in unum sarciunt corpus.

(De praescr. haer. 39.3–5)

Today you see completely different stories being composed out of Virgil, as they construct their material according to his verses and his verses according to their material. Indeed, Hosidius Geta sucked the entirety of his tragedy, the *Medea,* out of Virgil. Even my relative set out, among the other compositions of his leisure, the *Pinax* of Cebes out of the same poet. There are also the ones we call *Homerocentones,* which fix up into a single unit, from Homer's poems, their own work in a patchwork manner, out of the many pieces drawn together from here and there.

Whatever Tertullian thinks of the cento as a literary pursuit,[111] he definitely thinks of it as a secondary text that must be read in light of its peculiar form of composition. Although the cento is a completely different story ("fabula in totum alia"), it retains the traces of its former existence. For Tertullian, a cento is a new, though perhaps not wholly legitimate, text.

Jerome was more aggressively opposed to centonic poetry, partly because by his time centos had been written on Christian as well as secular themes.[112] His main argument against centonic poetry is that it misrepresents the (Vergilian) text. In letter 53, Jerome discusses the proper interpretation of the scriptures and condemns those who, out of a lack of understanding, force a text to say what it did not originally mean:

Sola scripturarum ars est, quam sibi omnes passim vindicent: "scribimus indocti doctique poemata passim." hanc garrula anus, hanc delirus senex, hanc soloecista verbosus, hanc universi praesumunt, lacerant, docent, antequam discant. . . . taceo de meis similibus, qui si forte ad scripturas sanctas post saeculares litteras venerint et sermone composito aurem populi mulserint, quicquid dixerint, hoc legem dei putant nec scire dignantur, quid prophetae, quid apostoli senserint, sed ad sensum

---

110. The name Hosidius Geta is corrupt in the manuscripts. On its reconstruction, see Lamacchia 1981.

111. McGill suggests that Tertullian and Jerome react only to the misreading of the Bible and not to the cento form itself (2005, xvi–xvii).

112. On Jerome and centonic poetry, see McGill 2007.

suum incongrua aptant testimonia, quasi grande sit et non vitiosissi-
mum dicendi genus depravare sententias et ad voluntatem suam scrip-
turam trahere repugnantem, quasi non legerimus Homerocentonas et
Vergiliocentonas ac non sic etiam Maronem sine Christo possimus di-
cere Christianum, quia scripserit: "iam redit et virgo, redeunt Saturnia
regna, iam nova progenies caelo demittitur alto"; et patrem loquentem
ad filium, "nate, meae vires, mea magna potentia solus"; et post verba
salvatoris in cruce, "talia perstabat memorans fixusque manebat." puer-
ilia sunt haec et circulatorum ludo similia, docere, quod ignores.

(Ep. 53.7)

The art of the scriptures is the only one which all people claim as
their own: "We write poems without discrimination, the learned and
unlearned."[113] A garrulous old woman, a crazy old man, a wordy
bumbler, everyone presumes to this art; they mangle it; they teach
before they have learned. . . . I am not talking about my peers, who, if
they should come to the holy scriptures after secular literature and
should tickle the people's ears with a contrived sermon, think that
whatever they say is the law of God. And they do not even bother to
learn what the prophets and apostles intended. Instead, they adapt in-
congruous testimonies to their own interpretation, as if distorting one's
meaning and forcing scripture, against its will, to their own desires is
something grand and not a most vicious form of speaking, as if we
have not read the Homeric and Vergilian centos, and as if[114] we could
not say in this way that even Vergil was a Christian, on account of his
having written: "Now the girl also returns, the kingdom of Saturn
returns, now a new progeny is sent down from on high";[115] and the
father speaking to his son: "You alone, son, are my strength, my great
force";[116] and then the words of the Savior on the cross: "He endured
such things in thought and remained fixed."[117] These things are child-
ish and like carnival games, teaching what you do not know.

---

113. Hor. *Epist.* 2.1.117.

114. I take *ac* as introducing a second subordinate clause dependent on *quasi* (pace McGill 2007).
Herzog and Schmidt print *ac si non sic* (as an emendation?) when they cite this passage (1989,
5:340). *Ac si* may be correct, but it would create an even longer (and abnormal) string of conjunc-
tions and adverbs.

115. Verg. *Ecl.* 4.6–7.

116. *Aen.* 1.664.

117. *Aen.* 2.650.

The *garrula anus* whom Jerome attacks is probably none other than Proba herself, for in her cento she used two of the Vergilian lines whose Christian interpretation Jerome condemns.[118] The forcefulness of Jerome's response reveals a real difference of opinion between himself and those whom he represents as the unlearned majority. Those who write "Christian centos," those who want to read Vergil as a Christian, and those who force scripture to their own interpretation ("ad sensum suum") are all strong readers who look beyond the original meaning of a text. The extreme case of the cento, which constantly invites the reader to acknowledge its Vergilian subtext, met with strong resistance from Jerome. But Jerome's resistance is unsurprising since he is a model proponent of authorship in the strongest of terms.[119] Jerome's strong dismissal of the cento proves only that the full ability of a cento to reshape its source was already recognized in late antiquity.

The *Cento Probae*, which provides an overview of history from creation to the ascension of Christ, was probably written in the middle of the fourth century by Faltonia Betitia Proba (*PLRE* 2).[120] In the proem to her *Cento*, Proba declares the technique of her poem (note that this line is not drawn from Vergil; Proba begins the cento proper only at line 24):[121]

Vergilium cecinisse loquar pia munera Christi.

(23)

I will say that Vergil sang the kind gifts of Christ.

Proba transforms Vergil by saying that he actually sang of Christ. But *loquar* makes her statement subjective and indistinguishable from the poetic moment of the text. For that reason, I do not think that Proba makes any sort of argument about the actual content of Vergil's poetry. In this respect, I differ from McGill, who concludes (largely because of the tense of *cecinisse*) that Proba employs "an idiosyncratic allegorical approach" to "bring out the Christian in Virgil, rather than impose Christian material on him" (2007, 176). Proba performs her own reading of Vergil; and she does not

---

118. *Aen.* 1.664 appears at *Cento Probae* 403, and *Aen.* 2.650 at 624. Hers is the only extant cento that uses *Aen.* 2.650 of Christ on the cross (E. A. Clark and Hatch 1981, 104–5). Additionally, Vessey is confident that Ambrose was one of the rhetors condemned by Jerome (2007, 43n44).

119. See Vessey 1994 and Foucault 1979, both cited in Conybeare 2000, 44.

120. On the controversy surrounding Proba's identity, see Green 2008.

121. For full discussion of the proem to Proba's *Cento*, see Green 1997 and Bažil 2009, 116–24. Sineri 2011 is a good commentary on the entire poem.

much care about Vergil's original meaning (*sensus suus*, as Jerome would say). Rather, she explains that her cento will turn Vergil into a poet who already did sing of Christ. And the form of the cento allows her to do this in literally every line. If Jerome thought that Proba was actually concerned about whether or not Vergil wrote of Christ, he seems to have been mistaken.[122] Proba writes for and within a community of readers who value their own role in shaping the texts they encounter.

Between 395 and 397,[123] an anonymous scribe appended a fifteen-line dedication to Proba's Vergilian cento.[124] After addressing the emperor and before describing the contents of the cento, this dedication asks that the poem be read intertextually:

> dignare Maronem
> mutatum in melius divino agnoscere sensu,
> scribendum famulo quem iusseras.
>
> (*Cento Probae*, praef. 3–5)

> Please recognize Vergil
> turned to the better by a divine meaning,
> whom you had ordered your servant to write.

The preface requests ("dignare") that Vergil's presence be recognized within the words of Proba's poem. A proper reading of the cento, from this point of view, depends on the reader's participation in the poet's intertextuality. Moreover, the reader is asked to recognize a Vergil who has been changed for the better. The cento, therefore, depends on the reader's acknowledgment of the original text that lies beneath the cento. The instrument that produces the new Vergil is a *divinus sensus*, a secondary (nonauthorial) meaning imposed upon the text.[125] Centonic poetry most clearly reveals the instability of the poetic text in the face of future readings. And the concluding

---

122. To be more precise, Proba qua centonist is not concerned with that question; qua poet, she emulatively rejects Vergil's poetics. On her rejection of Vergil, see Bažil 2009, 116–21.

123. For the date of this preface, see Mastandrea 2001, 566–69.

124. This poem is included in Schenkl's edition of Proba's *Cento* and as number 735 in Riese's *Anthologia Latina*. The argument in Mastandrea 2001 in favor of identifying this scribe as Flavius Anicius Petronius Probus (*PLRE* 11) is intriguing but by no means certain.

125. *Sensu* is ambiguous between the faculty of perception and its content. I take that ambiguity to be indicative of the scribe's equation of meaning with the point of reception. On the possible meanings of *sensu* here, compare McGill 2007, 175; and Mastandrea 2001, 566.

lines of this preface are precisely concerned with the reading and transmission of Proba's cento:

> haec relegas servesque diu tradasque minori
> Arcadio, haec ille suo semini,[126] haec tua semper
> accipiat doceatque suos augusta propago.
>
> (Proba, Cento Probae, praef. 13–15)

> Read these over, keep them a while, and hand them on to the
>   younger
> Arcadius.[127] And may he pass them on to his children; and may your
>   solemn descendants always receive and teach them to their family.

These closing lines of the preface reemphasize the need for careful study, rereading, preservation, and interpretation of the poetic text. Like any other text, a cento depends on its reception; and this scribe hopes that his audience will be watchful. By describing Vergil as "mutatum in melius," the scribe acknowledges even more clearly than Proba that her work aims to transform Vergil. He also recognizes that the success of that transformation is dependent on its reception.

Ausonius, Tertullian, Jerome, Proba, and her anonymous scribe all agree that a cento permits new and powerful readings of its source. Proba and her scribe also welcome the transformations imposed upon that source. Ausonius plays most fully with the ambiguity of his cento, which both is and is not Vergilian. These contemporary readers confirm that the cento is a form of poetry dependent in late antiquity on powerful readings imposed on the text.

Centonic poetry, therefore, creates a fragmented text that remains for the reader to interpret. The form was popular in late antiquity, and it depends on treating Vergil's poems as an open text and on the reader's willingness to explore the poem and to create connections between its various layers. In this way, the cento, like the figural poetry of Optatian and the allegory of Prudentius, shows the openness of late antique texts. If one were to read the centos as if they were fixed and closed texts, the potential and the vitality of the form would be lost. To put it differently, the centonists expect to be read in the same way in which they have read Vergil.

---

126. With some hesitation, Riese prints *generi* in favor of the manuscripts' unmetrical *semini*.

127. It is most likely that "Arcadio minori" refers to the as-yet-unborn first child of Arcadius and Eudoxia, who, as it turned out, was a girl and was named Flacilla (see Green 1995, 561–62; and Mastandrea 2001, 567–69).

From Fragmentation to Interpretation

Optatian, Prudentius, and the centonists compel their readers to trace the various strands latent in their poetry and then to make something of those strands, to join them together in a way that the text can at most only suggest. The verbal surface of their poetry conceals a variety of meanings that must be encountered and either accepted or rejected. Because the textual layers compel the reader to look for connections and significance beneath the surface ("aliud verbis, aliud sensu"), they draw the reader into the text so that she may participate in making the poem's words and lines mean in some way.

The poems I have discussed in this chapter are fragmented by their different layers. The poems of Optatian are a literal grid. Prudentius's allegory creates a meaning that is distinct and even separable from its narrative. The centos are composed entirely of fragments. On the surface, this is not surprising, for Michael Roberts describes the poetry of late antiquity as characterized by a jeweled style, by fragmentary narrative and tessellated description. However, in his seminal work from 1989, Roberts does not inquire into the openness of these texts or the potential meanings to be drawn from any readerly text. The form of the poem and the talent of the author motivated Roberts's view of late antiquity. This is his analysis of the cento, of the miniaturization of late antique poetry, and of the rhetorical delight in hard words:

> Words are viewed as possessing a physical presence of their own, distinct from any considerations of sense or syntax. They may be moved like building blocks or pieces in a puzzle to create ever new formal constructs. It is this sense of the physical existence of words and of meter as their structural matrix that underlies the ingenious verbal patterns of Optatianus Porfyrius and the *Technopaegnion* of Ausonius.[128]

By treating these works as open poetry, I have shown that "considerations of sense" are in fact essential. More than creating ingenious patterns, the late antique poet creates a series of meanings that are purposefully and intentionally fluid. By being open to the reader, late antique poetry defers a

---

128. Roberts 1989, 58. Compare ibid., 64–65: "The placing and ordering of words within the text fragmented by *leptologia* was a matter of *variatio*. And the individual elements to be varied were increasingly viewed as brilliant, multicolored flowers or jewels. The art of the poet lay in setting the variegated pieces off against each other to best effect."

sense of textual coherence, which is to be found only in an individual's momentary interpretation.[129] Thus the figure of the reader closes the gaps inherent in open poetry and offers the sense that meaning can and must be established here and now.

The figural poetry of Optatian, the *Psychomachia*, and the centos are extreme texts. Nevertheless, they reveal something central to late antique poetry as a whole. In the same way in which their fragmentation leaves the work of interpretation up to the reader, late antique poetry in general demands to be read not as a closed and permanent artifact but as a potential script. The gaps and fragmentation in the text are opportunities for the reader. To be understood in their own context or at all, these late antique poems must be approached as open texts.

---

129. Compare Roberts's explanation of architectural spoliation, which he connects to the poetry of late antiquity: "It is the Late Antique aesthetic of discontinuity—the emphasis on the part, as object of ornamentation, rather than on the whole—that permits such unclassical use of the classical inheritance" (ibid., 97).

✒ CHAPTER 4

The Presence of the Reader
Allusion in Late Antiquity

Like contemporary texts and paratexts, the hypertextuality of late antiquity was directed toward active readers.[1] When late antique poets allude to classical texts, they often do so in ways that create space for reading. Because late antique allusions lie on the surface of the text, they create a sense of the reader's presence. And the particular dynamics of allusion in late antiquity mark the distance between classical and late antique poetry. They reveal the pastness of the past, and they call for an appreciative engagement in the processes of interpretation. I will begin by discussing, as a baseline, the ways in which allusion was employed by classical poets; then I will treat allusions from late antiquity that are progressively more exposed to the presence of their reader. Because late antique allusions do not need to be read as referential, the referentiality (or not) of allusion will serve as a pivot between classical and late antique poetics. Instead of asserting their control over the tradition, late antique poets present their work as a fragmented and open text: they juxtapose independent fragments of classical poetry, they set these units in apposition to their own words, and they avoid emulation. In so doing, they reveal themselves as readers and allow their audience to engage in the continuing play of interpretation.

---

1. For the distinction between hypertext and hypotext, I am indebted to Gérard Genette's *Palimpsestes: La littérature au second degré* (1982).

☙ The Referentiality of Classical Allusion

The allusions of classical Latin poetry recall an earlier text and construct their meaning through this hypotext. It is important that they work as references back to a different context. Scholars agree that classical poets directly engage, through allusion, the context of their hypotext. And although various theories and approaches have been applied to allusion, they agree that its basic function is to refer to or interact with another text. But—as I will go on to show—late antique allusions do not necessarily fit this mold.

Most of the scholarship on allusion within classical studies can be traced back to Giorgio Pasquali's 1942 article "Arte allusiva." Pasquali began his groundbreaking piece by invoking the voice of his detractors. They thought that Pasquali was engaged in source criticism: "Dicono: «Tu, quando spieghi i classici antichi . . . li soffochi con i confronti, dimentico che la fonte della poesia è sempre nell'anima del poeta e mai in libri che possa aver letto. La tua è fatica vana»" (1942, 185). Pasquali responds by demonstrating that allusions are integral to a proper understanding of poetry since a knowledge of the source of an allusion clarifies the meaning of the poem. He explains the difference between an inert source and an allusion: "Le reminiscenze possono essere inconsapevoli; le imitazioni, il poeta può desiderare che sfuggano al pubblico; le allusioni non producono l'effetto voluto se non su un lettore che si ricordi chiaramente del testo cui si riferiscono" (1942, 185). By distinguishing so sharply between reminiscences on one end and allusions on the other, Pasquali distances the practice of allusion from simple repetition.

Although he recognizes the importance for allusion of a knowledgeable reader, Pasquali retains a focus upon the author's desire and the text's referentiality, and consequently upon *aemulatio*, a particularly authorial form of allusion.[2] Despite privileging the poet's agency, Pasquali does present three striking cases of a poet's exact and extended repetition of his hypotext. He cites one line of the *Eclogues* drawn entirely from the *De morte* of Vergil's friend Varius Rufus,[3] a line from the astrological section of the *Georgics* drawn from Terentius

---

2. Gian Biagio Conte criticizes Pasquali for emphasizing *aemulatio*, which privileges strong poets, rather than the system itself (1986, 26, 28, 36, and 51). As Joseph Pucci points out, Pasquali also placed the author within the context of his literary past and of his reading public (thereby deemphasizing the role of the author), but that strand of Pasquali's thought was not significantly advanced until Conte himself appropriated Pasquali's approach (1998, 13–14).

3. *Ecl.* 8.88. Pasquali analyzes this as a case of *variatio*, on account of the change in context (1942, 186). We know of this allusion because it was cited by Macrobius (*Sat.* 6.2.20).

Varro Atacinus's *Ephemeris*,[4] and a near-complete line of the *Aeneid* also drawn from the *De morte* of Varius Rufus and allusively comparing Marc Antony to the treacherous sinners of hell. This last allusion most eloquently confirms Pasquali's observation that Vergil's poetry depends on a clear remembrance of the text to which the poet refers. In his description of the worst of Hades's dead, Vergil reuses nearly an entire line from his friend's poem[5]:

vendidit hic auro patriam dominumque potentem
imposuit, *fixit leges pretio atque refixit.*

(6.622)

He sold his country for gold and laid on it
a controlling master; he set laws for a price and even reset them.

Varius wrote:

vendidit hic Latium populis agrosque Quiritum
eripuit, *fixit leges pretio atque refixit.*

He sold citizenship to the peoples, and the land of the citizens
he stole; he set laws for a price and even reset them.

Vergil's lines refer to an anonymous sinner; Varius's lines referred to Antony. Although Vergil does not name Antony, his reference to Varius's text allows him to portray Antony in the company of the unjust dead.[6] The political allusion is activated only when the reader compares Vergil's words to their context in Varius's lines.

Pasquali's discussion emphasizes the poet's references back to a particular source rather than the fact that these prior words are present within the

---

4. G. 1.377. Pasquali demonstrates that in the surrounding lines Vergil improves upon Varro's translation of Aratus (1942, 187). On *Ephemeris* as the title of this work by Varro, see Courtney 1993, 246. Servius quotes the line in question and its context (*Ad G.* 1.377). In his commentary on the *Georgics*, Richard Thomas (ad loc.) says that this kind of repetition is "as far as can be known an extreme rarity for Vergil," although Thomas also refers to G. 2.404, on which Servius comments, "Varronis hic versus est" (Thomas 1988). But note H. D. Jocelyn's reservations concerning the literal accuracy of such statements in the (late antique) grammarians and in the case of this statement in particular (1964–1965, 15:141–42).

5. Discussed by Pasquali at 1942, 186. Macrobius cites Varius's lines as being from his *De morte* (*Sat.* 6.1.39).

6. This is the interpretation proposed by Servius (ad loc.) and supported by Pasquali. Alternatively, Vergil's lines can be read as referring to the Caesarean Curio, in which case the political point of the allusion would be anti-Augustan (see R. Thomas 2001, 89–92). For my purposes, Vergil's politics do not matter because the allusion works in the same way in either case.

hypertext. And I do not dispute his interpretation, because the Vergilian allusions considered by Pasquali do—as far as we can tell from hypotexts that survive only in fragments—interact directly with their sources. But by focusing on the poet's relation to his predecessor, Pasquali obviates the need to consider such basic figures of repetition as the centonic quotation, which he dismisses, presumably because of its lack of referentiality: "Dei centoni omerici e virgiliani, della tarda antichità, esercizi scolastici inferiori, qui vogliamo tacere" (1942, 185). In opposition to the cento, Pasquali considers as true allusions those reminiscences that display the skill of the author who can interact directly with another poet. The referentiality of the allusion allows the poet to create meaning and the critic to engage in something higher than source criticism.

Gian Biagio Conte's *Rhetoric of Imitation* (1986) applies the insights of structuralism to the poetics of Latin intertextuality.[7] Although Conte draws inspiration from Pasquali, his structuralism keeps him from viewing imitation as a contest between strong authors. Rather, he focuses on the textual system of Latin poetry and distinguishes two types of allusion, "reflective" and "integrative." The reflective allusion plays "with the relationship between poetry as an autonomous reality and the literary process which constructs that reality—in other words, with the relationship between poetry's inner space and its utilization of the space outside itself" (1986, 63). While the reflective allusion plays with the pastness of poetry, the integrative allusion shapes the hypertext through its relation to a hypotext. Conte compares the integrative allusion to metaphor, a trope that works by displacing the customary meaning of a word or phrase with a new, poetic meaning; he compares the reflective allusion to the simile, which he emphatically says is not a trope.[8] He then ranks these two kinds of allusion in terms of their ability to disrupt the settled sense of poetic memory:

> [A] range of disturbances of transparency will be created in allusion . . .
> stretching between the high values characteristic of integrative allusion,
> when poetic memory contains an intrinsic surplus of sense, and the low

---

7. This publication is an adaptation and translation of two essays originally published in Italian (Conte 1974, 1984). For an insightful discussion of Conte's approach, see Charles Segal's foreword in Conte 1986.

8. For allusion as the trope of metaphor, see Conte 1986, 38–39 and 50–57; for the dissociation of trope and simile, see 67–68. Since Conte makes it clear that allusion itself may be likened to a metaphor (52–53), he seems paradoxically to place "reflective allusion" beyond the bounds of allusion proper.

values characteristic of reflective allusion, when poetic memory increases its meaning by attaching itself to an external source of sense.

(1986, 69)

The higher kind of poetry is thus the one characterized by the integrative allusion, which operates by creating, in cooperation with the old text, a new meaning. By engaging in this way with the systematic structure of poetry, the classical poet makes himself a part of his tradition; as Conte says, "The classical conception of art . . . encourages an awareness of the literary tradition as a whole rather than an awareness of the individual text" (1986, 69). Conte thereby relates the integrative allusion to the poetics of classicism. Because the postclassical poets (and Ovid in the first place)[9] view themselves as outside the tradition, it is not surprising that they should tend toward what Conte calls reflective allusion.

While an integrative allusion may display the poet's artistry directly (by emphasizing the poet's ability to improve his material), a reflective allusion more often repeats the words of a predecessor. Because it tends toward repetition, reflective allusion is a better test case for the referentiality of classical allusion. Conte's primary example of reflective allusion is a statement made by Mars to Jupiter in both Ovid's *Fasti* and *Metamorphoses* (1986, 57–59). In the *Metamorphoses*, Mars reminds Jupiter that he had agreed to make Romulus a god:

tu mihi concilio quondam praesente deorum
(nam memoro memorique animo pia verba notavi)
"unus erit, quem tu tolles in caerula caeli"
dixisti: rata sit verborum summa tuorum!

(*Met.* 14.812–15)

You once said, and the council of the gods was there,
(for I remember, I made note of your words, and my mind remembers)
"There will be one, whom you will raise to the heights of heaven."
May the whole of your words stand firm!

9. In the foreword to his translation of Conte's work, Charles Segal explained Conte's Vergil and Ovid as embodying "two complementary modes of literary allusiveness. The Virgilian 'integration' . . . blends the allusion into a new synthesis that minimizes the juncture; the Ovidian mode is to call attention to the artifice involved in the allusion, to break the frame and make the enframing structure visible" (Conte 1986, 12).

In a similar passage from the *Fasti*, Mars again reminds Jupiter of the same statement:

> Redde patri natum: quamvis intercidit alter,
>   pro se proque Remo, qui mihi restat, erit.
> *"Unus erit, quem tu tolles in caerula caeli"*
>   tu mihi dixisti: sint rata dicta Iovis.
>
> (Fast. 2.485–88)

> Return the son to his father: Although my other son died,
>   he who remains will be good for himself and for Remus.
> *"There will be one, whom you will raise to the heights of heaven,"*
>   you said that to me. May the words of Jove stand firm.

Both of these passages refer to Ennius's *Annales* 54–55 (Skutsch), which is preserved in Varro (*Ling.* 7.5):

> *Unus erit quem tu tolles in caerula caeli*
> Templa.

> There will be one whom you will raise to the dark heights
> of heaven.

In both of Ovid's poems, Mars quotes back to Jupiter his promise from the *Annales* of Ennius. And in both poems, the word *dixisti* marks the reference and sets the words within reported speech. The context of Mars's address in the *Annales* authorizes its use in Ovid's poems because Ovid's allusion derives its power from the fact that Jupiter had made this promise before in the course of Latin poetry. This reflective allusion is effective because it repeats Mars's words in a similar context. In both the *Metamorphoses* and the *Fasti*, Ovid playfully compels the reader to imagine Latin poetry as a closed and comprehensible system, in which a god may remember in one poem his words from another. His allusion is reflective because it juxtaposes an old and a new text without allowing the old text to alter the internal coherence of the new one. Rather than alter the meaning of the hypertext, Ovid's citation plays with the literary tradition and exposes the fact that his poetry responds directly to Ennius.

By focusing upon the structure of poetic memory, Conte shows that allusion functions beyond the emulative ambitions of intentional poets. However, his emphasis on allusion's ability to create new meaning still privileges the hypertext's ability to integrate and thereby replace its hypotext. Although it is clear that Conte's integrative allusion is central to classical poetics (with its erasure of temporal distance), reflective allusion is central to any system that would create closure or separation between traditions. For, in the hands of a postclassical poet, allusion creates distance between the post-classical and the classical text. In any case, both integrative and reflective allusions depend for their meaning upon the context of their hypotext. And although Conte excludes the author from his analysis of allusion and de-scribes instead the workings of poetic memory, he nevertheless focuses on the direct interaction of a text and its context. While he inscribes the refer-entiality of allusion within the textual system rather than within the mind of the author, he does view intertextuality as an essentially referential system.

Richard Thomas was also influenced by Pasquali's work on allusion. In "Virgil's *Georgics* and the Art of Reference," Thomas describes the reader's precise memory of the evoked text as an essential component of allusion. To emphasize this, Thomas uses the term "reference" in place of "allusion" in order to draw out its recursive nature.[10] Thomas studies the *Georgics* in that article because he finds them to be representative of (classical) Latin poetry as a whole.[11] And Thomas ranks allusions in terms of their artfulness, with "casual references" on one end of the spectrum and "conflation" or "multiple references" on the other. Throughout his article, Thomas focuses on the au-thor's ability to control his allusion and thereby shape the literary tradition.

Before considering references themselves, Thomas dispenses with what he calls parallels, an "accidental (and inevitable) linguistic confluence" (1986, 174). He ascribes to this category the rare collocation "immensi maris" (from *G.* 1.29), which finds an exact parallel in Pindar's ἀμετρήτας ἀλός (*Isthm.* 1.53). Since there is no demonstrable reason for a reference to Pindar's ode at this point in the *Georgics*, Thomas concludes that this collocation is uninten-tional and unimportant. The accidental confluence is excluded from the cat-egory of allusion because it is not "susceptible of interpretation" (1986, 174).

Thomas also considers "casual references," which are references that refer to the general tone of an antecedent rather than to a specific hypotext. The phrase "nonne vides" is used by Lucretius fifteen times to introduce an example that will support his teaching; Vergil uses the phrase three times in the *Georgics* in order to recall Lucretius's didacticism (1986, 175). These

---

10. Thomas explains his choice as follows: "Virgil is not so much 'playing' with his models but constantly intends that his reader be 'sent back' to them, consulting them through memory or physically, and that he then return and apply his observation to the Virgilian text; the word *allusion* has implications far too frivolous to suit this process" (1986, 172n8). In more recent work, Thomas has not insisted on the word "reference" and uses "intertextuality" both in deference to modern usage and because it more fully captures the range of Latin allusivity (R. Thomas 1999, 1–2).

11. R. Thomas 1986, 173 and 198; 1999, 6.

references are casual because they do not necessitate an exact comparison of any source and because they do not inform Vergil's art. Thomas notes how rare it is for Vergil, or any other Alexandrian poet, to echo or refer casually to an antecedent (177n20).

Thomas goes on to consider in turn the "single reference," "self-reference," and "correction" (1986, 177–89). In a single reference, an author refers the reader back to a single, previous text. In a self-reference, the poet refers to one of his own earlier poems; thus Vergil at times repeats even an entire line from one of his earlier poems or within a single work.[12] As the name implies, however, the self-reference is confined to the poet's own corpus. For that reason, it does not allow the poet to alter the literary system or even present himself differently within it. The "correction," however, is the next type of reference presented by Thomas. The correction is "the quintessentially Alexandrian type of reference" and "reveals the polemical attitudes that lie close beneath the surface of much of the best poetry of Rome" (1986, 185). For example, in book 2 of the *Georgics*, Vergil describes the attack by Otus and Ephialtes on Jupiter:[13]

> ter sunt conati imponere Pelio Ossam
> scilicet atque Ossae frondosum involvere Olympum.
>
> (G. 1.281–82)

> Three times they tried to set Ossa on Pelion,
> yes and to roll leafy Olympus on to Ossa

Vergil's lines correspond directly to *Odyssey* 11.315–16:

> Ὄσσαν ἐπ᾽ Οὐλύμπῳ μέμασαν θέμεν, αὐτὰρ ἐπ᾽ Ὄσσῃ
> Πήλιον εἰνοσίφυλλον.

> They tried to put Ossa on Olympus, and on Ossa
> leafy Pelion.

Vergil "corrected" the order of the mountains so that the giants would no longer be stacking Ossa and Pelion on Olympus (since Olympus was presumably the goal of their project, it could not have been the lowest of the mountains). His allusion makes sense when the reader recognizes that the Roman poet wanted to give an account of the giants' activity that would

---

12. Thomas discusses the well-known example of *Aen.* 2.473–75 and G. 3.437–39. An "internal" self-reference operates within a single work (R. Thomas 1986, 184–85).

13. See ibid., 186, for a discussion of this passage.

be more plausible than Homer's. As in previous cases, the point of Vergil's lines is understood only when they are compared with their hypotext, in this case the *Odyssey*. After the reader makes that comparison, Vergil's point and rhetorical superiority are evident.

After considering "apparent references," in which the poet seems to allude to one text but actually refers to another, Thomas investigates Vergilian "conflation" or "multiple reference."[14] He calls this "the most complex type of reference in Virgil" and suggests that "its function is to revise the tradition" (1986, 193). *Georgics* 1.138 describes three of the constellations through language borrowed from Homer and Callimachus: "Pleiades, Hyadas, claramque Lycaonis Arcton." In his description of Achilles's shield, Homer wrote Πληιάδας θ' Ὑάδας τε (*Il.* 18.486); and line 41 of Callimachus's *Hymn to Zeus* ends Λυκαονίης ἄρκτοιο. Vergil, therefore, alludes to both archaic and Hellenistic poetry and thereby subsumes both of them within his own project. By alluding to both authors, Vergil appropriates their poetry and creates a work that is more complete or, as Thomas says, that is "master of its tradition" (1986, 198). In cases such as this, the conflation refers to an author or his corpus rather than to a specific context. However, more developed conflations do refer to a specific context, and all such conflations present the author as in control of his new text. In that sense, Vergil's conflations are systematic and integrative. The difference of language between Vergil and his Greek sources is also important. It moves these allusions away from repetition and towards transposition[15] and also involves them in the Roman discourse of Hellenism. The multiple reference, therefore, integrates its sources into its new context. And like his other varieties of reference, Thomas's most complex form of allusion compels the reader to recognize the author's skill in manipulating his source. Each of Thomas's forms of reference, therefore, constructs a more or less direct link between the allusive text and its referent.

Stephen Hinds's *Allusion and Intertext* draws on Conte's work in order to develop for Latin philology a "spacious" and "pluralist" account of intertextual theory (1998, xi–xii). In particular, Hinds explores the strengths and weaknesses of a discourse focused on the intentions of an alluding author (47–49 and 144). He rejects Thomas's term "reference" because it detracts

---

14. Ibid., 190–93 and 193–98, respectively.

15. The exception to this rule is *Aen.* 9.767 ("Alcandrumque Haliumque Noemonaque Prytanimque"), which exactly transliterates *Il.* 5.678 (Ἀλκανδρόν θ' Ἅλιόν τε Νοήμονά τε Πρύτανίν τε). On this transliteration (which is the only case in which Vergil exactly repeats a line from Homer), see Hardie 1994, ad loc. and Farrell 2005, 100. Ovid noticed and repeated Vergil's transliteration at *Met.* 13.258. For Ovid's line and a convincing argument that each poet refers to Odysseus, see A. Smith 1997, 47–48.

from the undecidability of allusion and because there is often no way to verify that an allusion actually refers to any given hypotext (17–25). For example, the phrase "me miserum" appears in Ovid's *Amores* 1.1.25–26:[16]

> me miserum! certus habuit puer ille sagittas.
>   uror, et in vacuo pectore regnat Amor.

> I'm miserable! That boy sure knew how to use his arrows.
>   I'm on fire, and Love reigns in my empty heart.

As Hinds explains, "me miserum" is a lament commonly found in comedy, rhetoric, colloquial discourse, and also elegy. The multiplicity of subtexts complicates any interpretation of Ovid's words. But despite the fact that "me miserum" is a common phrase, there are strong reasons to read Ovid as alluding to Propertius 1.1.1–2:

> Cynthia prima suis miserum me cepit ocellis,
>   contactum nullis ante cupidinibus.

> Cynthia was the first to capture miserable me with her eyes,
>   though I had never before been touched with desire.

The strongest reason for reading an allusion here is that Ovid, in the first of his elegies, could be expected to refer to the famous opening of Propertius's first book of elegies. And by reading this line as an allusion, we can see Ovid figuring himself as the typical lover of elegy, even though the very words with which he portrays himself as a particularly elegiac lover are also used in non-elegiac contexts. In this case, the multiple contexts of Ovid's phrase produce, within his singular text, a multiplicity of readings and voices; and the reader may refer his words to different contexts. Thus Ovid's allusion complicates the idea that allusions are references back to a single hypotext. However, Hinds does not contest that the reader will refer Ovid's words to another context; he merely points out that readers can interpret Ovid's allusion in any number of ways depending on which context they have in mind. The outcome of this intertextual approach is that interpretation is always possible (or, put differently, that referentiality is always active). Hinds concludes: "The fact that language renders us always acculturated guarantees that there is no such thing as a wholly non-negotiable conflu-

---

16. Hinds discusses this allusion at 1998, 29–34.

ence, no such thing as zero-interpretability."[17] Hinds, therefore, removes the necessity for an alluding author but still asserts that any allusion works through the comparison of two contexts as one text impacts our interpretation of another.

In the same year in which Hinds's work appeared, Joseph Pucci published *The Full-Knowing Reader: Allusion and the Power of the Reader in the Western Literary Tradition*. Pucci presents the reader as the essential receiver of allusion and thereby reorients the referentiality of allusion. He explains the three premises of his study as follows:

> [F]irst, that allusion is an essential literary figure, retrievable in roughly the same form and performing roughly the same functions in Homer as in hip-hop; second, that the most important feature of this essentialism is a powerful reader, possessed of discrete and unique competencies; and third, that a sensitivity to this reader and her competencies is fundamental to an understanding of allusion historically in the Western literary tradition.
>
> (1998, xv)

Pucci traces the role of allusion from Catullus to Ezra Pound and shows that it has played an important role throughout Western literature. Further, he argues that the reader, rather than the text or the author, controls the allusion. The full-knowing reader of Pucci's title has the power to activate the allusive function of the author's words. In this way, Pucci moves away from focusing exclusively on either the figure of the author or the text itself. Further, Pucci distinguishes the referentiality of the allusion from either the intention of the author or the textual system (1998, 32–38). Instead, he "argues for a less ideal situation, in which a meaning is constituted for the allusion in the mind of the reader—and quite apart from the systems of referentiality that give rise to it" (1998, 38). The play of allusion, therefore, consists in the reader's use of two similar texts. Thus Pucci concurs that allusions are referential, but he shows the full importance of the reader in identifying and interpreting their referentiality. He also traces the history of allusion within ancient literary theory and concludes that allusion was accepted as a category of literary criticism only after late antiquity's legitimation of the reader's active and powerful intervention in the text (1998, 63–82).

---

17. Ibid., 34. Thomas has pointed out that Hinds did not discuss his own analysis of Vergil's "immensi maris" (R. Thomas 1999, 7n10).

Classical authors were more circumspect when they discussed the reader's role in controlling the referentiality of allusion.

Although an allusion always depends on a strong reader for its activation, the classical forms of allusion occlude the role of the reader and ostensibly set either the author or the textual system itself in a position to declare the meaning of the allusion; for the classical allusion is on the whole integrative, systematic, and penetrating. And though there are times at which a classical poet exactly repeats the words of a predecessor, those words are made to fit seamlessly within their new context. In a field as complex and divided as Latin intertextuality, it is remarkable that there is widespread agreement that an allusion essentially brings an old and a new context into creative conflict. This agreement on the referentiality of allusion, however, has been obscured by concerns about attributing or denying intentionality to the author of a text. In allusion as practiced in classical Latin poetry, it is either the specific context of the antecedent that gives new meaning to the allusion or (as in the case of casual references) the general tone of a predecessor's work that the new poet borrows. And, as Pasquali noted, a precise knowledge of the source text is necessary in order to read the allusion. Thus this intertextuality depends not just on the specific words that are repeated but also on their previous, textually encoded meaning. Pucci's work on allusion, however, shifts the burden of referentiality away from the text and onto the shoulders of the reader. I will show later in this chapter that a particularly late antique form of allusion reveals the necessity of that shift: a number of late antique allusions do not interact directly with their hypotext, and they should not be read primarily in terms of their author. But first I will explain how this late antique move away from referentiality has been obscured by a scholarly focus upon strong authors and purposeful *aemulatio*.

✍ Current Approaches to Allusion in Late Antique Poetry

The study of allusion in late antique poetry has been driven by the research on allusion in classical poetry.[18] In particular, Pasquali's "Arte allusiva" has directly affected the study of Ausonius's use of allusion. Thus Maria Posani, in a thorough study published in 1962, applied Pasquali's understanding of allusion to the *Mosella* of Ausonius.[19] Before she could discuss Ausonius's

---

18. The exception to this rule involves Christian and specifically biblical poetry.

19. The article is entitled "Remiscenze di poeti latini nella «Mosella» di Ausonio." Posani prominently cites Pasquali's "Arte allusiva" (1962, 35).

allusions, Posani had to deal with Ausonius's reminiscences. Posani reluc-
tantly acknowledges that Ausonius was a centonist and says that in the *Mosella* (as in his *Cento nuptialis*) Ausonius sometimes incorporated fragments
of earlier poetry into his own work without always ensuring that their contexts were similar.[20] Then Posani distinguishes sharply between reminiscences that do not depend on a direct engagement with their source and
reminiscences that evoke their source; only those that directly engage their
source qualify as allusions (1962, 35–38). She dispenses quickly with allusions that are not integrative.[21] Allusion itself, though, is divided into allusion per se and *aemulatio*. The purpose of an allusion proper is to evoke
"un'immagine, un'atmosfera, una tonalità diversa e lontana e creare così una
particolare tensione," but *aemulatio* produces "in simile atmosfera, in simile
tonalità, qualche cosa di nuovo, qualche cosa di bello" (1962, 51). Posani
shows that Ausonius skillfully employs every kind of allusion in the *Mosella*,
although she makes it very clear that centonic reminiscences stand, in her
estimation, at the lowest level of artistic merit and that *aemulatio* displays the
activity and originality of the poet.[22] In order to explain Ausonius's penchant for centonic poetry, Posani envisions her poet as desperately protect-
ing his Roman heritage: "Si direbbe che Ausonio, il quale, come Rutilio
Namaziano, guarda a Roma con l'amore di un figlio che vede un genitore
in pericolo, ma anche con la reverenza e la gratitudine di un barbaro adot-
tato che si sente onorato per questa adozione, veda in queste citazioni un
mezzo di nobilitare la sua poesia" (1962, 65). Given Posani's own demon-
stration of Ausonius's ability to emulate his predecessors successfully, one
wonders why the consul Ausonius should have used citations to ennoble his
poetry. Because she views tradition as a given inheritance rather than as the
active discovery of each period, Posani finds Ausonius's repetition slavish.
And by emphasizing both the importance of originality in allusion and of
Ausonius's "passive" reception of classical poetry, she avoids explaining what
his centonic reminiscences actually achieve.

Two more articles on the *Mosella* have demonstrated, in greater depth
than Posani, that Ausonius engaged his predecessors in ways that are both
complex and emulative. First, Woldemar Görler's "Vergilzitate in Ausonius'
Mosella" (1969) argues that the *Mosella* alludes systematically to book 6 of

---

20. On Ausonius the centonist, see Posani 1962, 33, 36, 38, and 64–66.

21. See ibid., 38–40, for examples of centonic reminiscences.

22. Ibid., 64: "Sia che si tratti del più meccanico inserimento nel poemetto di espressioni o frasi
prese da altri poeti, sia che si tratti della più alta e legittima forma di imitazione, l'*aemulatio*, Ausonio
in questo ricordare dimostra sempre una grandissima abilità, una prestigiosa sicurezza."

the *Aeneid* and to the *laudes Italiae* of book 2 of the *Georgics*. By showing that a series of allusions from different places in the *Mosella* refer to these Vergilian passages (and that Ausonius therefore meant his poem to be read as a renewal and an improvement upon that Vergilian material), Görler draws attention to Ausonius's systematic use of Vergil. In his conclusion, Görler summarizes his approach to allusion:

> In jedem einzelnen Fall ist zu fragen, welche Funktion ein Zitat in seinem Zusammenhang ausübt. Es mag Anklänge geben, hinter denen sich nichts verbirgt; es steht fest, daß es daneben—man mag es Rätselsucht nennen oder Raffinesse—ganze Gruppen von Anspielungen und Zitaten gibt, mit deren richtiger Interpretation das Verständnis des Gedichts steht und fällt.
>
> (1969, 114)

Görler focuses on the complex allusions that are not apparent at first sight but that conceal the proper meaning of the poem; he does not bother with Ausonius's direct quotations of Vergil.

Another study of Ausonius's allusive strategy in the *Mosella* is Carole Newlands's 1988 article "*Naturae mirabor opus*: Ausonius' Challenge to Statius in the *Mosella*." Although she does not use the word *aemulatio*, she focuses on passages in which Ausonius challenges Statius. Whereas Statius had described man's development of nature as positive and beneficial, Ausonius describes nature as ideal on its own, apart from the intrusion of humanity. Newlands shows that by means of direct, allusive engagement with Statius's descriptions from the *Silvae* of scenes from a river, of villas, and of Baiae, Ausonius intends to improve upon Statius's presentation of nature.[23] It is this sense of improvement that makes me say that Newlands focuses in her article on *aemulatio*. In explaining Ausonius's practice of allusion, Newlands herself says that his allusions are "heuristic" and that "Ausonius uses imitation in order to revise classical values, not to perpetuate them."[24] Although the term "heuristic" would appear to be congenial to the role of the reader

---

23. Posani notes that Ausonius's instances of *aemulatio* most often engage Statius, whereas (in Posani's words) "per brevissimi tratti Ausonio osa *certare* con il sommo e amatissimo Virgilio" (ibid., 66). If *aemulatio* characterizes the relation of poets writing within the same literary system, it is not surprising that a postclassical poet should emulate Statius more directly than Vergil.

24. Newlands 1988, 404. The term "heuristic allusion" derives from T. M. Greene's *The Light in Troy*. Greene explains what he means by the term as follows: "Heuristic imitations come to us advertising their derivation from the subtexts they carry with them, but having done that, they proceed to distance themselves from the subtext and force us to recognize the poetic distance traversed" (1982, 40). The Renaissance poets who are the focus of Greene's study had a different approach to the classics than their late antique predecessors (they sought to erase the gap between themselves

in allusion, Newlands's sharp distinction between revision and perpetuation would drive a wedge through the dynamic interplay that allows Ausonius to simultaneously revise and perpetuate his models.

We may imagine that Roger Green had the studies of Görler and Newlands in mind when he wrote, that "Much is lost if one adopts the approach of Hosius, for whom the *Moselle* was a patchwork of reminiscences, or that of Posani, who sees the technique of the centonist as prevalent."[25] What is lost is an awareness of Ausonius's complex and emulative engagement with his predecessors. On the other hand, if Ausonius's centonic composition is ignored, one loses his nonemulative and readerly engagement with the past. What is needed, therefore, is a method of analyzing Ausonius's allusions that leaves room for *aemulatio* while also acknowledging the importance of his centonic quotations.

In the same way in which Posani distinguished sharply between Ausonius's reminiscences and allusions, Maria Lühken has drawn a sharp line between Prudentius's formal reminiscences and his apparently more meaningful uses of imitation.[26] Her *Christianorum Maro et Flaccus: Zur Vergil- und Horazrezeption des Prudentius* (2002) is a careful and important study of Prudentius's poetry. Nevertheless, she dispenses with formal reminiscences in two short, introductory chapters and then gives priority to his more polemical and integrative imitations. She describes the most significant of these as cases of *Kontrastimitation*, a form of allusion that distinguishes sharply between Christian and pagan poetry.[27] In this regard, *Kontrastimitation* can be grouped with *aemulatio*, although the contrast is typically said to be theological rather than stylistic.[28] The new text is engaged in a polemical relationship with the old text, and there is a clear winner and loser.

---

and the ancients, the gap that was created in late antiquity), but his insights are stimulating reading for any student of allusion.

25. Green 1991, xx. Hosius wrote (1926, *ad Mosellam* 77): "Diese Worte lehren trefflich, wie Auson zuweilen arbeitet; kaum ein oder zwei Ausdrücke sind sein ausschliessliches Eigentum; der Rest ist ein aus Reminiscenzen an antike Muster zusammengestoppeltes Flickwerk." Hosius exaggerates, but he does touch on an important aspect of Ausonius's poetry.

26. Likewise, Anne-Marie Palmer distinguishes sharply between "the crude technique of the centonist" and allusions that ask of the reader "a sophisticated appreciation of the poet's technique" (1989, 106).

27. Lühken 2002, 29 and 273–75. In his influential essay on epic poetry in the *Reallexikon für Antike und Christentum*, Klaus Thraede defined *Kontrastimitation* as "die Übernahme von Junkturen zum Zwecke gegenteiliger Aussagen" (1962, 1039).

28. I am grateful to the anonymous reviewer for Cornell University Press who expressed disagreement on this point. To my mind, *Kontrastimitation* and *aemulatio* are comparable because they both work to replace or outmode a prior text.

Lühken defines formal reminiscences in terms of a lack of relevance to their new context (2002, 33). She then discusses lexical reminiscences of a single word, repeated phrases and figures, metrical reminiscences, and structural reminiscences.[29] These are dealt with briefly because they offer the poet less room to construct his art; and she discusses only shorter phrases because she says that the longer ones are more fully integrated within their text.[30] She describes reminiscences, therefore, as being both nonreferential and not meaningful. Although Lühken does not describe every creative imitation as a case of *Kontrastimitation*, she does draw a sharp distinction between formal reminiscences that demand less of her attention and more creative imitations, which find their meaning in the interaction between an allusion and the context of its hypotext. These examples of *Kontrastimitation* are the reminiscences that are most disruptive of their source. They set the new Christian poetry against its pagan past. Because she focuses on such cases, Lühken does not discuss some of Prudentius's most extended reminiscences. Although she is too aware of how intertextuality works to be completely carried away by a simple appeal to the author's *aemulatio*,[31] Lühken does downplay Prudentius's repetitions in favor of his more active reshaping of traditional material.

Because previous scholarship has shown how *aemulatio* and other complex forms of allusion were used in later Latin poetry, late antique poetry can no longer be described as simply derivative. However, the emphasis of these scholars on *aemulatio* has obscured what is most distinctively late antique within these poems. In the following sections, I will show that nonreferential allusions are important within late antique poetry because they are meaningful beyond the strictly narrow limits of their context. A focus on the reader will reveal that late antique poets were both more active and less emulative than has been thought. Whereas a classical poet imagines a textual world devoid of temporality, the late antique poet's quotations of Latin poetry allow him to present his work *sub specie praeteritatis*. This aspect of allusion in the poetry of late antiquity has been overlooked because *aemulatio* has been emphasized and repetition marginalized.

---

29. Lühken 2002, 33–43 and 185–92, on reminiscences of Vergil and Horace, respectively.

30. "Im Verlauf der Darstellung wird sich zeigen, daß Prudentius sehr häufig vergilische Verse und Halbverse unverändert übernimmt. In der Regel sind solche rhythmisch unveränderten wörtlichen Reminiszenzen, die um so mehr ins Auge springen, je größer ihr Ümfang ist, auch von Bedeutung für die Aussage des Textes" (ibid., 39). Despite this, a number of Prudentius's more extended reminiscences are discussed, if at all, only in footnotes.

31. See ibid., 23–30.

✎ Nonreferential Allusions

A number of late antique allusions do not function as references back to their sources.[32] In saying this, I do not mean that a reader could not find some connection between the passages I will discuss and their sources. It is certainly possible that another reader will find a reference where I have not; that is in the nature of allusion. Nor do I mean that these allusions do not reveal their source. Even in order to say that they are nonreferential, it is necessary to compare their contexts. I am asserting that the following allusions leave their own referentiality undefined; the link between the context of their text and its hypotext is undetermined. In this, the practice of late antique poets diverges from that of classical poets.

In his *Apotheosis*, Prudentius uses a half line from the *Aeneid* as he transitions from his discussion of Jesus's multiplication of food to the raising of Lazarus from the dead.[33] I discuss this allusion first because it is entirely certain and because it is not a reference back to the original context in which its words were found. In changing subjects, Prudentius asks the following rhetorical question:

> *Sed quid ego haec autem* titubanti voce retexo,
> indignus qui sancta canam?
>
> > (*Apoth.* 741–42)

> But why then do I repeat these things in faltering speech,
> I who am unworthy to sing what is holy?

This transitional hesitation was also used by Vergil's Sinon, the treacherous Greek who had paused, for rhetorical effect, before going on to persuade the Trojans to bring the horse into their city:[34]

> *Sed quid ego haec autem* nequiquam ingrata revolvo,
> quidve moror?
>
> > (*Aen.* 2.101)

> But why then do I go over these unpleasant things in vain,
> And why do I delay?

---

32. Michael Roberts has observed in a different context that the poetry of late antiquity displays "a retreat from referentiality" (2007, 147).

33. On Prudentius's use of allusion, see Lühken 2002, with extensive bibliography; Heinz 2007; and Mastrangelo 2008, 14–40.

34. Lühken (2002) cites Prudentius's allusion in her index of reminiscences but does not discuss it.

I do not think that Prudentius is comparing himself to Sinon, but the repetition is not fortuitous. The phrase "sed quid ego haec autem" occurs nowhere else in Latin literature;[35] it was found at a memorable point in the *Aeneid*, and it occurs in the same metrical position in Prudentius's poem as it had in the *Aeneid*. Further, Prudentius's "retexo" both recalls Vergil's "revolvo" and signals the presence of his allusion.[36] However, I can find no good reason to think that Prudentius is comparing himself to one of the most despised characters in the *Aeneid*. This allusion is as certain as can be, and it does not interact significantly with the original context of Vergil's poem. Instead, Prudentius's allusion is his own creative use of the earlier poet's words. He alludes, but not to Vergil's context.

The next allusion I discuss is similarly unmotivated by the context of its hypotext. I draw this example from Claudian's[37] mythological epic *De raptu Proserpinae* in order to emphasize that nonreferential allusions are found even in the "higher" genres and in poetry whose subject matter is classical, although Claudian does seem to use such centonic allusions less conspicuously than his contemporaries. In Claudian's *De Raptu Proserpinae*, Proserpina calls to Jupiter for help, as she is being dragged to the underworld by Pluto. Among her complaints, she asks the following:

> Cur non torsisti *manibus fabricata Cyclopum*
> in nos tela, pater?
>
> (2.250–51)

> Why, father, did you not throw at me those spears
> made by the hands of the Cyclopes?

The phrase "manibus fabricata Cyclopum" is from Ovid's *Metamorphoses* 1.259, a passage in which Ovid describes Jupiter's destruction of the world by a flood rather than by lightning. The strong caesura preceding "manibus fabricata Cyclopum" sets it off from the rest of the line, and the quoted words create a gap between the verb "torsisti" and its object "tela." Thus Claudian's

---

35. I base this statement on an electronic search of the Library of Latin Texts and of the Bibliotheca Teubneriana Latina. The coverage of the two databases is not the same. Although the Library of Latin Texts is extremely useful, it is not always reliable; for example, the compilers have mistranscribed the beginning of line 741 of the *Apotheosis* so that it reads "sed qui ego haec autem." The absence of a critical apparatus makes such mistakes especially dangerous.

36. I am grateful to Carole Newlands and Christopher Polt, each of whom suggested that I give more consideration to Prudentius's use of this verb here.

37. On Claudian's use of allusion, see Gruzelier 1989; Keudel 1970; and Cameron 1970b, 279–84 and 315–21.

pause and hyperbaton serve to isolate Ovid's words within his text. Because they are a discrete unit set within Claudian's narrative, Ovid's words call attention to their difference. At the same time, only a reader who is familiar with book 1 of the *Metamorphoses* will be aware that the phrase derives from that work. Although the context of Ovid's words does not add meaning to Claudian's description,[38] a reader who recognizes the quotation will appreciate Claudian's juxtaposition of old and new poetry. Thus the nonreferential allusion calls attention to a similarity on the verbal level while declining to engage its hypertext's original context. Put differently, this allusion tells us as much about Claudian's method of composition as about Proserpina's character. Claudian uses Ovid's words, not because he does not have words of his own to express the same thought, but because he would rather recall the poetic past shared by both author and reader. In this respect, "manibus fabricata Cyclopum" might seem to function like Conte's reflexive allusion. However, in Conte's reflexive allusion, the hypertext and the hypotext share a similarity of character or situation on the level of the narrative, and thus the reflexive allusion performs a narrative function. In Claudian's quotation of Ovid, the allusion does not function at the level of the narrative; it does not tell us anything more about the character of Proserpina or about her plight. Rather, Claudian's allusion reveals something about his construction of poetry: as a reader of Ovid, Claudian creates his own poetry through Ovid's words. Claudian's reader, in turn, appreciates the poet's use of an ancient and fragmentary phrase.

Two passages from the poetry of Paulinus of Nola will show the danger of reading allusions from late antiquity as referential, even when it is possible to do so.[39] Near the end of the second of the *Natalicia* (a series of poems composed in honor of the martyr Felix), Paulinus asks Felix to pray for his safe arrival in heaven. In doing so, he uses Vergil's words from the *Eclogues* and from the *Aeneid*:

> *sis bonus o felixque tuis dominumque potentem*
> exores, liceat placati munere Christi
> post pelagi fluctus mundi quoque fluctibus actis
> in statione tua placido consistere portu.

(*Carm.* 13.31–34)

---

38. But some readers will disagree here and may point to the importance for Claudian of the gigantomachy. I am grateful to Catherine Ware for sharing her thoughts on this allusion.

39. On Paulinus's use of allusion, see Ruggiero 1996, 45–54; and Green 1971, 41–60.

Be kind, yes and favorable to your own, and the lord powerful
do pray, that I, by the gift of Christ's satisfaction,
and after the turbulence of the world's sea and the driven surf,
may gain a calm harbor in your resting place.

The words "sis bonus o felixque tuis" are is from Vergil, *Eclogues* 5.65, where they express Menalcas's cry to the recently deified Daphnis. The transference could, of course, be read as Paulinus's Christianization of pagan prayer; and *felix* is a pun on the saint's name. The second half of the line (*Aeneid* 6.621) has already been discussed in reference to Vergil's reuse of Varius's poetry. Vergil describes those punished in the afterlife for such offenses as selling one's country and handing it over to a harsh master. It would be incredible to read Paulinus's allusion as portraying Christ through the lens of this tyrant from Tartarus. Rather than refer to the specific context of its hypotext, this second allusion ("dominumque potentem") is composed of a distinct fragment transferred on its own without calling to mind its original meaning. Despite the difficulty of determining a meaning for this allusion, its presence is confirmed by the more extensive "sis bonus o felixque tuis." Just as the first allusion confirms the presence of the second one, the second allusion's lack of referentiality calls into question the referentiality of the first allusion and therefore the relevance of a Christianizing reading of this passage. Thus the inert and fragmentary reuse of Vergil's words does not constitute an act of Christianization as much as it portrays Paulinus's reading.

Paulinus's poem 27 employs fragments of Vergilian poetry that have been pulled out of their original context and set within a new and different frame. The passage in question immediately precedes an extended poetic discussion of divine song. The following series of allusions, in which Paulinus employs Vergil's words in four out of five lines, is significant not only because it calls attention to itself but also because it introduces Paulinus's reflections on the use and importance of poetry. In this passage, Paulinus describes Pentecost and the disciples speaking in tongues:

hoc sollemne dies sequitur (septem numeramus
hebdomadas, et lux populis festiva recurrit),
qua sanctus quondam *caelo demissus ab alto*
spiritus ignito divisit lumine linguas,
unus et ipse deus diversa *per ora cucurrit*
omnigenasque uno sonuit tunc *ore loquellas*,
omnibus ignotas tribuens *expromere voces*,
quisque suam ut gentem peregrino agnosceret ore

externamque suo nesciret in ore loquellam.
barbarus ipse sibi non notis nota canebat
verba, suis aliena loquens; sed in omnibus unum
voce deum varia laudabat spiritus unus.
ut citharis modulans unius verbere plectri
dissona fila movet.

(Carm. 27.60–73)

This solemnity is followed by the day (we count off seven
weeks, and the festal day comes round for the crowds),
on which, at one time, the Holy who descended from high heaven
Spirit[40] set out tongues of blazing light,
the real and single God ran through each mouth
and then spoke all sorts of words from his one mouth,
as he gave all of them to express voices they did not understand.
And so each of them recognized his own nation in a foreigner's
    mouth
but did not understand the alien speech in his own mouth.
Even a barbarian would sing words that were understandable, though
not understood by him, speaking others' words in his own; but in all
it was one spirit that praised one God in a changing voice.
As one who plays the lyre moves different strings
in the movement of a single pick.

The Vergilian contexts are not relevant to Paulinus's poem, and the last three allusions all seem to have been chosen only because they describe speech. "Expromere voces" is from Aeneas's description of Hector's appearance to him in a dream:

ultro flens ipse videbar
compellare virum et maestas *expromere voces.*
(Aen. 2.279–80)

Vergil used the phrase "ore loquelas" in the *Aeneid* to describe Sleep bewitching Palinurus:

puppique deus consedit in alta
Phorbanti similis funditque has *ore loquelas.*
(Aen. 5.841–42)

---

40. Note the hyperbaton and "quondam" ("at one time"), which acts as a "signpost" of the allusion (on signposting, see note 56).

He used "per ora cucurrit" to describe the report to the Latins of the news that Diomedes would not fight on their side:[41]

Vix ea legati, variusque *per ora cucurrit*
Ausonidum turbata fremor.
(*Aen.* 11.296–97)

The partial exception to the rule that these allusions are nonreferential is "caelo demissus ab alto," in part derived from *Aeneid* 4.575, which describes the appearance of Hermes to Aeneas ("deus *aethere missus ab alto*"),[42] but also reminiscent of *Eclogues* 4.7: "iam nova progenies caelo demittitur alto," from Vergil's "messianic" eclogue. The Vergilian context of this last phrase is the one that could most easily be interpreted as relevant to Paulinus's description of the coming of the Holy Spirit, but even in this case, there is not much to make of the similarity. Although the fourth *Eclogue* was often read in reference to Christ's birth, it was not otherwise used in the context of Pentecost.[43] We can easily conclude that the original Vergilian context was less important than Paulinus's agency in placing this phrase alongside three parallel phrases from his model. Even in the one case where a reference could be read, Paulinus's practice in the following lines leads us not to look for a reference. Despite the absence of a direct reference, each allusion is rather obvious: they each occur in the same metrical position as they did in Vergil, and their appearance together removes the possibility that any one of them is the result of a random confluence.[44] These allusions are nonreferential, and yet they draw attention to themselves. Moreover, they are significant to Paulinus's poetry and not mere reminiscences, as is evident in the following lines of his poem.

Paulinus goes on in the immediately succeeding portion of this poem to compare God's inspiration of human voices to the harmonies created by a player at his lyre. While the harmony created by the dissonant strings of a

---

41. "Per ora cucurrit" is also used at *Aen.* 12.66 to describe Lavinia's blush before her mother's declaration of loyalty to Turnus. I quote the earlier passage because the hypertext describes speech rather than color.

42. And perhaps *Aen.* 1.297 as well: "genitum demittit ab alto" (in reference to Cupid).

43. For readings of the fourth *Eclogue* in reference to Christ, see Courcelle 1957, 295–300; and Benko 1980, 670–78. The anonymous cento *De verbi incarnatione* applies the phrase "caelo demissus ab alto" to the Holy Spirit's role in the annunciation (at line 15), perhaps in memory of this passage from Paulinus.

44. Paul. Nol. *Carm.* 33.61–72 presents a similar exaggeration of Vergilian phrases (but the authenticity of this poem has been called into question; see Trout 1999, 272). Prudent. *Apoth.* 393–96 also gathers a series of allusive fragments (see Heinz 2007, 136–39).

lyre is a metaphor for God's inspiration, it is also a metaphor for Paulinus's activity as a poet.[45] When Paulinus describes the inspiration of the Holy Spirit through the words of Vergil, he allows classical Latin poetry a voice within his poem. The voice of classical poetry becomes like the Christians at Pentecost who did not understand their own words, while Paulinus—like the Holy Spirit—makes Vergil's words meaningful within his poem. The closest this passage comes to presenting a polemical interpretation of classical poetry is in the line "barbarus ipse sibi non notis nota canebat." But even if we were to read Vergil as a *Christianus barbarus*, Paulinus would still be implying that Vergil should be understood correctly and not that he should be dismissed. That is, Paulinus provides a reading and interpretation of the words of classical poetry. Paulinus's description of Pentecost, moreover, considers the nature of language and the poet's ability to shape his words; for Paulinus, "suis aliena loquens," sang of Pentecost but replaced the glossolalia of the narrative with his own historical sense. The reader will appreciate the juxtaposition of old and new words but also understand in it Paulinus's investigation of the formal emptiness of the signifying word; his allusions demand authentication and interpretation, but not from Vergil's poetry. These nonreferential allusions, therefore, allow Paulinus to explore the use and meaning of language.

I have now argued that some late antique allusions are nonreferential. It would be possible to examine further cases, but the passages already considered should demonstrate that the late antique poets employed allusions differently than their classical predecessors. In each of these cases, the poet alludes to a specific antecedent but does not ask the reader to interpret a given hypertext through the context of its hypotext. Since a comparison of the two texts would only show that the poet used his quotation in a new sense, the late antique poet alludes to the poetic past and to his own ability to rewrite Latin poetry. Because they call attention to themselves and invite interpretation, the nonreferential allusions of the late antique poet should be taken seriously. Therefore, I will turn now to the positive function of such undefined allusions within the textual world of late antiquity.

---

45. For the importance to Christian poetry of the idea of "harmony in diversity," see Roberts 1989, 145–46; Heinz 2007, 165–67; and especially J. Fontaine 1973, who explores the theme of the lyre in the poetry of Paulinus.

✦ Juxtaposed Fragments of Classical Poetry

The two passages from Paulinus that I discussed in the preceding section are (in addition to being nonreferential) instances of the juxtaposition of disparate, allusive fragments. Such juxtapositions betray an interest in the hypotextual fragment for its own sake, and they present a hermeneutic puzzle to the reader who will piece together their bits of text.[46] This centonic technique displays the otherness of the poet's material and, therefore, presents the tradition as malleable and liable to reuse. Because late antique poetry brings out the constituent elements in its text, it has often been compared to art contemporary with it, and mosaics in particular.[47] Michael Roberts has shown that a late antique poem resembles a mosaic in its staccato phrasing and in the manipulation of its verbal surface. In *The Jeweled Style*, he considers the formal elements of the late antique poem, apart from its intertextual units of composition.[48] Before Roberts, Reinhart Herzog had already discussed the imitative reuse of classical material by Christian, biblical poets. Herzog speaks of the late antique poet's penchant for neutralizing the meaning of a classical text and then interpreting the old poet's words in a new sense (1975, 185–211). I differ from Herzog insofar as I question the necessity of forcing an allusion to neutralize and thereby dismiss the meaning of the original text, but his work is certainly stimulating reading, especially in his discussion of the exegetical function of late antique poetry. What remains is to show the ways in which late antique poetry employed a jeweled style of allusion. The poet, by devising allusions in the jeweled style, engaged both with the past and with contemporary readers in order to create fragments whose potential remained to be actualized. In this way, late antique poets wrote allusions in which the referentiality of the borrowed text yielded to the reader's active participation in determining the meaning of both texts on their own terms.

As a first case of juxtaposition, Prudentius merges two half lines from book eight of the *Aeneid* into his description of pagan Rome before its Christianization.

---

46. On bits of text in late antique poetry, compare the first preface to Ausonius's *Technopaegnion*: "quae lecturus es monosyllaba sunt, quasi quaedam puncta sermonum, in quibus nullus facundiae locus est, sensuum nulla conceptio, propositio, redditio, conclusio aliaque sophistica, quae in uno versu esse non possunt, sed cohaerent ita ut circuli catenarum separati" (Auson. *Technop.* 1).

47. See Roberts 1989, 57 and 70–73, with further references. Patricia Cox Miller also discusses the use of juxtaposition in late antiquity (2009, 42–61).

48. But Roberts does acknowledge the importance of *imitatio* (1989, 57–58; 2002).

Romanumque forum et Capitolia celsa tenebant.

(*Symm.* 1.534)

They held the Roman forum and the lofty Capitol.

At *Aeneid* 8.361, Vergil describes the future Rome through which Evander and Aeneas walk with the phrase "Romanoque foro et" (minor syntactic changes are not uncommon in the genre to which this sort of quotation is related, namely, the cento).[49] And "et Capitolia celsa tenebat" is used at *Aeneid* 8.653 to describe the portrayal on Aeneas's shield of Marcus Manlius guarding the Capitoline. The two phrases used together emphasize Prudentius's borrowing. This is a rather simple case of juxtaposed allusions, in which the positioning of these fragments within their new context is important quite apart from their source. Although these allusions are referential to some extent (after all, it is not irrelevant that Prudentius chose phrases that had, at programmatic moments of the *Aeneid*, described the glory of Rome), their juxtaposition operates on its own within Prudentius's text. By using two quotations side by side, Prudentius draws attention to his reuse of the phrases and thus distances them from their specific meaning within Vergil's text.

A second and similar case comes from Ausonius's[50] *Cupido cruciatus.*

Aeris in campis, memorat quos Musa Maronis,
myrteus amentes ubi lucus opacat amantes,
orgia ducebant heroides et sua quaeque,
ut quondam occiderant, leti argumenta gerebant,
errantes silva in magna et *sub luce maligna*
inter harundineasque comas gravidumque papaver.

(*Cupido* 1–6)

In the gloomy plains that the Muse of Maro recalls,
where a myrtle grove shades the mindless lovers,
the heroines held their revels, and each told
how she had died once, the story of her own death,
as they wandered in the great forest and under a barren light
between leaves and their reeds and the laden poppy. . . .

---

49. See Bažil 2009, 187–89. Such substitutions are a deferral of the centonic effect and are therefore less effective than direct quotation.

50. On Ausonius's use of allusion, see Pucci 2002, 2000; Nugent 1990; Newlands 1988; Benedetti 1980; Green 1977; Görler 1969; and Posani 1962. On Ausonius and Vergil, see O'Daly 2004.

Ausonius begins his poem with "aeris in campis" (from *Aen.* 6.887) and by stating explicitly his debt to the Muse of Maro. So it is clear from the first line that the *Cupido cruciatus* will engage closely with the poetry of the *Aeneid* and with book 6 in particular.[51] However, the juxtaposed allusions in line 5 are what is of interest here. "Errabat silva in magna" was used to describe Dido wandering in the underworld (*Aen.* 6.451), and "sub luce maligna" described Aeneas's descent to the underworld (*Aen.* 6.270). These Vergilian fragments are not unrelated to Ausonius's poem (they are from book 6, after all), but the relevance of their prior context is not what matters here. Ausonius's "et" functions rather nicely to draw attention to the logic of his two fragments, for it shows that the poetry of line 5 consists in Ausonius's juxtaposition of two Vergilian half lines. The work of the poet is to link together prior material. Moreover, the effect of the line depends on the reader's appreciation of Ausonius's explicit awareness of his own part in representing Vergil's poetry. Rather than being deferential to Vergil and the tradition he established, Ausonius plays with the fact that his own poetry will be read through Vergil. Ausonius does not need to prove that he knows Vergil's text, and he does not need to justify his own poem in any simpleminded way, but he does actively engage the reader in his involvement with earlier Latin poetry. Whereas Vergil used allusions to improve on his Hellenistic competitors, Ausonius leaves Vergil his space and then goes on to tell his own story. Juxtaposed allusions, therefore, dismiss *aemulatio* as the motivation for allusion; instead, allusion becomes a pretext for the poet's recognition of the literary past.[52]

A third and more extended use of juxtaposed allusions is found in the *Mosella* of Ausonius.[53] Near the end of his poem, Ausonius proclaims that he will someday compose an even greater poem in praise of the Moselle:

---

51. On this poem and its engagement with Vergil, see Nugent 1990, 41–42; Davis 1994; and Pucci 2009, 66.

52. I have discussed examples of Ausonius, Prudentius, and Paulinus each constructing entire lines of poetry by juxtaposing two fragments of (Vergil's) poetry. Claudian does not seem to have written an entire line in this way. Auson. *Cupido* 82 ("*terrorem ingeminat stimulisque* accendit *amaris*") and Paul. Nol. *Carm.* 22.9 ("*heia age tende chelym, fecundum concute pectus*") seem to be the only other cases from these poets of entire lines formed from two or more nonreferential fragments ("Terrorem ingeminat" is from *Aen.* 7.578, and "stimulisque agitabat amaris" is from *Aen.* 11.337; "Heia age" is found at *Aen.* 4.569, "tendo chelyn" at *Theb.* 1.33, and "fecundum concute pectus" at *Aen.* 7.338). There are more numerous cases of juxtaposed allusions that do not take up an entire line.

53. In *Epist.* 13.4–5, Ausonius again juxtaposes a whole line and a half line from Vergil, and Paulinus does so at *Carm.* 18.126–27.

addam felices ripa ex utraque colonos
teque inter medios *hominumque boumque labores*
stringentem ripas et pinguia culta secantem.

(Mos. 458–60)

I'll add happy farmers on each bank,
and you, amid the intervening labors of men and oxen
brushing past the banks and halving their fertile fields.

"Hominumque boumque labores" comes from Vergil's *Georgics* 1.118, and it is notable that Ausonius describes his river as being amid (*inter*) those Vergilian labors. "Stringentem ripas et pinguia culta secantem," from *Aeneid* 8.63, described the Tiber. By indicating the literary context of its project, these fragments further the promise of a future poem that will extend the fame of the Moselle.[54] Of course, such a work was never written, and the hope of (another) Vergilian poem remains a promise for the future. But in the present time of the poem Ausonius's juxtaposed allusions point to the song's ability to remember Vergil, to renew his classical poetry and to set it within a new context. Thus readers of the *Mosella* could recognize in Ausonius's renewal of Vergil's words a model for their own discovery of meaning within the words of another. The juxtaposition of these Vergilian fragments draws attention to their individual unity and to the reader's reinterpretation of their meaning within a foreign context. By juxtaposing more than one nonreferential allusion, the poet reveals that what is at stake is the ability to revise and recompose these fragments of poetry.

A fourth case of juxtaposition is found in Claudian's programmatic allusions to Vergil and Statius in the first line of the narrative section of *De raptu Proserpinae*. By alluding to both poets, Claudian acknowledges that his poem should be read in light of those epics. In this case, Claudian juxtaposes both fragments of Latin poetry and the epic traditions for which they stand:

Dux Erebi quondam *tumidas exarsit in iras*
proelia moturus superis quod solus egeret
conubiis sterilesque diu consumeret annos.

(Rapt. 1.32–34)

The leader of Erebos once blazed out in swelling anger
(he was about to make war on the Olympians) because he alone had no

---

54. This passage is also comparable to Vergil's promise at the beginning of book 3 of the *Georgics* to erect a temple in honor of Augustus. At line 454, Ausonius clearly alludes to G. 3.30.

> share in marriage and he had long squandered his years in
> sterility. . . .

Statius called Pluto the "dux Erebi" at *Thebaid* 8.22, at the beginning of his description of Hades.[55] Vergil used the phrase "exarsit in iras" to describe Allecto's reaction to Turnus's lack of interest in her advice (*Aen.* 7.445). Further, Jean-Louis Charlet has suggested that "tumidas" with "iras" derives from "tumida ex ira" of *Aeneid* 6.407 (1991, 93). "Quondam" alerts the reader to the prior history of Claudian's words; it thereby serves as a signpost of his allusions.[56] Because Claudian's allusive phrases are circumscribed (they are distinct syntactic units, and they fall within the same metrical position as in their sources), they call attention to the fact that they are repeated fragments. Therefore, these juxtaposed allusions to Statius and Vergil demonstrate Claudian's ability to reshape the tradition of Latin poetry through his reading of it. They highlight the verbal surface of his poetry and offer a model by which the reader may understand Claudian's poem through his use of both classical and imperial epic. In that sense, these juxtaposed allusions are programmatic for Claudian's poem and his poetics.

Juxtaposed allusions prominently display the different layers of a text, its composite nature. Because they are not defined by the meaning of any prior context, they make the need for a strong form of reading explicit. When readers confront juxtaposed allusions, they make them cohere within their new location. At the same time, such allusions reveal the poet's ability to revise the past and to use its words in a new sense. For this reason, Giovanni Polara has compared the allusivity of the cento to antanaclasis, the figure of speech in which a word is repeated in a different sense (1981 and 1989). Because the late antique poets go out of their way—beyond the limits of their centos—to employ the words of their predecessors in a new sense, Polara's analogy of centonic allusion to antanaclasis can also be applied to noncentonic composition in late antiquity. By repeating the words of a predecessor with a different meaning, the poet plays with his or her own ability to reinterpret the text. As does the cento, the juxtaposed allusion reveals the reception of the text and not its original meaning or context, because the juxtaposition of disparate fragments foregrounds the reader's presence in the text. Although this aspect of allusion is most evident when the poet juxta-

---

55. On the underworld opening of Claudian's epic, see Wheeler 1995.

56. On the signposting of allusions, see Hinds 1998, 1–3; for this use of *quondam*, compare Ov. *Met.* 14.812, Auson. *Cupido* 4, and Paul. Nol. *Carm.* 27.62 (each discussed earlier), and Auson. *Praef.* 4.2 (discussed later).

poses two disparate fragments, it operates whenever an allusion allows itself to be defined by the reader.

✒ The Apposed Allusion in Late Antiquity

Whereas juxtaposed allusions permit two fragmentary intertexts to refract each other's presence and thereby work together to reveal the discontinuities between text and intertext, a single allusion apposed to the text disrupts, on its own, the verbal surface of the poem. In this way, an apposed allusion marks itself off as distinct from its text without the need for more than one fragment. Because a single apposed allusion can also show the space between ancient and modern, it can take part in the same dynamic employed in juxtaposed allusions. And because the repeated words must still be integrated within their new context, the space between the text and intertext remains as the domain of the reader. While every allusion disrupts the verbal surface of the text, an apposed allusion isolates the foreign element within it. Rather than integrating that previous voice into its new context, an apposed allusion draws attention to the ventriloquism of the intertext. In so doing, it reveals the necessary presence of an interpretive reader.

In his *Hymnus ante cibum*, Prudentius incorporates half a line from the *Aeneid* and also alludes more traditionally to Aeneas's return from the underworld.

> *Credo equidem (neque vana fides)*
> corpora vivere more animae:
> nam modo corporeum memini
> de Flegetonte *gradu facili*
> *ad superos remeasse* deum.
>
> <div align="right">(<i>Cath.</i> 3.196–200)</div>

> I believe (and my confidence is not in vain)
> that our bodies will live like our souls:
> for just now I recall that it was in bodily form
> and out from Phlegethon, walking easily,
> that God returned to those above.

In book 4 of the *Aeneid*, Dido explains to her sister Anna her passion for Aeneas:

> Anna soror, quae me suspensam insomnia terrent!
> quis novus hic nostris successit sedibus hospes,

quem sese ore ferens, quam forti pectore et armis!
credo equidem, nec vana fides, genus esse deorum.

(4.9–12)

Anna, my sister, what dreams these are that terrify me!
Who is this new guest who showed up in our home,
how he carries himself in speech, in strength, and in arms!
I believe (and my confidence is not in vain) that he is divine.

And in his encounter with the Sibyl, Aeneas is warned that a return from the underworld is difficult:

> *facilis* descensus Averno:
> noctes atque dies patet atri ianua Ditis;
> sed *revocare gradum superas*que evadere *ad* auras,
> hoc opus, hic labor est.

(*Aen.* 6.126–29)

> It is easy to get down to Avernus:
> The gate of dread Dis stands open day and night;
> but to turn back your step and to get out to the upper air,
> this is the work, this is the labor.

Prudentius's "memini" in line 198 prepares the reader for the second allusion, and the references to Aeneas portray Christ's return from Hades through Aeneas's journey. Lühken characterizes this passage as an example of *Kontrastimitation* because the Christian resurrection was corporeal, unlike the afterlife portrayed by Vergil (2002, 149). Prudentius's "corporeum" ensures that the journey in mind is a physical thing, but Christ's journey is not, for that reason, opposed to Aeneas's trip through Hades. Despite the poetic ambiguity introduced by the gates of sleep at the end of book 6, Aeneas also went to and returned from the underworld in his physical body. Instead of contrasting his poetry to Vergil's, Prudentius portrays Aeneas as a type of Christ, and his allusion to Aeneas is integrative (in Conte's sense) because it creates a complex image out of the interplay between Christ's harrowing of hell and Aeneas's visit to the underworld. Prudentius, therefore, minimizes the contrast between his own portrayal of Hades and Vergil's book 6 of the *Aeneid*. Prudentius's Christian reading of the *Aeneid* may even extend to the second half of *Aeneid* 4.12: "*credo equidem, nec vana fides*, genus esse deorum." Of course, Dido's words are flippant, but it is possible to read a parallel between Aeneas's descent from the gods and Christ's birth. In that case, Aeneas would be an even clearer type of Christ.

Because Prudentius draws attention to the similarities between Christ and Aeneas, I find it hard to read these allusions as either emulative or contrastive.

While the allusions to book 6 of the *Aeneid* are integrative, the quotation from book 4 repeats Vergil's words with only the slightest of changes (from *nec* to *neque*). Lühken describes the quotation as only a set piece and a marker of the following allusions (2002, 148–49). Although it does prepare the reader for the following allusions, Prudentius's quotation is primarily emblematic of his reading of Vergil. For "credo equidem neque vana fides" stands as a fragment of Vergilian speech within Prudentius's poem, and the art of Prudentius's allusion consists in his ability to employ Vergil's words in a new sense. As do juxtaposed allusions, this apposed allusion calls attention to the difference between Vergil's text and Prudentius's. By retaining Vergil's words and by allowing them an entire line to themselves, Prudentius invites reflection on their previous sense and his new use of them. Thus Prudentius allows Vergil to speak even as he displays his own appropriation of Vergil's words. An exact quotation most neatly embodies the poet's reading, and this apposed allusion isolates Vergil's words within Prudentius's text.

Just as Prudentius places Vergil's words at the head of his stanza, Paulinus begins his paraphrase of Psalm 1 with a quotation from Horace.[57] In Horace's poetry, such an allusion at the beginning of a poem has been called a motto, but whereas Horace either translates or adapts his mottoes, Paulinus incorporates Horace verbatim.[58] Paulinus's fifty-one-line development of Psalm 1 adds ethical and rhetorical details that befit a Christian poet, but the first four words are a direct quotation of the opening of Horace, *Epodes* 2.1, in which Horace presented a banker's dream of life in the countryside. This allusion is significant because it draws attention to itself, introduces Paulinus's poem, and complicates the relationship between the Christian and classical ideals.

> *Beatus ille qui procul* vitam suam
> ab inpiorum segregarit coetibus
> et in via peccantium non manserit
> nec in cathedra pestilenti sederit.
>
> (*Carm.* 7.1–4)

---

57. On the practice of paraphrase in late antique Latin poetry, see Roberts 1985. "Paraphrase" is now the common term, although "metaphrasis" was sometimes used in antiquity to distinguish a more elaborate reworking of a hypotext (Roberts 1985, 25–26).

58. On the Horatian motto, see Cavarzere 1996. The closest adaptation among Horace's mottoes is the opening of *Odes* 1.37: "nunc est bibendum," which translates Alcaeus fr. 332 (Lobel and Page): νῦν χρῆ μεθύσθην. Though Horace adapts Alcaeus closely, his motto is a translation, not an exact repetition. On this motto, see Cavarzere 1996, 193–97; and Fraenkel 1957, 159.

Happy is he who far away leads
his own life from the gatherings of the wicked,
and who does not stay in the path of sinners
or sit in a foul chair.

Horace's epode began:

Beatus ille qui procul negotiis,
    ut prisca gens mortalium,
paterna rura bobus exercet suis,
    solutus omni faenore.

(*Epod.* 2.1–4)

Happy is he who far away from business,
    like the olden race of mortals,
works his ancestral land with his own oxen,
    free from every debt.

Paulinus transfers Horace's words into his version of Psalm 1 but also contaminates them with the Latin translation of the Psalm, which begins "Beatus vir qui."[59] By alluding to Psalm 1 at the same time as he quotes Horace, Paulinus further complicates his use of Horace's words. Paulinus changes the meaning of Horace's words along with their context, but his technique (exact repetition) makes it more difficult to see in them any kind of emulative or corrective engagement with his source. Therefore, Paulinus's quotation of Horace adds a further, and in some ways incoherent, layer to his poem. Even in formal terms, the hyperbaton of *procul* and *ab* reinforces the separation of Horace's phrase. In Horace's poem, *procul* goes directly with the ablative *negotiis*, but Paulinus uses it with *ab* to govern *coetibus*, and the imposition of *vitam suam* breaks the easy flow of his words. Like Prudentius, Paulinus sets aside his own poetry in favor of repeating the words of a classical poet. Also like Prudentius, Paulinus allows Horace's words to stand on their own and to blend or not into his own poetry. Paulinus's allusion is a very simple form of intertextuality, in which the hypotext can stand on its own within the hypertext. Paulinus allows it to remain, not because he cannot integrate it more fully, but because he wants the reader to appreciate the harmony of two poetic voices. The voice of a single author would disguise the need for a reader; the imposition of a nonauthorial voice (or rather the

---

59. On *contaminatio*, see Farrell 1991, 94–104. Heinz 2007 considers Prudentius's *contaminatio* of biblical and classical sources.

voices of a second and a third author) brings forward the question of how and why these words are being read. Paulinus's quotation has been read as constructing a Christian version of the classical *secessus in villam*, a version intended to surpass and replace Horace's poem (Nazzaro 1982, 99–100). A quotation, however, is precisely the form of allusion that complicates such a reading. Paulinus's quotation depends for its effect upon a reader who appreciates the poet's repetition of classical poetry. By using an integrative or emulative allusion, Paulinus could have revised Horace's words to fit his poem. If Paulinus had rewritten Horace in that way, he would have presented his own version of Horace's phrase. Instead, Paulinus incorporates Horace's phrase on its own and without criticism. And though his poem does present a different version of beatitude than the one found in the classical poem, Paulinus does not reduce the impact within his poem of Horace's voice.

The exact and extended allusions presented here reduce the difference between an allusion and a quotation. A quotation typically acknowledges its source explicitly, but these apposed allusions also call attention to their source and make no attempt to conceal their borrowing. Because these late antique allusions do (implicitly but clearly) acknowledge their borrowing, they could almost be called quotations and even more so because explicit quotations are not absent from late antique poetry. Catullus, Horace, and Vergil are each quoted by Ausonius.[60] I will consider here Ausonius's quotation of the first line of Catullus's first poem, which Ausonius sets at the beginning of a preface addressed to Latinius Pacatus Drepanius and appended to some collection of his poetry:[61]

---

60. Auson. *Prof.* 6.50–54 quotes Hor. *Carm.* 2.16.27–28: "quam fatiloquo dicta profatu versus Horati: 'nihil est ab omni parte beati.'" Auson. *Ecl.* 19.19–21 quotes Verg. *Aen.* 12.879–80: "Iuturna reclamat: / 'quo vitam dedit aeternam? cur mortis adempta est / condicio?'" Auson. *Ecl.* 19.18–23 is omitted by V (the oldest of Ausonius's manuscripts) but is probably genuine (Green 1991, ad loc.). There is perhaps a first-century analogue to Ausonius's quotation. Persius seems to quote Ennius at *Sat.* 6.9–10: "Lunai portum, est operae, cognoscite cives, / cor iubet hoc Enni." The evidence that Persius has actually quoted this line from Ennius is the disjunction of the line from its context, Persius's phrase "cor iubet hoc Enni," and the scholium to this line of Persius's *Saturae*: "hunc versum ad suum carmen de Ennii carminibus transtulit." The scholium's "transtulit," however, need not imply quotation: H. D. Jocelyn has collected a series of scholia to Vergil in which the scholiast's language (and specifically the verb *transferre*) seems to imply that Vergil has taken a whole line from a source when he has actually either adapted freely or borrowed a few words (Jocelyn 1965, 139–44). Whether or not Persius explicitly quoted an entire line from Ennius, this line does stand out from the rest of his poem and is therefore a close analogue to Ausonius's quotation of Catullus. Both Ausonius's and Persius's quotations are discussed together at Conte 1986, 59–60.

61. In the manuscript, this preface comes before a series of "eclogues," but Green does not think that they are an introduction to the poems they precede (1991, 242).

"Cui dono lepidum novum libellum?"
Veronensis ait poeta quondam
inventoque dedit statim Nepoti.
at nos illepidum rudem libellum,
burras quisquilias ineptiasque,
credemus gremio cui fovendum?

(Praef. 4.1–6)

"To whom should I give my pretty new book?"
the poet from Verona once said,
and he gave it to Nepos, whom he found on the spot.
But I have an ugly and rude book,
ridiculous, trash, absurdity,
to whom will I give it to be loved on their lap?

Ausonius acknowledges that he is quoting a line from Catullus and then gives the reader a brief summary of Catullus's poem. By explicitly acknowledging his quotation, Ausonius sets the first line apart from the rest of his poem and thereby plays on the difference between himself and Catullus, but he also juxtaposes Catullus's poem and his own. Though Ausonius could have composed a different first line for his dedicatory poem, it would not have perpetuated the category of the classical in the same way that his invocation of Catullus does. Rather than simply playing on the cultural capital of Catullus's poetry, Ausonius reinvigorates that poetry by placing it within the context of his own dedication. His poem ironically reads Catullus's situation as though it were not analogous to his own, although the dedicatee, at least, would want Ausonius's quotation to be read as though it were appropriate to this *libellus*. This type of appositional allusion, a quotation in which the source is acknowledged explicitly, is an extreme example of how to incorporate a fragment of previous poetry. Although it is an explicit quotation, I call it an allusion and discuss it here because it stands on a continuum with the allusions I have discussed from Prudentius's *Hymnus ante cibum* and Paulinus's poem 7. Even the use of *quondam* is analogous to the signposting of a more normal allusion. Because Ausonius plays with the literary past and allows his reader to play with the meaning of Catullus's words within his own, his quotation is in fact allusive. The only difference between the apposed allusions of Prudentius or Paulinus and Ausonius's quotation is that Ausonius names his source explicitly. In the simplest sense, Ausonius appropriates Catullus's words, for they are now a part of his poetry. And because this allusion is explicit, Ausonius is able to dramatize the response that is only implicit when he quotes a classical poet without acknowledgment. Although it is usually the reader who would have recognized the secondary voice within the text, Ausonius plays the part of the reader in these lines.

By setting an allusion in apposition to their own poetry, late antique poets invite readers to consider their use of previous material. My understanding of these apposed allusions diverges sharply from Conte's explanation of such quotations. Since Conte cites Ausonius's quotation of Catullus in order to distinguish between his reflective and integrative types of allusion, it will be helpful to quote his entire analysis of Ausonius's quotation. He touches on what is different about the function of allusion in late antiquity:

> [The quoting text] openly acknowledge[s] the work of another, so that no tension is established between the two texts. No "expropriation" of an older text occurs, because the new verbal segment does not rework the old one dialectically; it simply inserts the old text statically within itself. Thus no interpenetration occurs between the two texts—no violence is done to the "propriety" of the old text, and the new text sets up no new meaning to add to its own evident sense (so that there is no complication of sense or of the artistic process).
>
> (1986, 60)

What Ausonius's allusion lacks in textual interpenetration is repaid in the hermeneutic puzzle that it sets for the reader. Whereas the integrative allusion accomplishes the interpretation of the hypotext on its own, the quotation leaves the prior text untouched, still open to the reader's control. Instead of expropriating its hypotext, the quotation encourages a sense of ease, a more level and productive relationship between the poet and his tradition. Of course, a productive relationship depends upon having a reader who wants to explore the past through the present. Both Ausonius and Pacatus were apparently readers who desired just that sort of relationship. The quotation is an extreme form of allusion, but in a way that is characteristic of allusion in late antiquity. The quotation prevents a strong author from expropriating the literary past. And so, instead of erasing the evidence of his predecessor's influence, the late antique poet presents a layered text in which the words of a prior poet can still find their place.

✐ Devising the Classical Canon

The late antique poet was able to appropriate his exemplar without violence because of the poetic distance between himself and his classical models. We should measure this distance first in terms of general reading habits and then through certain programmatic statements made by Ausonius and some of his contemporaries. I will return presently to the question of *aemulatio*.

During the fourth century, a broad shift occurred in the reading habits of educated Romans. Whereas earlier writers had studied, quoted, and alluded to authors from republican Rome, in the fourth century writers were unlikely to read or cite most republican authors. They became much more likely to cite an imperial poet, such as Lucan, Statius, or Juvenal, rather than Ennius, Accius, or Lucilius. Servius in particular, in his commentary on Vergil, replaced a number of references to Vergil's republican predecessors with references to his imperial successors.[62] Vergil came to be cited alongside republican authors as one of the *antiqui* or *maiores*, and early imperial authors were cited as *veteres* and *idonei auctores*.[63] The grammatical habit of late antiquity created "a gap between the past and the present," and Vergil was the central figure on the far side of that gap.[64] That imperial rather than republican authors were read in late antiquity lengthened the distance between Vergil and poets such as Ausonius or Prudentius. The other result of this shift was that Latin literature came to have a thick history on its own, quite apart from the Greek sources of a Vergil or a Horace. Because these Latin authors were now sources in their own right, they were read as inspiring a definitively Latin tradition. Because he was considered an ancient poet, Vergil was read as the source of Roman poetry. Therefore, authors could set his poetry apart as being other, as anterior or simply different from their own work. By setting Vergil's words apart in their allusions, the late antique poets allowed themselves to play with the cultural distance between the contemporary context and their classical sources.

Ausonius and his contemporaries imagined themselves as separate from their classical models. In a letter to an unnamed friend, Ausonius invites the

---

62. See Cameron 2011, 399–420. See also the reading curriculum mentioned in a late antique school text printed by Dionisotti (1982, 100); the Latin authors cited by name are Terence, Cicero, Sallust, Vergil, Lucan, Persius, and Statius.

63. Chin 2008, 21–24; Kaster 1978; and Uhl 1998, 419–21.

64. Chin 2008, 23. Chin locates the "transformative potential of grammar" in its ability to construct "narratives that ultimately conjure readers as actors in the movement from past to present" (170).

recipient to his villa but asks him not to bring the books that would slow down his journey. For the Muses, Ausonius says, are a great burden:

> attamen ut citius venias leviusque vehare,
> historiam mimos carmina linque domi.
> grande onus in Musis; tot saecula condita chartis,
> quae sua vix tolerant tempora, nostra gravant.

(Epist. 8.21–24)

> But to come more quickly and to travel more lightly,
> leave at home history, mimes, and poetry.
> There's a great burden in the Muses, so many ages committed to paper,
> they're scarcely tolerable to their own times, heavy to ours.

Green calls this description of the Muses "[a]n illuminating half-serious comment from one of the fourth century's most learned men" (1991, 618). It is also an important text for any description of classicizing poetry in late antiquity. In *Epistles* 4, a separate invitation to Axius Paulus, Ausonius makes a similar list of ancient genres. In that letter, Ausonius asks his recipient to bring his books; but he still describes them as mere luggage for his wagon. By listing and objectifying his friends' readings, Ausonius separates himself from his classical models.[65]

In his *Protrepticus ad nepotem*, Ausonius constructed a curriculum of readings for his young grandson. He lists Homer, Menander, Horace, Vergil, Terence, and Sallust as the principal Greek and Roman authors. As he transitions to his list of Latin authors, Ausonius wonders when his grandson will introduce him again to poetry:

> ecquando ista meae contingent dona senectae?
> quando oblita mihi tot carmina totque per aevum
> conexa historiae, soccos aulaeaque regum
> et melicos lyricosque modos profando novabis
> obductosque seni facies puerascere sensus?

(Protr. 51–55)

---

65. On the role of such moves in creating an idea of the classical, compare ibid., 11: "Learning to read is always a matter of learning to read *something*. Late ancient grammarians formed their discipline by teaching their students how to read the classics—or rather, by teaching their students how to read in a way that created classics."

Oh, when will these gifts befall my old age?
When will you make new for me as you recite them
so many forgotten poems and so many links through time of history,
and comedy and the curtains of kings
and the melodious and lyric meters,
and when will you make an old man's wrinkled senses[66] grow young?

The contrast between Ausonius's old age and his grandson's youth is emphasized throughout, and that contrast draws attention to the ways in which classical poetry needs to be renewed, both for the grandson and for the grandfather. As though to emphasize that his forgetfulness is a trope, Ausonius describes himself in words borrowed from Vergil: "oblita mihi tot carmina" is from *Eclogue* 9, where the goatherd Moeris laments that he cannot even remember the poetry he once sang as a boy.[67] Thus Ausonius's protreptic creates an image of the past as something to be restored through individual acts of reinscription.[68] By playing with the contrast between age / forgetfulness and youth / education Ausonius is able to approach the past as both a distant observer and also as a ready participant. For Ausonius, the classical authors become approachable as they are distanced from the present.

Rather than set themselves up as rivals to the classical poets, Ausonius and his peers often played with the similarities and the differences between themselves and their noted predecessors. In his *Epitaphia heroum qui bello Troico interfuerunt*, Ausonius wrote a two-line epitaph for Odysseus; instead of describing Odysseus, he tells those who are curious to read through the *Odyssey*.[69] In his epigram for Deiphobus, the hero himself declares that his only tomb is the one that Aeneas and Vergil composed for him.[70] Thus Ausonius ostentatiously refers the reader back to the canonical treatments of Odysseus and Deiphobus. In the same way, Paulinus begins his panegyric on John the Baptist by declaring that he will have nothing new or original to say; his material comes straight from the biblical authors.[71]

---

66. Would it be too much to translate "obductos sensus" as "covered meanings"?

67. "[S]aepe ego longos / cantando puerum memini me condere soles. / nunc *oblita mihi tot carmina*" (E. 9.51–53). In listing his canon in this poem, Ausonius employs a series of similar allusions, so that his poetry embodies the ideal of a continuous tradition.

68. And perhaps there was something to Symmachus's playful request for a didascalic poem from Ausonius (Symm. *Ep.* 1.31.2).

69. *Epit.* 5.2: "perlege Odyssian omnia nosse volens."

70. *Epit.* 13.3–4: "non habeo tumulum, nisi quem mihi voce vocantis / et pius Aeneas et Maro composuit."

71. "Nec nova nunc aut nostra canam; dixere prophetae / cuncta prius" (*Carm.* 6.14–15).

While they sometimes advertised their dependence on their sources, late antique poets were also described as the equals of their classical models. Thus Symmachus compared Ausonius's *Mosella* to Vergil's poetry.[72] Paulinus compared Ausonius to Vergil and Cicero.[73] On an honorary statue, the Senate compared Claudian to both Homer and Vergil.[74] In the *Mosella*, Ausonius himself combines deference and confidence. He compares his river to the famous rivers in the *Iliad* and the *Aeneid*:

> quod si tibi, dia Mosella,
> Smyrna suum vatem vel Mantua clara dedisset,
> cederet Iliacis Simois memoratus in oris
> nec praeferre suos auderet Thybris honores.
>
> (*Mos.* 374–77)

> [B]ut if, divine Moselle, to you
> Smyrna or glorious Mantua had given their own poet,
> the Simois, famous on the shores of Ilion, would give way;
> and the Tiber would not dare to prefer its honors.

Although Ausonius claims that Homer and Vergil would have praised the Moselle more successfully than he has, he also implies that his river is in fact preferable. That combination of deference and assurance mirrors the contemporary praise of Ausonius's poetry. In introducing the classical authors as though they also had written poems about a river, Ausonius both reinforces the idea of the classical and elevates his own vision of contemporary poetry.[75] Because the classical poets were separate and distant, Ausonius could advertise their greatness without diminishing his own stature. Because he returns to these sources, Ausonius lends Vergil a voice and an influence within his poem. Thus the canonicity of the classical poets allows them to be appropriated without the textual violence that is characteristic of emulative allusions.

---

72. Symm. *Ep.* 1.14.5: "ego hoc tuum carmen libris Maronis adiungo."

73. *Carm.* 11.38–39: "vix Tullius et Maro tecum / sustineant aequale iugum."

74. Εἰν ἑνὶ Βιργιλίοιο νόον καὶ μοῦσαν Ὁμήρου / Κλαυδιανὸν Ῥώμη καὶ βασιλῆς ἔθεσαν (*CIL* VI, 1710).

75. This ostentatious display of deference recalls Statius's command to the *Thebaid* to follow the *Aeneid* at a respectful distance: "nec tu divinam Aeneida tempta, / sed longe sequere et vestigia semper adora" (*Theb.* 12.816–17). On this passage and Statian "secondariness," see Hinds 1998, 91–95. Unlike Statius, Ausonius did not write a heroic epic. Ausonius's use of Vergil and Homer is radically tendentious because he shifts the field of epic poetry from heroes to rivers.

✒ Toward a New Theory of Appropriation

We may now address directly the question of *aemulatio*, which was raised earlier both by Paulinus's striking reuse of Horace and by Prudentius's allusions to Aeneas's *katabasis* in book 6 of the *Aeneid*. An emulative allusion portrays its hypertext and author in opposition to an earlier and outmoded hypotext and author; and earlier in this chapter, I discussed the trend within scholarship towards reading such late antique allusions as emulative. Although this model of allusion fits Vergil's engagement with Hellenistic poetry, I propose that poetic quotations be read through their reader rather than through the competitive systems of author and text. Because a quotation is exactly repetitive, it distances allusion from *aemulatio* and allows the reader to consider both texts on their own, as well as together.[76] Thus, if we think again of Paulinus's use of *Epode* 2, a reader may appreciate the two poems at different times (Horace and Paulinus); and he or she may read an earlier poem through a later one (Horace through Paulinus); moreover, when the reader has finished the later poem, the reader may still return to the earlier poem as it was (Horace without Paulinus remains an option). A quotation reveals the independence of the reader most clearly, for it allows the two texts to remain distinct. Already in this chapter, I have introduced the nonreferential allusions of late antiquity, I have explained them through the figure of a strong reader, and I have placed that reader within the context of the canonical Augustan poets. Although it is certainly not the case that all of the allusions discussed here exclude referentiality, they do all make the reader aware in the first place of the present instantiation of the text and of the historical distance between the hypertext and its source. Moreover, they make readers aware of their role in the current presentation of the text, by which I mean the reader's present enjoyment (through activation) of its poetry. Therefore, the reader's enjoyment of a quotation admits of referentiality while still resisting the movement to integration.[77]

Prudentius's *Psychomachia* begins with an obvious allusion to Vergil's *Aeneid*. It has been read as emulative, but I would argue that it actually reflects Prudentius's creative reading of Vergil.

---

76. Compare Pucci 1998, 86: "[*Aemulatio*] might be useful to explain the psychology of the allusive author, or the dynamics of a literary culture that would seem to place heavy emphasis on tradition. But it does not explicate allusion, for allusion is not exclusively (if at all) an emulative or competitive form. It requires an engagement of the older work at issue, not a conjuring up of its best features in order to be outdone by a newer version."

77. In terms of Conte's integrative allusion, discussed earlier in this chapter.

Christe, *gravis* hominum *semper miserate labores*,
qui patria virtute cluis propriaque sed una
(unum namque deum colimus de nomine utroque,
non tamen et solum, quia tu deus ex patre, Christe),
dissere, rex noster, quo milite pellere culpas
mens armata queat nostri de pectoris antro.

(*Psych.* 1–6)

Christ, you have always pitied the hard labors of men,
who are famous in the power that is the father's and yours, but still
    one
(for we worship one God in either name,
though again not single, since you, Christ, are God from the father),
speak out, our king, by what soldiery an armed mind
may drive blemishes from the cave of our heart.

Prudentius echoes the beginning of Aeneas's prayer to Apollo from book 6 of the *Aeneid*:

Phoebe, *gravis* Troiae *semper miserate labores*.

(*Aen.* 6.56)

Phoebus, you have always pitied the hard labors of Troy.

Prudentius changes the addressee of the prayer and writes "hominum" instead of "Troiae." Although the changes are meaningful, the similarities are more concerted. Prudentius selected a line from the *Aeneid* that he could adapt, with only minimal changes, as the opening line of this poem on the soul's struggle against vice. Maria Lühken reads those slight changes as indicative of *aemulatio*, as a *Kontrastimitation*.[78] For her, Prudentius's "Christe" and "hominum" are decisive because "[d]er Gott der Christen ist Hoffnung auf Erlösung für alle Menschen; deshalb muß er—und nicht der heidnische Gott Apollo—im Gebet um sein Erbarmen angefleht werden" (2002, 46). No one would deny that there are differences between Christ and Apollo, or that Prudentius does differentiate (at times sharply) between Roman paganism and Christian theology. But this is not one of the cases in which he makes a sharp distinction between past and present. In this passage, Prudentius repeats the words of Vergil, and the form of allusion he chooses prevents him from marginalizing Vergil's text. Macklin Smith, in his chapter

---

78. Herzog also read this as a case of correction (1975, 193).

titled "The Assault upon Vergil," also reads this allusion as an attack on the *Aeneid* (1976, 271–76), but Smith went further than Lühken and claimed that the sense of Prudentius's allusion is parodic. In the case of a similar allusion (Prudentius's quotations of Vergil in his description of the battle between Pudicitia and Libido), Smith describes Prudentius's use of Vergil as an insult: "The insult is repeated every time Prudentius uses Vergil thus irrelevantly or irreverently: it is as if Prudentius were flaunting his lack of respect for Vergil's content, as if he were saying, 'I can use you for any purpose whatever.'"[79] For Smith, use implies insult rather than play. And Smith thinks that Prudentius means to contrast Apollo and Christ absolutely, so that either Aeneas's prayer will be approved poetically and theologically or Prudentius's prayer will win the day.[80] The emulative readings of this allusion see a sharp contrast between Prudentius's and Vergil's lines.

The difference of content between Vergil and Prudentius need not imply a strong contrast in the case of this particular allusion. Prudentius went out of his way here to portray Christ through Apollo. In fact, Marc Mastrangelo has read this line as the first of a series of passages in the *Psychomachia* in which Prudentius figures Aeneas as a type of the reader whose struggle has become interior and spiritual rather than national and material (2008, 15–20). Mastrangelo therefore reads Prudentius as using Vergil in a positive sense, to portray Christ and his prayer through his reader's prior knowledge of the *Aeneid*. In this way, Prudentius can be read as alluding to Vergil without the motive of *aemulatio*.

It is important to note that Prudentius performs this typological reading of Aeneas by quoting nearly an entire line from Vergil. Because Prudentius allows Vergil's words to stand so starkly within his poem, he enables the reader to consider Vergil's words in a new light and to make new sense of them without setting up a contrast between the two poets. Prudentius's quotation— repeating exactly the words of a predecessor in a manner which clearly reveals the hypotext and distances its words from the hypertext—resists the movement towards *aemulatio*. Instead of inventing his own invocation to counter Vergil's invocation of Apollo, Prudentius remembers and incorporates Vergil's

---

79. M. Smith 1976, 288. Actual parody is rare in the allusive quotations of late antiquity, although Ausonius does use Vergil to mock a woman named Crispa: "Crispa tamen cunctas exercet corpore in uno: / deglubit, fellat, molitur per utramque cavernam, / *ne quid inexpertum frustra moritura relinquat*" (*Epigr.* 75.6–8). The final line plays with the more serious meaning of *Aen.* 4.415.

80. Macklin Smith sets Prudentius within the context of a violent literary struggle between paganism and Christianity. Just a year after Smith published his study, Alan Cameron deconstructed the idea of the circle of Symmachus and of a vicious conflict between paganism and Christianity at the end of the fourth century (Cameron 1977).

words. The result is a poetic text that embraces its layers of meaning and invites the reading that will make sense of it. *Aemulatio* recedes in favor of a more balanced awareness of the history of both texts, and the reader may appreciate both the *Aeneid* in its own way and the *Psychomachia* for what it is. In alluding to Vergil in this way at the beginning of his poem, Prudentius invites the reader to consider the difference between the poems (and they are radically different poems) and even to read the *Aeneid* through the *Psychomachia*, but Prudentius does not directly rival Vergil. Instead, his quotation connects the two poems and invites further readings both of the *Psychomachia* and of the *Aeneid*.

In a quotation, a poet both repeats the words of a predecessor and appropriates them in a new sense. Both of those actions are important. At the end of his bilingual letter to Axius Paulus, Ausonius appends to his poem two lines from Horace's *Carmina* 2.3. The difference between this case and those already considered is that Ausonius also translated the second line from Latin into Greek. In translating Horace into Greek, Ausonius acknowledges his ability to retain and transform the poet's words. Because both the retention and the transformation of Horace are active choices, Ausonius's quotation alludes to the poet's present shaping of prior poetry, even in the case of exact quotation. *Aemulatio* is excluded from this allusion for two reasons: Ausonius repeats exactly the sense of Horace, and his translation into Greek does not challenge the Latin poetry of his predecessor.[81] Ausonius ends his invitation to Paulus as follows:

ambo igitur nostrae παραθέλξομεν otia vitae,
>   dum res et aetas et sororum
>   νήματα πορφύρεα πλέκηται.

>   (*Epist.* 6.43–45)

We will both then charm the idleness of our life,
>   As long as there's money and time and the sisters
>   Weave the dark thread.

The next-to-last line is Horace, *Carmina* 2.3.15. Anyone who did not immediately notice the quotation would be brought to attention by the sudden break in meter, the imposition of the closing lines of an Alcaic strophe, apposed to forty-three of Ausonius's hexameter verses. Further, Ausonius's

---

81. But Horace does criticize Lucilius in *Epist.* 1.10 precisely for combining Latin and Greek, and Ausonius does offer in this bilingual letter an alternative to the Horatian poetics of linguistic and imaginative unity.

final line translates Horace's *Carmina* 2.3.16 into rather stately Greek. Ausonius elsewhere incorporates fragments of classical texts into his narratives in such a way as to distance his creation from theirs and to create new meanings for those fragments, but nowhere else does he accomplishes those twin steps of dislocation and translation more clearly or more emphatically. He makes Horace new within a new context and a new idiom, and at the same time he consigns the Latin text of the old Horace to a footnote.[82] Ausonius's letter to Axius Paulus is programmatic of his own approach to Latin poetry, an invitation to his villa and an invitation to his poetics. Ausonius, therefore, enacts his ability as a reader to transform these classical fragments into something new. This apposed allusion to Horace draws attention to the distance between Ausonius and his source and compels Ausonius's reader to make sense of its presence. As in the case of juxtaposed allusions, the apposed allusion depends for its effect upon a mediation which neither the narrative nor the text can provide. The reader, therefore, is tasked with construing the link between Horace and Ausonius. Such transitive reading makes sense of a quotation, just as Ausonius himself makes new sense of Horace by translating the second line of his quotation into Greek. The change occasions less a sense of competition than an awareness of the poetic distance traversed through the poet's new reading of the past.

Because the late antique poets designate their sources as other and foreign, they often feel no need to challenge their predecessors. In this respect, they are different from the classical Latin poets. David West and Tony Woodman's influential collection of essays, *Creative Imitation and Latin Literature* (1979), demonstrated the artistry of Latin literature against its Greek originals. In his introductory essay to that volume, Donald Russell gives what he calls "five principles" of imitation as it was generally understood in antiquity. He derives these principles from Longinus and other ancient critics. Because they outline classical poetics so neatly, Russell's five principles set the differences of late antiquity in high relief. I quote them in full:

(i) The object must be worth imitating.

(ii) The spirit rather than the letter must be reproduced.

(iii) The imitation must be tacitly acknowledged, on the understanding that the informed reader will recognize and approve the borrowing.

(iv) The borrowing must be "made one's own," by individual treatment and assimilation to its new place and purpose.

---

82. "Fila trium patiuntur atra."

(v) The imitator must think of himself as competing with his model,
even if he knows he cannot win.

("*De Imitatione*," 1979, 16)

Although Russell's theory works for classical poetry, it fails to account for
the use of allusion in late antiquity; for (1) while such allusions are usually
drawn from an esteemed source, there is no assurance that the particular
context of that source is "worth imitating"; (2) though not in every case,
the late antique poet often reproduces the letter rather than the spirit of his
source; (3) Ausonius, at the least, does acknowledge several of his quotations
explicitly and not tacitly; (4) the allusive quotation works within its new
context, but it works by resisting the poet's inclination to make it his own;
and (5) the late antique poet who alludes to a classical author may think that
he could win a competition with his model, but the quotation is precisely
the point at which he silences his competitive instincts. Russell's five principles of *imitatio* mark a baseline of agreement on classical allusion, an agreement that centers around the creative reuse and emulative strategies of the
classical Latin poets. But his principles are inadequate to treat the concerns
of these late antique poets who had their own methods of reading classical
poetry.

When Ausonius or Prudentius quote Vergil, they often are not meaning
to compete with their source. Instead, they create a poetry that embraces
the differences within its units of composition and which thereby compels
their reader to engage in its interpretation.[83] Of course, not all allusions
from Ausonius, Prudentius, or their contemporaries fit this category. These
poets (I repeat myself for emphasis) are very good at composing more traditional allusions and at rivaling their peers and their tradition. But they also
employ allusions to celebrate their own direct repetition of the past. When
late antique poets want to write an allusion, they often appropriate directly
the words of their classical predecessor while ignoring their original context. By alluding to the past in such a way as to emphasize the difference
between these prior words and their present use, the late antique poet creates
out of the text a strong reader, charged with navigating the meaning of that
difference. While every allusion depends for its activation upon this strong
reader, late antique allusions bring that dependence into focus. The allusive
techniques discussed in this chapter allow the poet to enact—on the level of

---

83. This interest in the intertextual units of composition is paralleled by the late antique poets'
awareness of the verbal surface of their texts; compare Roberts's description of *leptologia*, which
"directs attention to the differences within the repeated units" (1989, 44).

the text and through the reader—his own appropriation of classical Latin poetry. Insofar as they resist the movement toward intertextuality, these allusions work in ways that are counter to received notions of the dynamics of appropriation in Latin poetry. Because the inclusion of classical fragments draws attention to the individual unit of composition, this centonic composition resists the allusion's ability to integrate old and new contexts. And that resistance creates a gap between the ancient context and its new use. Thus the late antique poets created an ideal of classical poetry against which they were able to write their own poetry. In the history of the reception of Latin poetry, their quotations mark the first attempt to read that tradition from the outside. They create, therefore, a presence for their reader and for the idea of late antique poetry.

Conclusion

The figure of the reader lends a sense of co-
herence and meaning to the Latin poetry from late antiquity. I have described four ways in which the reader structures the textual world of this
period. In interpretive and theoretical works, contemporary prose authors
presented the reader's involvement as central to the present instantiation of
literature. In their prefaces, late antique poets mediated the eventual reception of their poems through a particular reading of the work in question. In
figural poetry, allegory, and centos, late antique poets compelled the reader
to navigate the multiple, parallel layers of the text. And by juxtaposing allusive fragments of classical poetry within their texts, they made room for
the reader on the level of the text and so made the role of the reader obvious. In the long fourth century, Latin poets explored the interaction between text, meaning, and interpretation, and the most distinctive forms of
late antique poetry reflect upon this interplay between source and reading.
Moreover, as the reader came to play a central role in mediating the presence of the text, the poetics of late antiquity stand out in high relief against
the classicisms of Augustan Rome.

The "presence of the text" consists in the sense that the poem remains
to be heard, interpreted, and lived in the particular moment at which it is
encountered by the reader. This sense of the reader's presence is what
Hans Ulrich Gumbrecht describes in *The Production of Presence* (2004) as

"presentification," the creation or performance of the subject's presence in the world. Because the late antique poet allows the reader space within the text, readers inhabit that space as it becomes present to them. A centonic allusion reveals that the reader is constantly at work sorting the text into coherent fragments. In this way, by invoking the reader's presence, the poet lends a virtual immediacy to the verbal (and therefore mediated) strands of his text. This effect of presence explains the particular coherence and vitality of late antique poetry. The repetitions, the gaps, the impressively verbal artistry of late antique poetry allowed the works to be present to their first readers. For this reason, many of the tropes that once struck classicists as frigid formalities are better read as markers of the text's ability to communicate a sense of presence to its contemporary audience. When poets enact through an allusion or a preface the presence of their reader, they reveal most directly the intention of the text to create a sense of transitive, tangible meaning. Therefore, the idea of presence as an effect of the text reveals the way in which different aspects of reading have come together in the poetry of late antiquity. Because the words of the poem appear as centonic fragments to be pieced together by the reader, readers come to enjoy their own role in receiving and enacting the poem that stands before them.

In *De raptu Proserpinae*, Claudian provides a vivid image both for the reader's presence and for the openness of his text. He does so in his description of Proserpina's unfinished embroidery. Since ecphrases are a privileged site of metapoetic reflection, it is hardly surprising that Proserpina's weaving should stand as a symbol of Claudian's poem.[1] But Proserpina never finishes the traditional boundary around her work. Although she meant to set the ocean around its margins, she did not finish her text:[2]

> coeperat et vitreis summo iam margine texti
> Oceanum sinuare vadis; sed cardine verso
> cernit adesse deas inperfectumque laborem
> deserit . . .
>
> (*Rapt.* 1.269–72)

She had begun also to bend now, on the very edge of the weaving,
Ocean with its glassy depths. But as the door opened

---

1. Michael von Albrecht (1989) has read Proserpina's weaving as a symbol of the poem's cosmic design, but he ignores the fact that her work is unfinished. The textual metaphor for poetry is common throughout antiquity (for a good introduction to this theme, see Scheid and Svenbro 1996). Gineste 2000 surveys the role of weaving within *De raptu Proserpinae*.

2. On closure in Claudian's poetry, compare Hinds 2013.

she sees the goddesses approach; and her unfinished work,
she leaves it behind . . .

The incompletion of Proserpina's work is not an idle detail, for Claudian had already drawn attention to it when he said that Proserpina was weaving this gift in vain ("inrita texebat rediturae munera matri," 1.247). But the incompletion of Proserpina's text only prepares the way for its rediscovery later in the epic.

In book 3 of *De raptu Proserpinae*, when Ceres discovers that her house on Sicily has been deserted, she encounters a spider at work on her daughter's unfinished weaving:

[Ceres] semirutas confuso stamine telas
atque interceptas agnoscit pectinis artes.
divinus perit ille labor, spatiumque relictum
audax sacrilego supplebat aranea textu.

(*Rapt.* 3.155–58)

Ceres recognizes the threads, half ruined around the fallen
weft, and also the stilled craft of the comb.
That divine work is lost, and the space that remained,
An audacious spider filled it in with her sacrilegious text.

Because of Ovid's Arachne, the spider could naturally be read as a metaphor for the artist.[3] Moreover, Claudian also describes his epic as "daring," both in the preface to his poem and in its proem ("ausus," praef. 3; "audacia," praef. 9; "audaci," 1.3). This spider, however, fills in the space that remains, the gaps open in the text. If Claudian is like this spider, he is a secondary author; if his poem is like Proserpina's text, its gaps remain for the reader to construe. As Claudian creates a supplemental work, he enables a profound sense of coherence between himself and his epic predecessors, but he also sets a fundamental gap between his work and theirs. Thus the late antique poet enacts his version of reading through a specific appropriation of classical Latin poetry. And in the interplay of presence and absence, the reader emerges as central to the textual strategies of Claudian's mythological epic.

I have limited myself in this book to a single century and to a single aspect of reading in late antiquity. Many questions remain for future study. How much can we say about the development of reading in the second and

---

3. Kellner (1997, 286–87) reads this audacious spider as a metaphor for the political and religious aspects of Claudian's poem.

third centuries CE? What is the relation of late antique Latin poetry to Hellenistic poetry, and to the rhetoric of the Second Sophistic, or even to silver Latin poetry? How does the textual construction of reading in late antiquity relate to the material and social realities of reading? More broadly, how does the construction of reading within late antiquity help us to understand the modern theoretical turn towards the reader? These and other questions would reward further study.

As late antique readers enshrined the poetry of classical Rome, they handed on to their successors a revised version of Latin literature. The tradition of Latin poetry came to include the more active reader of late antiquity, and the meaning of the text came to play a more influential role in its reception. Because the meaning of the text continued to be a source of its presence in the world, we should also ask how reading was figured after the fourth century. Specifically, how does the poetry of the fifth and sixth centuries respond to the concerns of the fourth? Or what do poets such as Sedulius, Sidonius, and Ennodius expect of their readers? And how do they construct their authority in the shadows of Ausonius and Claudian? This is a different story, one that begins with the continuing transformations of literature and interpretation in the emerging medieval world. Thus, at the very end of the *Expositio Virgilianae continentiae*, Fulgentius warns the reader to be attentive: "Farewell, dear sir," he says, "and read the thickets of my heart carefully" ("vale domine, et mei tribulos pectoris cautius lege"). By warning his reader, Fulgentius admits that his allegorical treatise is a tendentious appropriation of Vergil's epic. Even more than Macrobius or Ausonius, Fulgentius acknowledges the need for a cautious interpretation. The presence of the reader continued to structure Latin literature after the fourth century. Poets continued to return to the same textual strategies, and they continued to create through the reader a sense of the poem's presence in the world.

✒ References

Abel, Karlhans. 1955. *Die Plautusprologe*. Mülheim: C. Fabri.

Agamben, Giorgio. 2010. *Categorie italiane: Studi di poetica e di letteratura*. Rome: GLF editori Laterza.

Albrecht, Michael von. 1989. "Proserpina's Tapestry in Claudian's *De raptu*: Tradition and Design." *Illinois Classical Studies* 14:383–90.

———. 1994. *Geschichte der römischen Literatur: Von Andronicus bis Boethius*. 2 vols. Munich: K. G. Saur.

Ando, Clifford. 1994. "Augustine on Language." *Revue des études augustiniennes* 40 (1): 45–78.

Auerbach, Eric. 1944. "Figura." In *Neue Dantestudien*, 11–71. Istanbul. This is a revised version of Auerbach 1938. "Figura." *Archivum Romanicum* 22 (4): 436–489.

Babcock, William S., trans. 1989. *Tyconius: The Book of Rules*. Atlanta: Scholars Press.

Baraz, Yelena. 2012. *A Written Republic: Cicero's Philosophical Politics*. Princeton, NJ: Princeton University Press.

Barnes, T. D. 1975. "Optatianus Porfyrius." *American Journal of Philology* 96 (2): 173–86.

Bažil, Martin. 2009. *Centones Christiani: Métamorphoses d'une forme intertextuelle dans la poésie latine chrétienne de l'Antiquité tardive*. Paris: Études Augustiniennes.

Beatrice, Pier Franco. 1971. "L'allegoria nella *Psychomachia* di Prudenzio." *Studia Patavina* 18:25–73.

Benedetti, Fabrizio. 1980. *La tecnica del «vertere» negli epigrammi di Ausonio*. Florence: L. S. Olschki.

Benko, Stephen. 1980. "Virgil's Fourth Eclogue in Christian Interpretation." In *Aufstieg und Niedergang der Römischen Welt*, 2.31.1:646–705. Berlin: Walter de Gruyter.

Bing, Peter. 1985. "Kastorion of Soloi's Hymn to Pan (*Supplementum Hellenisticum* 310)." *American Journal of Philology* 106 (4): 502–9.

Bochet, Isabelle. 2004a. "De l'exégèse à l'herméneutique augustinienne." *Revue d'études augustiniennes et patristiques* 50 (2): 349–69.

———. 2004b. *Le firmament de l'Ecriture: L'herméneutique augustinienne*. Paris: Études Augustiniennes.

Borges, Jorge Luis. 1925. *Inquisiciones*. Buenos Aires: Proa.

Borgo, Antonella. 2001. "La *Praefatio* del II libro di Marziale: La *brevitas* principio di poetica." *Bollettino di studi latini* 31 (2): 497–506.

Bright, Pamela. 1988. *The "Book of Rules" of Tyconius: Its Purpose and Inner Logic.* Notre Dame, IN: University of Notre Dame Press.

———, ed. and trans. 1999. *Augustine and the Bible.* Notre Dame, IN: University of Notre Dame Press.

Brittain, Charles. 2011. "Augustine as a Reader of Cicero." In *Tolle, lege: Essays in Honor of Roland J. Teske, S.J.*, edited by Richard C. Taylor, David Twetten, and Michael Wreen, 81–114. Milwaukee, WI: Marquette University Press.

Brown, Dennis. 1992. *Vir Trilinguis: A Study in the Biblical Exegesis of Saint Jerome.* Kampen: Kok Pharos.

Brown, Peter. 1971. *The World of Late Antiquity: From Marcus Aurelius to Muhammad.* London: Thames & Hudson.

Bruhat, Marie-Odile. 1999. "Les *Carmina Figurata* de Publilius Optatianus Porfyrius: La métamorphose d'un genre et l'invention d'une poésie liturgique impériale sous Constantin." Thèse de doctorat, Paris-Sorbonne.

Cain, Andrew. 2009. *The Letters of Jerome: Asceticism, Biblical Exegesis, and the Construction of Christian Authority in Late Antiquity.* Oxford: Oxford University Press.

Camastra, Palma. 1998. *Il "Liber Regularum" di Ticonio.* Rome: Vivere in.

Cameron, Alan. 1970a. "Pap. Ant. iii. 15 and the Iambic Preface in Late Greek Poetry." *Classical Quarterly* 20 (1): 119–29.

———. 1970b. *Poetry and Propaganda at the Court of Honorius.* Oxford: Oxford University Press.

———. 1977. "Paganism and Literature in Late Fourth Century Rome." In *Christianisme et formes littéraires de l'antiquité tardive en occident*, 1–30. Vandoeuvres-Geneva: Fondation Hardt.

———. 1980. "*Poetae Novelli.*" *Harvard Studies in Classical Philology* 84:127–75.

———. 2011. *The Last Pagans of Rome.* New York: Oxford University Press.

Castelnérac, Benoît. 2007. "The Method of 'Eclecticism' in Plutarch and Seneca." *Hermathena* 182:135–63.

Cavallo, Guiglielmo, and Roger Chartier, eds. 1999. *A History of Reading in the West: Studies in Print Culture and the History of the Book.* Translated by Lydia G. Cochrane. Amherst: University of Massachusetts Press.

Cavarzere, Alberto. 1996. *Sul limitare: Il «motto» e la poesia di Orazio.* Bologna: Pàtron.

Charity, A. C. 1966. *Events and Their Afterlife: The Dialectics of Christian Typology in the Bible and Dante.* Cambridge: Cambridge University Press.

Charlet, Jean-Louis. 1988. "Aesthetic Trends in Late Latin Poetry (325–410)." *Philologus* 132:74–85.

———. 1991. *Claudien: Oeuvres.* Vol. 1, *Le rapt de Proserpine.* Paris: Les Belles Lettres.

———. 2000. "Comment lire le «De raptu Proserpinae» de Claudien." *Revue des études latines* 78:180–94.

———. 2003. "Signification de la préface à la *Psychomachia* de Prudence." *Revue des études latines* 81:232–51.

Chin, Catherine M. 2008. *Grammar and Christianity in the Late Roman World.* Philadelphia: University of Pennsylvania Press.

Citroni, Mario. 1995. *Poesia e lettori in Roma antica: Forme della comunicazione letteraria.* Rome: Editori Laterza.

Clark, Elizabeth A., and Diane F. Hatch. 1981. *The Golden Bough, the Oaken Cross: The Virgilian Cento of Faltonia Betitia Proba.* Chico, CA: Scholars Press.

Clark, Gillian. 2011. *Late Antiquity: A Very Short Introduction.* Oxford: Oxford University Press.

Comparetti, Domenico. 1997. *Vergil in the Middle Ages.* Reprinted with a new introduction by Jan M. Ziolkowski. Translated by E. F. M. Benecke. Princeton, NJ: Princeton University Press.

Consolino, Franca Ela. 2005. "Il senso del passato: Generi letterari e rapporti con la tradizione nella 'parafrasi biblica' latina." In *Nuovo e antico nella cultura Greco-Latin di IV–VI secolo*, edited by Isabella Gualandri, Fabrizio Conca, and Raffaele Passarella, 447–526. Milan: Cisalpino.

Conte, Gian Biagio. 1974. *Memoria dei poeti e sistema letterario: Catullo, Virgilio, Ovidio, Lucano.* Turin: G. Einaudi.

——. 1984. *Il genere e i suoi confini: Cinque studi sulla poesia di Virgilio.* Turin: Stampatori.

——. 1986. *The Rhetoric of Imitation.* Translated and edited by Charles Segal. Ithaca, NY: Cornell University Press.

Conybeare, Catherine. 2000. *Paulinus Noster: Self and Symbols in the Letters of Paulinus of Nola.* Oxford: Oxford University Press.

——. 2007. "*Sanctum, lector, percense volumen*: Snakes, Readers, and the Whole Text in Prudentius's *Hamartigenia.*" In *The Early Christian Book*, edited by William E. Klingshirn and Linda Safran, 225–40. Washington, DC: Catholic University of America Press.

Copeland, Rita, and Peter T. Struck. 2010. *The Cambridge Companion to Allegory.* Cambridge: Cambridge University Press.

Cotogni, Laura. 1936. "Sovrapposizione di visioni e di allegorie nella *Psychomachia* de Prudenzio." *Rendiconti della R. Accademia Nazionale dei Lincei, classe di scienze morali, storiche e filologiche* 12:441–61.

Coulter, James A. 1976. *The Literary Microcosm: Theories of Interpretation of the Later Neoplatonists.* Leiden: Brill.

Courcelle, Pierre. 1957. "Les exégèses chrétiennes de la quatrième églogue." *Revue des études anciennes* 59:294–319.

——. 1984. *Lecteurs païens et lecteurs chrétiens de l' "Énéide": Les témoignages littéraires.* Paris: Gauthier-Villars.

Courtney, Edward. 1993. *The Fragmentary Latin Poets.* Oxford: Clarendon Press.

Curtius, E. R. 1953. *European Literature and the Latin Middle Ages.* Translated by Willard R. Trask. New York: Pantheon Books.

Davis, N. Gregson. 1994. "Cupid at the Ivory Gates: Ausonius as a Reader of Vergil's *Aeneid.*" *Colby Quarterly* 30 (3): 162–70.

Dawson, David. 1992. *Allegorical Readers and Cultural Revision in Ancient Alexandria.* Berkeley: University of California Press.

——. 2002. *Christian Figural Reading and the Fashioning of Identity.* Berkeley: University of California Press.

De Rentiis, Dina. 1998. "Der Beitrag der Bienen: Überlegungen zum Bienengleichnis bei Seneca und Macrobius." *Rheinisches Museum für Philologie* 141:30–44.

Desbordes, Françoise. 1979. *Argonautica: Trois études sur l'imitation dans la littérature antique*. Brussels: Latomus.

Dionisotti, A. C. 1982. "From Ausonius' Schooldays? A Schoolbook and Its Relatives." *Journal of Roman Studies* 72:83–125.

Dorfbauer, Lukas J. 2010. "Die *praefationes* von Claudian und von Prudentius." In *Text und Bild*, edited by Victoria Zimmerl-Panagl and Dorothea Weber, 195–222. Vienna: Verlag der Österreichischen Akademie der Wissenschaften.

Dykes, Anthony. 2011. *Reading Sin in the World: The "Hamartigenia" of Prudentius and the Vocation of the Responsible Reader*. Cambridge: Cambridge University Press.

Eco, Umberto. 1979. *Lector in fabula: La cooperazione interpretativa nei testi narrativi*. Milan: Bompiani.

——. 1989. *The Open Work*. Translated by Anna Cancogni. Cambridge, MA: Harvard University Press. Originally published as *Opera aperta: Forma e indeterminazione nelle poetiche contemporanee*. Milan: Bompiani, 1962. The last revised Italian edition was published in 1976.

Edwards, John Stephan. 2005. "The *Carmina* of Publilius Optatianus Porphyrius and the Creative Process." In *Studies in Latin Literature and Roman History*, edited by Carl Deroux, 12:447–66. Brussels: Latomus.

Elsner, Jaś. 2000. "From the Culture of Spolia to the Cult of Relics: The Arch of Constantine and the Genesis of Late Antique Forms." *Papers of the British School at Rome* 68:149–84.

——. 2004. "Late Antique Art: The Problem of the Concept and the Cumulative Aesthetic." In *Approaching Late Antiquity: The Transformation from Early to Late Empire*, edited by Simon Swain and Mark Edwards, 271–309. Oxford: Oxford University Press.

Ernst, Ulrich. 1991. *Carmen Figuratum: Geschichte des Figurengedichts von den antiken Ursprüngen bis zum Ausgang des Mittelalters*. Cologne: Böhlau.

Farrell, Joseph. 1991. *Vergil's "Georgics" and the Traditions of Ancient Epic: The Art of Allusion in Literary History*. Oxford: Oxford University Press.

——. 2005. "Intention and Intertext." *Phoenix* 59 (1–2): 98–111.

Felgentreu, Fritz. 1999. *Claudians Praefationes: Bedingungen, Beschreibungen und Wirkungen einer poetischen Kleinform*. Stuttgart: Teubner.

Filosini, Stefania. 2008. *Paolino di Nola, Carmi 10 e 11: Introduzione, testo, traduzione e commento*. Rome: Herder.

Fitzgerald, William. 2007. *Martial: The World of the Epigram*. Chicago: University of Chicago Press.

Fontaine, Jacques. 1973. "Les symbolismes de la cythare dans la poésie de Paulin de Nole." In *Romanitas et Christianitas*, edited by W. den Boer, P. G. van der Nat, C. M. J. Sicking, and J. C. M. van Winden, 123–43. Amsterdam: North-Holland.

——. 1977. "Unité et diversité du mélange des genres et des tons chez quelques écrivains latins de la fin du IVe siècle: Ausone, Ambroise, Ammien." In *Christianisme et formes littéraires de l'antiquité tardive en occident*, edited by Manfred Fuhrmann, 425–82. Vandoeuvres-Geneva: Fondation Hardt.

Fontaine, Mike. 2013. "Dynamics of Appropriation in Roman Comedy: Menander's *Kolax* in Three Roman Receptions (Naevius, Plautus, and Terence's *Eunuchus*)." In *Ancient Comedy and Reception: Essays in Honor of Jeffrey Henderson*, edited by S. Douglas Olson, 180–202. Berlin: Walter de Gruyter.

Formisano, Marco. 2007. "Towards an Aesthetic Paradigm of Late Antiquity." *Antiquité tardive* 15:277–84.

———. 2012. "Late Antiquity, New Departures." In *The Oxford Handbook of Medieval Latin Literature*, edited by Ralph Hexter and David Townsend. Oxford: Oxford University Press.

Foucault, Michel. 1979. "What Is an Author?" In *Textual Strategies: Perspectives in Post-structuralist Criticism*, edited by Josué V. Harari, 141–60. Ithaca, NY: Cornell University Press.

Fraenkel, Eduard. 1957. *Horace*. Oxford: Clarendon Press.

Fredouille, Jean-Claude, Marie-Odile Goulet-Cazé, Philippe Hoffmann, and Pierre Petitmengin. 1997. *Titres et articulations du texte dans les oeuvres antiques: Actes du Colloque International de Chantilly, 13–15 décembre 1994*. Turnhout: Brepols.

Fuhrer, Theresa. 2008. "Augustine on the Power and Weakness of Words." In *Papers of the Langford Latin Seminar*, edited by Francis Cairns, 13:365–83. Cambridge: F. Cairns.

———. 2013. "Hypertexts and Auxiliary Texts: New Genres in Late Antiquity?" In *Generic Interfaces in Latin Literature*, edited by Theodore D. Papanghelis, Stephen J. Harrison, and Stavros Frangoulidis, 79–89. Berlin: Walter de Gruyter.

Gamble, Harry Y. 1995. *Books and Readers in the Early Church: A History of Early Christian Texts*. New Haven, CT: Yale University Press.

Genette, Gérard. 1982. *Palimpsestes: La littérature au second degré*. Paris: Seuil.

———. 1987. *Seuils*. Paris: Seuil.

Gibson, Bruce, ed. 2007. *Statius: Silvae 5*. Oxford: Oxford University Press.

Gillett, Andrew. 2012. "Epic Panegyric and Political Communication in the Fifth-Century West." In *Two Romes: Rome and Constantinople in Late Antiquity*, edited by Lucy Grig and Gavin Kelly, 265–90. Oxford: New York.

Gineste, Marie-France. 2000. "La signification du motif du tissage dans le *De raptu Proserpinae*." *Vita Latina* 157:48–56.

Gnilka, Christian. 2000–2003. *Prudentiana*. 3 vols. Munich: Saur.

Goldlust, Benjamin. 2009. "Un manifeste sur l'organicité littéraire: La préface des *Saturnales* de Macrobe." In *Manifestes littéraires dans la latinité tardive poétique et rhétorique: Actes du Colloque international de Paris, 23–24 mars 2007*, edited by Perrine Galand-Hallyn and Vincent Zarini, 279–96. Paris: Études Augustiniennes.

———. 2010. *Rhétorique et poétique de Macrobe dans les "Saturnales."* Turnhout: Brepols.

González Iglesias, Juan Antonio. 2000. "El intertexto absoluto: Optaciano Porfirio, entre Virgilio y Mallarmé." In *Intertextualidad en las literaturas griega y latina*, edited by V. Bécares, F. Pordomingo, R. Cortés Tovar, and J. C. Fernández Corte, 337–66. Madrid: Ediciones Clásicas.

Goold, G. P. 1970. "Servius and the Helen Episode." *Harvard Studies in Classical Philology* 74:101–68.

Görler, Woldemar. 1969. "Vergilzitate in Ausonius' Mosella." *Hermes* 97 (1): 94–114.

Grafton, Anthony, and Megan Williams. 2006. *Christianity and the Transformation of the Book: Origen, Eusebius, and the Library of Caesarea.* Cambridge, MA: Harvard University Press.

Green, Roger P. H. 1971. *The Poetry of Paulinus of Nola: A Study of His Latinity.* Brussels: Latomus.

——. 1977. "Ausonius' Use of the Classical Latin Poets: Some New Examples and Observations." *Classical Quarterly* 27 (2): 441–52.

——. 1991. *The Works of Ausonius: Edited with Introduction and Commentary.* Oxford: Clarendon Press.

——. 1995. "Proba's Cento: Its Date, Purpose and Reception." *Classical Quarterly* 45 (2): 551–63.

——. 1997. "Proba's Introduction to Her Cento." *Classical Quarterly* 47 (2): 548–59.

——, ed. 1999. *Ausonii Opera.* Oxford: Clarendon Press.

——. 2006. *Latin Epics of the New Testament: Juvencus, Sedulius, Arator.* Oxford: Oxford University Press.

——. 2008. "Which Proba Wrote the Cento?" *Classical Quarterly* 58 (1): 264–76.

Greene, Thomas M. 1982. *The Light in Troy: Imitation and Discovery in Renaissance Poetry.* New Haven, CT: Yale University Press.

Gruzelier, Claire. 1989. "Claudian and the Art of Imitatio in the *De raptu Proserpinae.*" *Prudentia* 21 (2): 15–24.

——, ed. 1993. *Claudian: De Raptu Proserpinae.* Oxford: Clarendon Press.

Gumbrecht, Hans Ulrich. 2004. *Production of Presence: What Meaning Cannot Convey.* Stanford, CA: Stanford University Press.

Gurd, Sean. 2012. *Work in Progress: Literary Revision as Social Performance in Ancient Rome.* New York: Oxford University Press.

Gutzwiller, Kathryn, ed. 2005. *The New Posidippus: A Hellenistic Poetry Book.* Oxford: Oxford University Press.

Hadas, Moses. 1952. *A History of Latin Literature.* New York: Columbia University Press.

Hadot, Pierre. 1979. "La division des parties de la philosophie dans l'Antiquité." *Museum Helveticum* 36 (4): 201–23.

Haines-Eitzen, Kim. 2000. *Guardians of Letters: Literacy, Power, and the Transmitters of Early Christian Literature.* Oxford: Oxford University Press.

Hall, J. B., ed. 1985. *Claudii Claudiani Carmina.* Leipzig: Teubner.

——. 1991. "Latin Poetry in Late Antiquity." Review of *The Jeweled Style*, by Michael Roberts. *Classical Review* 41 (2): 359–61.

Hansen, Maria Fabricius. 2003. *The Eloquence of Appropriation: Prolegomena to an Understanding of Spolia in Early Christian Rome.* Rome: L'Erma di Bretschneider.

Hardie, Philip. 1993. *The Epic Successors of Virgil: A Study in the Dynamics of a Tradition*. Cambridge: Cambridge University Press.

——, ed. 1994. *Virgil: Aeneid IX*. Cambridge: Cambridge University Press.

——. 2007. "Polyphony or Babel? Hosidius Geta's *Medea* and the Poetics of the Cento." In *Severan Culture*, edited by Simon Swain, Stephen Harrison, and Jaś Elsner, 168–76. Cambridge: Cambridge University Press.

Heinz, Carsten. 2007. *Mehrfache Intertextualität bei Prudentius*. Frankfurt am Main: Peter Lang.

Henderson, John. 2004. *Morals and Villas in Seneca's Letters: Places to Dwell*. Cambridge: Cambridge University Press.

Hernández Lobato, Jesús. 2007. "Ausonio ante el enigma del número tres: Política y poética en el *Griphus*." In *Munus quaesitum meritis*, edited by Gregorio Hinojo Andrés and José Carlos Fernández Corte, 455–62. Salamanca: Ediciones Universidad de Salamanca.

Herzog, Reinhart. 1966. *Die allegorische Dichtkunst des Prudentius*. Munich: Beck.

——. 1975. *Die Bibelepik der lateinischen Spätantike*. Munich: Fink.

Herzog, Reinhart, and Peter Lebrecht Schmidt, eds. 1989–. *Handbuch der lateinischen Literatur der Antike*. Munich: Beck.

Hexter, Ralph. 2006. "Literary History as a Provocation to Reception Studies." In *Classics and the Uses of Reception*, edited by Charles Martindale and Richard F. Thomas, 23–31. Malden, MA: Blackwell.

Higgins, Dick. 1987. *Pattern Poetry: Guide to an Unknown Literature*. Albany: State University of New York Press.

Hinds, Stephen. 1998. *Allusion and Intertext: Dynamics of Appropriation in Roman Poetry*. Cambridge: Cambridge University Press.

——. 2013. "Claudianism in the *De Raptu Proserpinae*." In *Generic Interfaces in Latin Literature*, edited by Theodore D. Papanghelis, Stephen J. Harrison, and Stavros Frangoulidis, 169–92. Berlin: Walter de Gruyter.

Holford-Strevens, Leofranc. 2003. *Aulus Gellius: An Antonine Scholar and His Achievement*. Rev. ed. Oxford: Oxford University Press.

Hose, Martin. 2007. "Konstantin und die Literatur—oder: Gibt es eine Konstantinische Literatur?" *Gymnasium* 114 (6): 535–58.

Hosius, Carl. 1926. *Die Moselgedichte des Decimus Magnus Ausonius und des Venantius Fortunatus*. 3rd ed. Marburg: Elwert.

Irvine, Martin. 1994. *The Making of Textual Culture: "Grammatica" and Literary Theory, 350–1100*. Cambridge: Cambridge University Press.

Jackson, Stephen. 1997. "Argo: The First Ship?" *Rheinisches Museum für Philologie* 140:249–57.

Jansen, Laura, ed. 2014. *The Roman Paratext: Frame, Texts, Readers*. Cambridge: Cambridge University Press.

Janson, Tore. 1964. *Latin Prose Prefaces*. Stockholm: Almqvist & Wiksell.

Jauss, Hans Robert. 1960. "Form und Auffassung der Allegorie in der Tradition der *Psychomachia*." In *Medium Aevum vivum: Festschrift für Walther Bulst*, edited by Hans Robert Jauss and Dieter Schaller, 179–206. Heidelberg: C. Winter.

——. 1968. "Enstehung und Strukturwandel der allegorischen Dichtung." In *La littérature didactique, allégorique et satirique*, edited by Hans Robert Jauss, vol. 1,

Partie historique, 146–244. Grundriss der Romanischen Literaturen des Mittelalters 6. Heidelberg: C. Winter.

——. 1982. *Toward an Aesthetic of Reception*. Translated by Timothy Bahti. Minneapolis: University of Minnesota Press.

Jay, Pierre. 1985. *L'exégèse de Saint Jérôme d'après son «Commentaire sur Isaïe»*. Paris: Études Augustiniennes.

——. 2004. "Jerome." In *Handbook of Patristic Exegesis: The Bible in Ancient Christianity*, edited by Charles Kannengiesser, 2:1094–1133. Leiden: Brill.

Jocelyn, H. D. 1964–1965. "Ancient Scholarship and Virgil's Use of Republican Latin Poetry." Pts. 1 and 2. *Classical Quarterly* 14 (2): 280–95; 15 (1): 126–44.

Johannsen, Nina. 2003. "Statius, Silvae 4, praef. und die Lokalisierung der *Praefationes*." *Rheinisches Museum für Philologie* 146 (1): 110–12.

——. 2006. *Dichter über ihre Gedichte: Die Prosavorreden in den »Epigrammaton libri« Martials und in den »Silvae« des Statius*. Göttingen: Vandenhoeck & Ruprecht.

Johnson, Scott Fitzgerald, ed. 2012. *The Oxford Handbook of Late Antiquity*. Oxford: Oxford University Press.

Johnson, William A. 2010. *Readers and Reading Culture in the High Roman Empire*. New York: Oxford University Press.

Johnson, William A., and Holt N. Parker. 2009. *Ancient Literacies: The Culture of Reading in Greece and Rome*. Oxford: Oxford University Press.

Jones, J. W., Jr. 1961. "Allegorical Interpretation in Servius." *Classical Journal* 56 (5): 217–26.

Kaster, Robert. 1978. "Servius and *idonei auctores*." *American Journal of Philology* 99 (2):181–209.

——. 1980. "Macrobius and Servius: Verecundia and the Grammarian's Function." *Harvard Studies in Classical Philology* 84:220–62.

——. 1988. *Guardians of Language: The Grammarian and Society in Late Antiquity*. Berkeley: University of California Press.

——, ed. and trans. 2011. *Macrobius: Saturnalia*. 3 vols. Cambridge, MA: Harvard University Press.

Keaney, J. J., and Robert Lamberton, eds. 1996. [Plutarch]. *Essay on the Life and Poetry of Homer*. Atlanta: Scholars Press.

Kellner, Thomas. 1997. *Die Göttergestalten in Claudians "De raptu Proserpinae": Polarität und Koinzidenz als anthropozentrische Dialektik mythologisch formulierter Weltvergewisserung*. Stuttgart: Teubner.

Kelly, Douglas. 1999. *The Conspiracy of Allusion: Description, Rewriting, and Authorship from Macrobius to Medieval Romance*. Leiden: Brill.

Kelly, Gavin. 2008. *Ammianus Marcellinus: The Allusive Historian*. Cambridge: Cambridge University Press.

Keudel, Ursula. 1970. *Poetische Vorläufer und Vorbilder in Claudians "De consulatu Stilichonis": Imitationskommentar*. Göttingen: Vandenhoeck & Ruprecht.

Kissel, Walter, ed. 1990. *Aules Persius Flaccus: Satiren*. Heidelberg: Carl Winter.

Kluge, Elsa. 1922. "Beiträge zur Chronologie der Geschichte Constantins des Grossen. *Historisches Jahrbuch der Görres Gesellschaft* 42:89–102.

Knorr, Ortwin. 2006. "Horace's Ship Ode (*Odes* 1.14) in Context: A Meta-phorical Love-Triangle." *Transactions of the American Philological Association* 136 (1): 149–69.

Konstan, David. 2004. "'The Birth of the Reader': Plutarch as a Literary Critic." *Scholia* 13:3–27.

———. 2006. "The Active Reader in Classical Antiquity." *Argos* 30:5–16.

Kwapisz, Jan. 2013. *The Greek Figure Poems.* Leuven: Peeters.

Laird, Andrew. 2003. "Figures of Allegory from Homer to Latin Epic." In *Metaphor, Allegory, and the Classical Tradition: Ancient Thought and Modern Revision*, edited by G. R. Boys-Stones, 151–75. Oxford: Oxford University Press.

Lamacchia, Rosa. 1958. "Dall' arte allusiva al centone." *Atene e Roma* 3:193–216.

———, ed. 1981. *Hosidius Geta. Medea: Cento Vergilianus.* Leipzig: Teubner.

Lamberton, Robert. 1986. *Homer the Theologian: Neoplatonist Allegorical Reading and the Growth of the Epic Tradition.* Berkeley: University of California Press.

———. 1992. "The Neoplatonists and the Spiritualization of Homer." In *Homer's Ancient Readers: The Hermeneutics of Greek Epic's Earliest Exegetes*, edited by Robert Lamberton and John J. Keaney, 115–33. Princeton, NJ: Princeton University Press.

Lamberton, Robert, and John J. Keaney, eds. 1992. *Homer's Ancient Readers: The Hermeneutics of Greek Epic's Earliest Exegetes.* Princeton, NJ: Princeton University Press.

Lardet, Pierre. 1993. *L'apologie de Jérôme contre Rufin: Un commentaire.* Leiden: Brill.

Laurenti, Joseph L., and Alberto Porqueras-Mayo. 1971. *Ensayo bibliografico del prologo en la literatura.* Madrid: C.S.I.C.

Lausberg, Marion. 1991. "Seneca und Platon (Calcidius) in der Vorrede zu den *Saturnalien* des Macrobius." *Rheinisches Museum für Philologie* 134:167–91.

Lavarenne, Maurice. 1948. *Prudence.* Vol. 3, *Psychomachie, Contre Symmaque.* 3rd ed., corrected and enlarged by Jean-Louis Charlet (1992). Paris: Les Belles Lettres.

Letrouit, Jean. 2007. "Pour une approche du *Carmen* XXV de P. Optatianus Porfyrius en terme de dénombrement." *Maia* 49 (1): 73–76.

Levitan, William. 1985. "Dancing at the End of the Rope: Optatian Porfyry and the Field of Roman Verse." *Transactions of the American Philological Association* 115:245–69.

Lowe, Dunstan. 2012. "Triple Tipple: Ausonius' *Griphus ternarii numeri*." In *The Muse at Play: Riddles and Wordplay in Greek and Latin Poetry*, edited by Jan Kwapisz, David Petrain, and Mikolaj Szymański, 335–52. Berlin: Walter de Gruyter.

Lühken, Maria. 2002. *Christianorum Maro et Flaccus: Zur Vergil- und Horazrezeption des Prudentius.* Göttingen: Vandenhoeck & Ruprecht.

Luz, Christine. 2010. *Technopaignia: Formspiele in der griechischen Dichtung.* Leiden: Brill.

Malamud, Martha. 2011. *The Origin of Sin: An English Translation of the "Hamartigenia."* Ithaca, NY: Cornell University Press.

Marinone, Nino. 1990. *Analecta graecolatina.* Bologna: Pàtron.

Markus, Robert. 1996. *Signs and Meanings: World and Text in Ancient Christianity.* Liverpool: Liverpool University Press.

Martin, Paul M. 2004. "La prosopopée de la patrie romaine dans la littérature latine." In *L'allégorie de l'antiquité à la renaissance*, edited by Brigitte Pérez-Jean and Patricia Eichek-Lojkine, 129–59. Paris: Champion.

Martindale, Charles. 1993. *Redeeming the Text: Latin Poetry and the Hermeneutics of Reception.* Cambridge: Cambridge University Press.

———. 1996. "Troping the Colours, or How (Not) to Write Literary History: The Case of Rome." *History of Human Sciences* 9:93–106.

Martindale, Charles, and Richard F. Thomas, eds. 2006. *Classics and the Uses of Reception.* Malden, MA: Blackwell.

Mastandrea, Paolo. 2001. "L'epigramma dedicatorio del «Cento Vergilianus» di Proba: Analisi del testo, ipotesi di datazione e identificazione dell'autore." *Bollettino di studi latini* 31 (2): 565–78.

Mastrangelo, Marc. 2008. *The Roman Self in Late Antiquity: Prudentius and the Poetics of the Soul.* Baltimore: Johns Hopkins University Press.

McGill, Scott. 2001. "*Poeta arte Christianus*: Pomponius' Cento *Versus ad Gratiam Domini* as an Early Example of Christian Bucolic." *Traditio* 56:15–26.

———. 2005. *Virgil Recomposed: The Mythological and Secular Centos in Antiquity.* New York: Oxford University Press.

———. 2007. "Virgil, Christianity, and the *Cento Probae*." In *Texts and Culture in Late Antiquity: Inheritance, Authority, and Change*, edited by J. H. D. Scourfield, 173–94. Swansea: Classical Press of Wales.

McKeown, J. C. 1987–1998. *Ovid: Amores: Text, Prolegomena and Commentary.* 3 vols. Liverpool: Cairns.

Miller, Patricia Cox. 1998. "'Differential Networks': Relics and Other Fragments in Late Antiquity." *Journal of Early Christian Studies* 6 (1): 113–38.

———. 2009. *The Corporeal Imagination: Signifying the Holy in Late Ancient Christianity.* Philadelphia: University of Pennsylvania Press.

Moreau, Madeleine, Isabelle Bochet, and Goulven Madec. 1997. *Augustin: La doctrine chrétienne. De doctrina christiana.* Bibliothèque augustinienne, vol. 11, pt. 2. Paris: Études Augustiniennes.

Morgan, Llewelyn. 1999. *Patterns of Redemption in Virgil's "Georgics."* Cambridge: Cambridge University Press.

Murgia, Charles E. 2003. "The Dating of Servius Revisited." *Classical Philology* 98 (1): 45–69.

Nauroy, Gérard, and Marie-Anne Vannier, eds. 2008. *Saint Augustin et la Bible: Actes du colloque de l'université Paul Verlaine-Metz (7–8 avril 2005).* Bern: Peter Lang.

Nazzaro, Antonio V. 1982. "La parafrasi salmica di Paolino di Nola." In *Atti del Convegno XXXI Cinquantenario della morte di S. Paolino di Nola (431–1981)*, 93–119. Rome: Herder.

Netz, Reviel, and William Noel. 2007. *The Archimedes Codex: How a Medieval Prayer Book Is Revealing the True Genius of Antiquity's Greatest Scientist.* Philadelphia: Da Capo.

Newlands, Carole. 1988. "*Naturae mirabor opus*: Ausonius' Challenge to Statius in the *Mosella*." *Transactions of the American Philological Association* 118:403–19.

——. 2009. "Statius' Prose Prefaces." *Materiali e discussioni per l'analisi dei testi classici* 61:229–42.

Niehoff, Maren R. 2011. *Jewish Exegesis and Homeric Scholarship in Alexandria.* Cambridge: Cambridge University Press.

Nisbet, R. G. M., and Margaret Hubbard. 1970. *A Commentary on Horace: Odes, Book I.* Oxford: Clarendon Press.

Nugent, S. Georgia. 1985. *Allegory and Poetics: The Structure and Imagery of Pruden-tius' "Psychomachia."* Frankfurt am Main: Peter Lang.

——. 1990. "Ausonius' 'Late-Antique' Poetics and 'Post-modern' Literary Theory." *Ramus* 19:26–50.

Nünlist, René. 2009. *The Ancient Critic at Work: Terms and Concepts of Literary Criticism in Greek Scholia.* Cambridge: Cambridge University Press.

O'Daly, Gerard. 2004. "*Sunt etiam Musis sua ludicra*: Vergil in Ausonius." In *Romane memento: Vergil in the Fourth Century*, edited by Roger Rees, 141–54. London: Duckworth.

Oliensis, Ellen. 1998. *Horace and the Rhetoric of Authority.* Cambridge: Cambridge University Press.

Pagán, Victoria E. 2010. "The Power of the Epistolary Preface from Statius to Pliny." *Classical Quarterly* 60 (1): 194–201.

Palmer, Anne-Marie. 1989. *Prudentius on the Martyrs.* Oxford: Clarendon Press.

Paolucci, Paola, ed. 2006. *Il centone virgiliano "Hippodamia" dell'"Anthologia latina": Introduzione, edizione critica, traduzione, commento.* Hildesheim: Georg Olms.

Parravicini, Achille. 1914. "Le prefazioni di Claudio Claudiano." *Athenaeum* 2:183–94.

Pasquali, Giorgio. 1942. "Arte allusiva." *Italia che scrive* 25:185–87. Reprinted in Giorgio Pasquali, *Stravaganze quarte e supreme*, 11–20. Venice: Pozza, 1951. Citations refer to the 1942 publication.

Pavlovskis, Zoja. 1967. "From Statius to Ennodius: A Brief History of Prose Prefaces to Poems." *Rendiconti dell'Istituto Lombardo* 101 (3): 535–67.

Paxson, James J. 1994. *The Poetics of Personification.* Cambridge: Cambridge University Press.

Pellizzari, Andrea. 2003. *Servio: Storia, cultura e istituzioni nell'opera di un grammatico tardoantico.* Florence: L. S. Olschki.

Pelttari, Aaron. 2011a. "Approaches to the Writing of Greek in Late Antique Latin Texts." *Greek, Roman, and Byzantine Studies* 51 (3): 461–82.

——. 2011b. "Symmachus' *Epistulae* 1.31 and Ausonius' Poetics of the Reader." *Classical Philology* 106 (2): 161–69.

Pépin, Jean. 1976. *Mythe et allégorie: Les origines grecques et les contestations judéo-chrétiennes.* 2nd ed. Paris: Études Augustiniennes.

Pernot, Laurent. 1993. *La rhétorique de l'éloge dans le monde gréco-romain.* 2 vols. Paris: Études Augustiniennes.

Perrelli, Raffaele. 1992. *I proemi claudianei: Tra epica ed epidittica.* Catania: Università di Catania.

Peuch, Aimé. 1888. *Prudence: Étude sur la poésie latine chrétienne au IVe siècle.* Paris: Hachette.

Pilch, Stanislaus. 1929. "Horatii C. I 14 quomodo sit interpretandum." *Eos* 32:449–72.

Pirovano, Luigi. 2006. *Le "Interpretationes Vergilianae" di Tiberio Claudio Donato: Problemi di retorica*. Rome: Herder.

Polara, Giovanni, ed. 1973. *Publilii Optatiani Porfyrii Carmina*. 2 vols. Turin: Paravia.

——. 1974–1975. "Cinquant'anni di studi su Optaziano." Pts. 1–3. *Vichiana* 3:110–24; 3:282–301; 4:97–115.

——. 1981. "Un aspetto della fortuna di Virgilio: Tra Virgilio, Ausonio e l'*Appendix Vergiliana*." *Koinonia* 5:48–62.

——. 1987. "Optaziano Porfirio tra il calligramma antico e il carme figurato di età medioevale." *Invigilata lucernis* 9:163–73.

——. 1989. "I centoni." In *Lo spazio letterario di Roma antica*, edited by Guglielmo Cavallo, Paolo Fedeli, and Andrea Giardina, vol. 3, *La ricezione del testo*, 245–75. Rome: Salerno.

——. 1991. "Le parole nella pagina: Grafica e contenuti nei carmi figurati latini." *Vetera Christianorum* 28:291–336. Reprinted in *Retorica ed esegesi biblica: Il rilievo dei contenuti attraverso le forme; Atti del II Seminario di Antichità Cristiane, Bari, 27–28 novembre 1991*, edited by Marcello Marin and Mario Girardi, 201–45. Bari: Edipuglia, 1996.

——. 2004. "Commenti di lettore e commenti d'autore." In *L'ultima parola: L'analisi dei testi; Teorie e pratiche nell'antichità greca e latina*, edited by Giancarlo Abbamonte, Ferruccio Conti Bizzarro, and Luigi Spina, 273–87. Naples: Arte tipografica.

Polara, Giovanni, and Enrico Flores. 1969. "Specimina di analisi applicate a strutture di 'Verspielerei' latina." *Rendiconti della Accademia di Archeologia Lettere e Belle Arti di Napoli* 44:111–36.

Pollmann, Karla. 1993. "Etymologie, Allegorese und epische Struktur. Zu den Toren der Träume bei Homer und Vergil." *Philologus* 137:232–51.

——. 1996. *Doctrina christiana: Untersuchungen zu den Anfängen der christlichen Hermeneutik unter besonderer Berücksichtigung von Augustinus*. Fribourg, Switzerland: Universitätsverlag.

——. 2004. "Sex and Salvation in the Vergilian Cento of the Fourth Century." In *Romane memento: Vergil in the Fourth Century*, edited by Roger Rees, 79–96. London: Duckworth.

——. 2009. "Exegesis without End: Forms, Methods, and Functions of Biblical Commentaries." In *A Companion to Late Antiquity*, edited by Philip Rousseau, 258–69. Malden, MA: Blackwell.

Porter, James I., ed. 2006. *Classical Pasts: The Classical Traditions of Greece and Rome*. Princeton, NJ: Princeton University Press.

Posani, Maria Rosa. 1962. "Reminiscenze di poeti latini nella «Mosella» di Ausonio." *Studi italiani di filologia classica* 34:31–69.

Pozzi, Giovanni. 1984. *Poesia per gioco: Prontuario di figure artificiose*. Bologna: Mulino.

——. 2002. *La parola dipinta*. 3rd ed. Milan: Adelphi.

Preminger, Alex, and T. V. F. Brogan, eds. 1993. *The New Princeton Encyclopedia of Poetry and Poetics*. Princeton, NJ: Princeton University Press.

Pucci, Joseph. 1998. *The Full-Knowing Reader: Allusion and the Power of the Reader in the Western Literary Tradition.* New Haven, CT: Yale University Press.

——. 2000. "Ausonius the Centaur: A Reading of the First Preface." *New England Classical Journal* 27 (3): 121–30.

——. 2002. "A Reading of Ausonius, *Professores* 1." In *Gestures: Essays in Ancient History, Literature, and Philosophy,* edited by Geoffrey W. Bakewell and James P. Sickinger, 87–101. Oxford: Oxbow.

——. 2009. "Ausonius' *Ephemeris* and the *Hermeneumata* Tradition." *Classical Philology* 104 (1): 50–68.

Quilligan, Maureen. 1979. *The Language of Allegory: Defining the Genre.* Ithaca, NY: Cornell University Press.

Raffaelli, Renato. 1980. "Prologhi, perioche, didascalie nel Terenzio Bembino (e nel Plauto Ambrosiano)." *Scrittura e civiltà* 4:41–101.

——. 2009. *Esercizi Plautini.* Urbino: Quattro venti.

Raspanti, Giacomo. 2009. "The Significance of Jerome's *Commentary on Galatians* in his Exegetical Production." In *Jerome of Stridon: His Life, Writing and Legacy,* edited by Andrew Cain and Josef Lössl, 163–71. Burlington, VT: Ashgate.

Rebillard, Éric. 2000. "A New Style of Argument in Christian Polemic: Augustine and the Use of Patristic Citations." *Journal of Early Christian Studies* 8 (4): 559–78.

Reckford, Kenneth J. 2009. *Recognizing Persius.* Princeton, NJ: Princeton University Press.

Rees, Roger, ed. 2004. *Romane memento: Vergil in the Fourth Century.* London: Duckworth.

Rigolot, François. 2000. "Le paratexte et l'émergence de la subjectivité littéraire." In *Paratextes: Études aux bords du texte,* edited by Mireille Calle-Gruber and Elisabeth Zawisza, 19–40. Paris: Harmattan.

Roberts, Michael. 1985. *Biblical Epic and Rhetorical Paraphrase in Late Antiquity.* Liverpool: Francis Cairns.

——. 1989. *The Jeweled Style: Poetry and Poetics in Late Antiquity.* Ithaca, NY: Cornell University Press.

——. 2002. "Creation in Ovid's *Metamorphoses* and the Latin Poets of Late Antiquity." *Arethusa* 35 (3): 403–15.

——. 2007. "Bringing Up the Rear: Continuity and Change in the Latin Poetry of Late Antiquity." In *Latinitas Perennis,* edited by Wim Verbaal, Yanick Maes, and Jan Papy, vol. 1, *The Continuity of Latin Literature,* 141–67. Leiden: Brill.

Rose, H. J. 1936. *A Handbook of Latin Literature: From the Earliest Times to the Death of St. Augustine.* London: Methuen.

Rosenblum, Morris. 1961. *Luxorius: A Latin Poet among the Vandals.* New York: Columbia University Press.

Rousseau, Philip, ed. 2009. *A Companion to Late Antiquity.* Malden, MA: Blackwell.

Ruggiero, Andrea, ed. 1996. *Paolino di Nola: I Carmi.* 2 vols. Naples: LER.

Rühl, Meike. 2003. "*Confer gemitus pariterque fleamus!*: Die Epikedien in den *Silven* des Statius." *Hyperboreus* 9 (1): 114–26.

Russell, Donald Andrew. 1979. "De Imitatione." In *Creative Imitation and Latin Literature*, edited by David West and Tony Woodman, 1–16. Cambridge: Cambridge University Press.

Salanitro, Giovanni. 1997. "Osidio Geta e la poesia centonaria." In *Aufstieg und Niedergang der römischen Welt*, 2.34.3:2314–60. Berlin: Walter de Gruyter.

Sánchez Salor, Eustaquio. 1976. "Hacia una poética de Ausonio." *Habis* 7:159–86. Translated by Frank Leinen as "Hinzu einer poetik des Ausonius" and reprinted in *Ausonius*, edited by Manfred Joachim Lossau, 112–45. Darmstadt: Wissenschaftliche Buchgesellschaft, 1991. Citations refer to the 1976 publication.

Scanzo, Roberto. 2006. "Leggere l'immagine, vedere la poesia: *Carmina Figurata* dall'antichità a Optaziano e Rabano Mauro, al «New Dada» e oltre." *Maia* 48 (2): 249–94.

Scheid, John, and Jesper Svenbro. 1996. *The Craft of Zeus: Myths of Weaving and Fabric*. Translated by Carol Volk. Cambridge, MA: Harvard University Press.

Schmidt, Peter Lebrecht. 1976. *Politik und Dichtung in der Panegyrik Claudians*. Constance: Universitäts-Verlag.

Schröder, Bianca-Jeanette. 1999. *Titel und Text: Zur Entwicklung lateinischer Gedichtüberschriften, mit Untersuchungen zu lateinischen Buchtiteln, Inhaltsverzeichnissen und anderen Gliederungsmitteln*. Berlin: Walter de Gruyter.

Seo, J. Mira. 2009. "Plagiarism and Poetic Identity in Martial." *American Journal of Philology* 130 (4): 567–93.

Setaioli, Aldo. 1966. "L'esegesi omerica nel commento di Macrobio al *Somnium Scipionis*." *Studi italiani di filologia classica* 38 (2): 154–98.

Sineri, Valentina. 2011. *Il Centone di Proba*. Acireale: Bonanno.

Smith, Alden. 1997. *Poetic Allusion and Poetic Embrace in Ovid and Virgil*. Ann Arbor: University of Michigan Press.

Smith, Macklin. 1976. *Prudentius' "Psychomachia": A Reexamination*. Princeton, NJ: Princeton University Press.

Springer, Carl P. E. 1988. *The Gospel as Epic in Late Antiquity: The "Paschale Carmen" of Sedulius*. Leiden: Brill.

Starr, Raymond J. 1987. "The Circulation of Literary Texts in the Roman World." *Classical Quarterly* 37 (1): 213–23.

———. 1992. "An Epic of Praise: Tiberius Claudius Donatus and Vergil's *Aeneid*." *Classical Antiquity* 11:159–74.

———. 2001. "The Flexibility of Literary Meaning and the Role of the Reader in Roman Antiquity." *Latomus* 60 (2): 433–45.

Stock, Brian. 1996. *Augustine the Reader: Meditation, Self-Knowledge, and the Ethics of Interpretation*. Cambridge, MA: Harvard University Press.

Struck, Peter T. 2004. *Birth of the Symbol: Ancient Readers at the Limits of Their Texts*. Princeton, NJ: Princeton University Press.

Thomas, Jean-François. 2004. "Le mot latin *allegoria*." In *L'allégorie de l'antiquité à la renaissance*, edited by Brigitte Pérez-Jean and Patricia Eichek-Lojkine, 75–92. Paris: Champion.

Thomas, Richard F. 1986. "Virgil's *Georgics* and the Art of Reference." *Harvard Studies in Classical Philology* 90:171–98.

——, ed. 1988. *Virgil: Georgics.* 2 vols. Cambridge: Cambridge University Press.

——. 1999. *Reading Virgil and His Texts: Studies in Intertextuality.* Ann Arbor: University of Michigan Press.

——. 2001. *Virgil and the Augustan Reception.* Cambridge: Cambridge University Press.

Thraede, Klaus. 1962. "Epos." In *Reallexikon für Antike und Christentum,* 5:983–1042. Stuttgart: Anton Hiersemann.

Timpanaro, Sebastiano. 2001. *Virgilianisti antichi e tradizione indiretta.* Florence: L. S. Olschki.

Trout, Dennis E. 1999. *Paulinus of Nola: Life, Letters, and Poems.* Berkeley: University of California Press.

Uhl, Anne. 1998. *Servius als Sprachlehrer: Zur Sprachrichtigkeit in der exegetischen Praxis des spätantiken Grammatikerunterrichts.* Göttingen: Vandenhoeck & Ruprecht.

Usher, Mark David. 1998. *Homeric Stitchings: The Homeric Centos of the Empress Eudocia.* Lanham, MD: Rowman & Littlefield.

——. 2003. "The Reception of Homer as Oral Poetry." *Oral Tradition* 18 (1): 79–81.

Vercruysse, Jean-Marc, ed. 2004. *Tyconius: Le livre des règles.* Sources chrétiennes 488. Paris: Editions du Cerf.

Vessey, Mark. 1993. "Jerome's Origen: The Making of a Christian Literary Persona." *Studia Patristica* 28:135–45.

——. 1994. "Erasmus' Jerome: The Publishing of a Christian Author." *Erasmus of Rotterdam Society Yearbook* 14:62–99.

——. 1996. "The Forging of Orthodoxy in Latin Christian Literature: A Case Study." *Journal of Early Christian Studies* 4 (4): 495–513.

——. 2002. "From *Cursus* to *Ductus*: Figures of Writing in Western Late Antiquity (Augustine, Jerome, Cassiodorus, Bede)." In *European Literary Careers: The Author from Antiquity to the Renaissance,* edited by Patrick Cheney and Frederick A. de Armas, 47–103. Toronto: University of Toronto Press.

——. 2007. "*Quid facit cum Horatio Hieronymus?* Christian Latin Poetry and Scriptural Poetics." In *Poetry and Exegesis in Premodern Latin Christianity: The Encounter between Classical and Christian Strategies of Interpretation,* edited by Willemien Otten and Karla Pollmann, 29–48. Leiden: Brill.

Viljamaa, Toivo. 1968. *Studies in Greek Encomiastic Poetry of the Early Byzantine Period.* Helsinki: Societas Scientiarum Fennica.

Vogt-Spira, Gregor. 2009. "Les *Saturnales* de Macrobe: Une poétique implicite de l'Antiquité tardive." In *Manifestes littéraires dans la latinité tardive poétique et rhétorique: Actes du Colloque international de Paris, 23–24 mars 2007,* edited by Perrine Galand-Hallyn and Vincent Zarini, 263–77. Paris: Études Augustiniennes.

Ware, Catherine. 2004. "Claudian: The Epic Poet in the Prefaces." In *Latin Epic and Didactic Poetry: Genre, Tradition and Individuality,* edited by Monica Gale, 181–201. Swansea: Classical Press of Wales.

——. 2012. *Claudian and the Roman Epic Tradition.* Cambridge: Cambridge University Press.

West, David, and Tony Woodman, eds. 1979. *Creative Imitation and Latin Literature.* Cambridge: Cambridge University Press.

Wheeler, Stephen M. 1995. "The Underworld Opening of Claudian's *De Raptu Proserpinae.*" *Transactions of the American Philological Association* 125:113–34.

Williams, Gordon. 1978. *Change and Decline: Roman Literature in the Early Empire.* Berkeley: University of California Press.

Williams, Megan Hale. 2006. *The Monk and the Book: Jerome and the Making of Christian Scholarship.* Chicago: University of Chicago Press.

Woodruff, Helen. 1930. *The Illustrated Manuscripts of Prudentius.* Cambridge, MA: Harvard University Press.

Young, Francis. 1994. "Typology." In *Crossing the Boundaries: Essays in Biblical Interpretation in Honour of Michael D. Goulder,* edited by Stanley E. Porter, Paul Joyce, and David E. Orton, 29–48. Leiden: Brill.

——. 1997. *Biblical Exegesis and the Formation of Christian Culture.* Cambridge: Cambridge University Press.

Zarini, Vincent. 2000. "Les préfaces des poèmes épico-panégyriques dans la latinité tardive (IVe–VIe siècles): Esquisse d'une synthèse." In *Le texte préfaciel,* edited by Laurence Kohn-Pireaux, 35–47. Nancy: Presses universitaires de Nancy.

Zetzel, James E. G. 1981. *Latin Textual Criticism in Antiquity.* Salem, NH: Ayer.

Ziolkowski, Jan M., and Michael C. J. Putnam, eds. 2008. *The Virgilian Tradition: The First Fifteen Hundred Years.* New Haven, CT: Yale University Press.

♨ GENERAL INDEX

Abraham, 60, 91, 94
acrostics, 4, 47n7, 80–81
aemulari, 30–31
aemulatio, 29, 116, 126–30, 140, 150,
    154–57
  See also *agon*; emulation
Aeneas, 34, 36, 102, 135–36, 139–40,
    143–44, 152, 154–56
agon, 29–30
Albrecht, Michael von, 85, 162n1
Alexandrian poetry. *See* Hellenistic poetry
allegoresis, 87–88, 90–91
allegorical poetry, 73–74, 84–96
allegory, 6–7, 92, 110, 112–13, 161, 164
  as defensive criticism, 12
  defined, 85–86
  Jewish tradition of, 87
  and Jerome, 14n5
  personification, 74, 84–85, 88–95
  and Vergil, 25, 32–41, 43, 164
  See also prefaces: allegorical; typology
allusion, 10, 115, 161
  apposed, 143–49
  classical, 116–126
  integrative, 118–21, 123, 127, 129,
    144–47, 149, 154n77
  juxtaposed, 138–43
  late antique, 126–30, 159–60
  nonreferential, 130–37, 154
  reflective, 118–21, 149
  signposts of, 142
  See also intertextuality; reminiscence;
    quotation
ambiguity, 18, 21, 24, 92
antanaclasis, 102, 142
antiqui, 150
anxiety (and originality), 6–7
Apollo, 38, 56–58, 82–84, 155–56
appropriation, 13, 25, 27, 67, 145, 158–60
Apuleius, 86
Arachne, 163

Archimedes, 53, 106n103
Athenaeus, 79
auctor, 26n49, 28–30, 104, 150
auctoritas, 20
audacity (Claudian's poetics), 6–7, 163
Augustan poetry, 11, 48–49, 72, 154, 161
  See also post–Augustan poetry
Augustine, 42n106
  the age of, 1–2
  on authors and readers, 9, 12–13, 17–24,
    44
Augustus, 39, 68n74, 141n
Ausonius, 2, 150–52, 158–59
  allusion in, 126–29, 139–41, 147–49,
    152–53, 157–58
  Cento nuptialis, 62, 64, 70–71, 97,
    101n88, 103n94–95, 104–7
  concinnatio, 106n107
  oxymora, 70, 105–7
  prefaces of, 62–72
author, 72, 123
  and allusion, 120–21
  human and divine, 20
  as reader, 17, 24, 32
  subjectivity of the, 46
  and text, 71
authority, 17, 25–32, 37, 57, 99, 110, 164
  auctoritas, 20
  of Vergil in late antiquity, 97–98
  constraints on, 48
authorship, 16, 25, 65, 110

Bažil, Martin, 97
biblical exempla, 95
biblical poetry, 10, 126n18, 138, 152
Borges, Jorge Luis, 32n66, 65n65
Brown, Peter, 2

Calcidius, 27
Callimachus, 4, 51–52, 123
Cameron, Alan, 12

✒ INDEX OF PASSAGES CITED